Publisher
Jim Scheikofer
The Family Handyman®

Director, Publication Services
Sue Baalman-Pohlman
Home Design Alternatives, Inc.

Editor
Kim Karsanbhai
Home Design Alternatives, Inc.

Newsstand Sales
David Algire
Reader's Digest Association, Inc.

John Crouse
Reader's Digest Association, Inc.

Marketing Manager
Andrea Vecchio
The Family Handyman

Production Manager
Judy Rodriguez
The Family Handyman

Plans Administrator
Curtis Cadenhead
Home Design Alternatives, Inc.

Copyright 2004 by
Home Service Publications, Inc.,
publishers of
The Family Handyman Magazine,
2915 Commers Drive, Suite 700,
Eagan, MN 55121.
Plan copyrights held by home
designer/architect.

Reader's Digest

The Family Handyman Contents

Vol. 18, No. 3

Featured Homes

Plan #706-0717 is featured on page 18.
Photo courtesy of Reinhold Construction, St. Louis, Missouri

Plan #706-DBI-1748-19 is featured on page 34.
Photo courtesy of Design Basics

On The Cover . . .

Plan #706-NDG-314 is featured on page 259.
Photo courtesy of Nelson Design Group, Mike Nelson, photographer.

Sections

The Family Handyman magazine and Home Design Alternatives (HDA, Inc.) are pleased to join together to bring you this collection of affordable home plans under 2,200 square feet from some of the nation's leading designers and architects.

Technical Specifications - At the time the construction drawings were prepared, every effort was made to ensure that these plan and specifications meet nationally recognized building codes (BOCA, Southern Building Code Congress and others). Because national building codes change or vary from area to area some drawing modifications and/or the assistance of a professional designer or architect may be necessary to comply with your local codes or to accommodate specific building conditions. We advise you to consult with your local building official for information regarding codes governing your area.

Functional Layout For Comfortable Living

1,360 total square feet of living area

Price Code A

Special features

- Kitchen/dining room features island work space and plenty of dining area
- Master bedroom with large walk-in closet and private bath
- Laundry room adjacent to the kitchen for easy access
- Convenient workshop in garage
- Large closets in secondary bedrooms
- 3 bedrooms, 2 baths, 2-car side entry garage
- Basement foundation, drawings also include crawl space and slab foundations

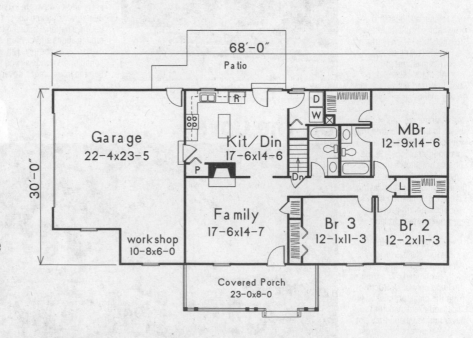

Garage 22-4x23-5

workshop 10-8x6-0

Patio

Kit/Din 17-6x14-6

Family 17-6x14-7

Covered Porch 23-0x8-0

MBr 12-9x14-6

Br 3 12-1x11-3

Br 2 12-2x11-3

68'-0"

30'-0"

2

TO ORDER BLUEPRINTS USE THE FORM ON PAGE 15 OR CALL TOLL-FREE 1-877-671-6036
View thousands more home plans online at www.familyhandyman.com/homeplans

Home.
The way nature
intended it to be.

Ask Sherwin-Williams.®

SHERWIN-WILLIAMS

1-800-4-SHERWIN   sherwin-williams.com

Classic Ranch Has Grand Appeal With Expansive Porch

1,400 total square feet of living area

Price Code B

Special features

- Master bedroom is secluded for privacy
- Large utility room with additional cabinet space
- Covered porch provides an outdoor seating area
- Roof dormers add great curb appeal
- Vaulted ceilings in living room and master bedroom
- Oversized two-car garage with storage
- 3 bedrooms, 2 baths, 2-car garage
- Basement foundation, drawings also include crawl space foundation

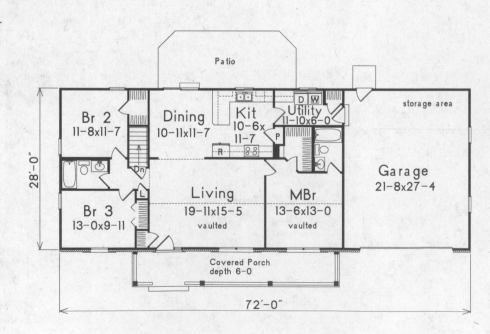

4

TO ORDER BLUEPRINTS USE THE FORM ON PAGE 15 OR CALL TOLL-FREE 1-877-671-6036
View thousands more home plans online at www.familyhandyman.com/homeplans

Enchanting Country Cottage

1,140 total square feet of living area

Price Code AA

Special features

- Open and spacious living and dining areas for family gatherings
- Well-organized kitchen with an abundance of cabinetry and a built-in pantry
- Roomy master bath features double-bowl vanity
- 3 bedrooms, 2 baths, 2-car drive under garage
- Basement foundation

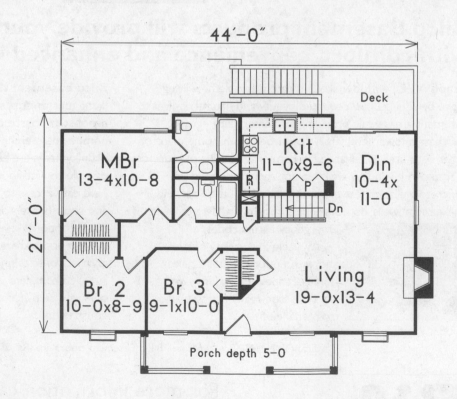

44'-0"

27'-0"

Deck

MBr 13-4x10-8

Kit 11-0x9-6

Din 10-4x 11-0

R
P
Dn
L

Br 2 10-0x8-9

Br 3 9-1x10-0

Living 19-0x13-4

Porch depth 5-0

The blinds will never get dirty. The rest of the house is another story.

Country-Style With Wrap-Around Porch

1,597 total square feet of living area

Price Code C

Special features

- Spacious family room includes fireplace and coat closet
- Open kitchen and dining room provide breakfast bar and access to the outdoors
- Convenient laundry area located near kitchen
- Secluded master suite with walk-in closet and private bath
- 4 bedrooms, 2 1/2 baths, 2-car detached garage
- Basement foundation

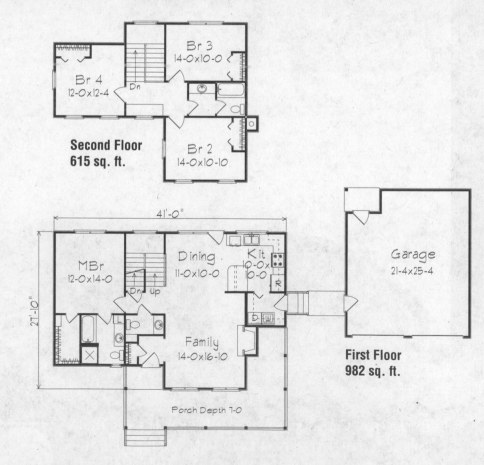

Second Floor 615 sq. ft.

Br 4 12-0x12-4

Br 3 14-0x10-0

Br 2 14-0x10-10

First Floor 982 sq. ft.

41'-0"

27'-10"

MBr 12-0x14-0

Dining 11-0x10-0

Kit 10-0x 10-0

Family 14-0x16-10

Garage 21-4x25-4

Porch Depth 7-0

TO ORDER BLUEPRINTS USE THE FORM ON PAGE 15 OR CALL TOLL-FREE 1-877-671-6036
View thousands more home plans online at www.familyhandyman.com/homeplans

Two surprisingly small speakers.
One remarkable surround sound experience.

Presenting the *newest* member of the 3·2·1 system family: the 3·2·1 *GS* system.

Introducing another step toward our goal: Good sound that's heard, not seen. We've made our award-winning 3·2·1 DVD system even smaller and better. Our new 3·2·1 *GS* DVD home entertainment system produces an enhanced surround sound experience from just two incredibly small speakers. With Bose® patented speaker technology and our latest signal processing, the two speakers deliver many of the benefits of a surround sound experience

without running wires to the back of your room. A hideaway Acoustimass® module (not shown) produces low notes that give impact to movies and music. The 3·2·1 *GS* system delivers the unique combination of simplicity and performance that won our original 3·2·1 system "Product of the Year" from *Electronic House*. Experience the power of two speakers with the 3·2·1 systems from Bose. They're just one of the reasons Bose is the most respected name in sound.

The 3·2·1 DVD home entertainment system.

The *new* 3·2·1 *GS* DVD home entertainment system.

BOSE®
Better sound through research®

Distinctive Country Porch

2,182 total square feet of living area

Price Code D

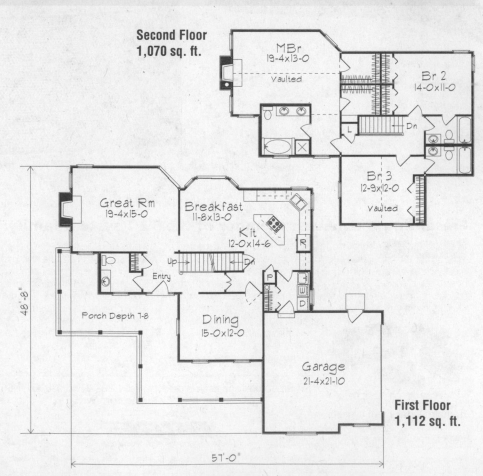

Second Floor
1,070 sq. ft.

MBr
19-4x13-0
Vaulted

Br 2
14-0x11-0

Br 3
12-9x12-0
Vaulted

Dn

L

Special features

- Meandering porch creates an inviting look

- Generous great room has four double-hung windows and gliding doors to exterior

- Highly functional kitchen features island/breakfast bar, menu desk and convenient pantry

- Each secondary bedroom includes generous closet and private bath

- 3 bedrooms, 3 1/2 baths, 2-car side entry garage

- Basement foundation

Great Rm
19-4x15-0

Breakfast
11-8x13-0

Kit
12-0x14-6

R

Up

Entry

Dn

F

W D

Dining
15-0x12-0

Porch Depth 7-8

Garage
21-4x21-10

48'-8"

57'-0"

First Floor
1,112 sq. ft.

Workshop Breakthrough!

You've GOT to see this!

Interchangeable workstation design lets you customize your shop for the type of work you'll be doing.

- Tools mount onto quick-change inserts. When you're ready to work, set the tool in place and lock it down. Changing tools takes just seconds!

- Save space. Store multiple benchtop tools in the Tool Rack.

- Tool accessories are within easy reach with blade and bit holders, built-in drawers, shelves and more.

- Rock-solid 18-gauge steel construction with 1-1/4" thick wood tops – designed to withstand hard use.

- Pick and choose the units that work best for your needs, and add on units as your workshop grows.

❝ Tool Dock is a GREAT product. I'm impressed with the quality. I really like the versatility of having my power tools mounted on changeable inserts, and being able to roll my projects into an open area. ❞

Jim Marteney
Tool Dock owner
Loves Park, IL

For complete details and an outlet near you:

www.tooldock.com

Or call toll-free: **1-866-866-5362**

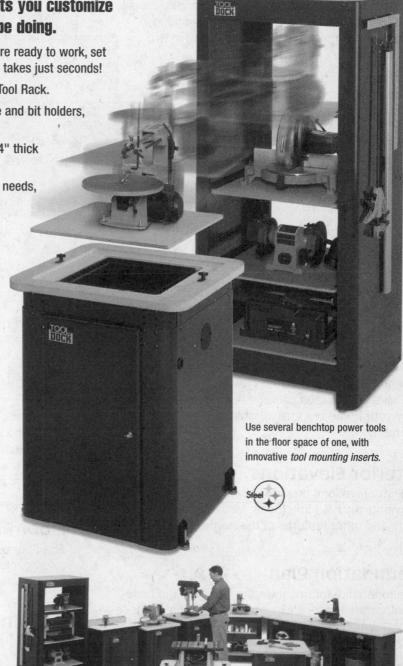

Use several benchtop power tools in the floor space of one, with innovative *tool mounting inserts*.

Steel

TOOL DOCK™

The Modular Workshop

Tools not included.

Our Blueprint Packages Offer...

Quality plans for building your future, with extras that provide unsurpassed value, ensure good construction and long-term enjoyment.

A quality home - one that looks good, functions well, and provides years of enjoyment - is a product of many things - design, materials, craftsmanship.

But it's also the result of outstanding blueprints - the actual plans and specifications that tell the builder exactly how to build your home.

And with our BLUEPRINT PACKAGES you get the absolute best. A complete set of blueprints is available for every design in this book. These "working drawings," are highly detailed, resulting in two key benefits:

- Better understanding by the contractor of how to build your home and...

- More accurate construction estimates.

When you purchase one of our designs, you'll receive all of the BLUEPRINT components shown here - elevations, foundation plan, floor plans, sections, and/or details. Other helpful building aids are also available to help make your dream home a reality.

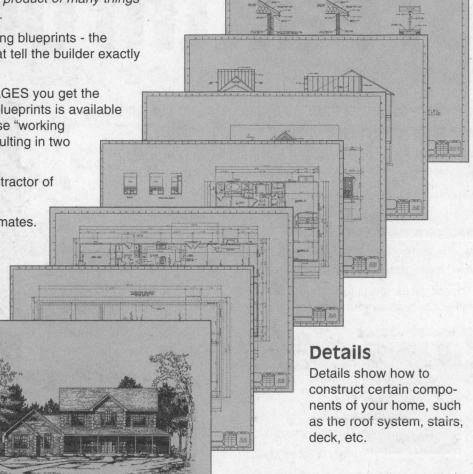

Cover Sheet

The cover sheet is the artist's rendering of the exterior of the home. It will give you an idea of how your home will look when completed and landscaped.

Interior Elevations

Interior elevations provide views of special interior elements such as fireplaces, kitchen cabinets, built-in units and other features of the home.

Foundation Plan

The foundation plan shows the layout of the basement, crawl space, slab or pier foundation. All necessary notations and dimensions are included. See plan page for the foundation types included. If the home plan you choose does not have your desired foundation type, our Customer Service Representatives can advise you on how to customize your foundation to suit your specific needs or site conditions.

Details

Details show how to construct certain components of your home, such as the roof system, stairs, deck, etc.

Sections

Sections show detail views of the home or portions of the home as if it were sliced from the roof to the foundation. This sheet shows important areas such as load-bearing walls, stairs, joists, trusses and other structural elements, which are critical for proper construction.

Floor Plans

The floor plans show the placement of walls, doors, closets, plumbing fixtures, electrical outlets, columns, and beams for each level of the home.

Exterior Elevations

Exterior elevations illustrate the front, rear and both sides of the house, with all details of exterior materials and the required dimensions.

DON'T LET YOUR Santa Fe Sky GET CLOUDY.

What Kind Of Plan Package Do You Need?

Now that you've found the home you've been looking for, here are some suggestions on how to make your Dream Home a reality. To get started, order the type of plans that fit your particular situation.

YOUR CHOICES

- **THE 1-SET STUDY PACKAGE -** We offer a 1-set plan package so you can study your home in detail. This one set is considered a study set and is marked "not for construction". It is a copyright violation to reproduce blueprints.

- **THE MINIMUM 5-SET PACKAGE -** If you're ready to start the construction process, this 5-set package is the minimum number of blueprint sets you will need. It will require keeping close track of each set so they can be used by multiple subcontractors and tradespeople.

- **THE STANDARD 8-SET PACKAGE -** For best results in terms of cost, schedule and quality of construction, we recommend you order eight (or more) sets of blueprints. Besides one set for yourself, additional sets of blueprints will be required by your mortgage lender, local building department, general contractor and all subcontractors working on foundation, electrical, plumbing, heating/air conditioning, carpentry work, etc.

- **REPRODUCIBLE MASTERS -** If you wish to make some minor design changes, you'll want to order reproducible masters. These drawings contain the same information as the blueprints but are printed on erasable and reproducible paper which clearly indicates your right to copy or reproduce. This will allow your builder or a local design professional to make the necessary drawing changes without the major expense of redrawing the plans. This package also allows you to print copies of the modified plans as needed. The right of building only one structure from these plans is licensed exclusively to the buyer. You may not use this design to build a second or multiple dwelling(s) without purchasing another blueprint. Each violation of the Copyright Law is punishable in a fine.

- **MIRROR REVERSE SETS -** Plans can be printed in mirror reverse. These plans are useful when the house would fit your site better if all the rooms were on the opposite side than shown. They are simply a mirror image of the original drawings causing the lettering and dimensions to read backwards. Therefore, when ordering mirror reverse drawings, you must purchase at least one set of right reading plans.

Other Helpful Building Aids...

Your Blueprint Package will contain the necessary construction information to build your home. We also offer the following products and services to save you time and money in the building process.

- **MATERIAL LIST -** Material lists are available for many of the plans in this book. Each list gives you the quantity, dimensions and description of the building materials necessary to construct your home. You'll get faster and more accurate bids from your contractor while saving money by paying for only the materials you need. See the Home Plans Index on page 16 for availability. Refer to the order form on page 15 for pricing.

- **DETAIL PLAN PACKAGES:** Framing, Plumbing & Electrical Plan Packages - Three separate packages offer homebuilders details for constructing various foundations; numerous floor, wall and roof framing techniques; simple to complex residential wiring; sump and water softener hookups; plumbing connection methods; installation of septic systems and more. Each package includes three-dimensional illustrations and a glossary of terms. Purchase one or all three. Cost: $20.00 each or all three for $40.00. Note: These drawings do not pertain to a specific home plan.

- **THE LEGAL KIT™ -** Our Legal Kit provides contracts and legal forms to help protect you from the potential pitfalls inherent in the building process. The Kit supplies commonly used forms and contracts suitable for homeowners and builders. It can save you a considerable amount of time and help protect you and your assets during and after construction. Cost: $35.00

- **EXPRESS DELIVERY -** Most orders are processed within 24 hours of receipt. Please allow 7-10 business days for delivery. If you need to place a rush order, please call us by 11:00 a.m. CST and ask for express service (allow 1-2 business days).

- **TECHNICAL ASSISTANCE-** If you have questions, call our technical support line at 1-314-770-2228 between 8:00 a.m. and 5:00 p.m. CST. Whether it involves design modifications or field assistance, our designers are extremely familiar with all of our designs and will be happy to help you. We want your home to be everything you expect it to be.

HD HOME DESIGN ALTERNATIVES, INC.

◆ **Exchange Policies -** Since blueprints are printed in response to your order, we cannot honor requests for refunds. However, if for some reason you find that the plan you have purchased does not meet your requirements, you may exchange that plan for another plan in our collection. At the time of the exchange, you will be charged a processing fee of 25% of your original plan package price, plus the difference in price between the plan packages (if applicable) and the cost to ship the new plans to you.

◆ **Building Codes & Requirements -** At the time the construction drawings were prepared, every effort was made to ensure that these plans and specifications meet nationally recognized codes. Our plans conform to most national building codes. Because building codes vary from area to area, some drawing modifications and/or the assistance of a professional designer or architect may be necessary to comply with your local codes or to accommodate specific building site conditions. We advise you to consult with your local building official for information regarding codes governing your area.

Please note: Reproducible drawings can only be exchanged if the package is unopened, and exchanges are allowed only within 90 days of purchase.

Questions? Call Our Customer Service Number
1-877-671-6036

BLUEPRINT PRICE SCHEDULE   *BEST VALUE*

Price Code	1-Set*	SAVE $110 5-Sets	SAVE $200 8-Sets	Material List**	Reproducible Masters
AAA	$225	$295	$340	$50	$440
AA	$275	$345	$390	$55	$490
A	$325	$395	$440	$60	$540
B	$375	$445	$490	$60	$590
C	$425	$495	$540	$65	$640
D	$475	$545	$590	$65	$690
E	$525	$595	$640	$70	$740
F	$575	$645	$690	$70	$790
G	$650	$720	$765	$75	$865
H	$755	$825	$870	$80	$970

Plan prices guaranteed through December 31, 2004.
Please note that plans are not refundable.

◆ **Additional Sets -** Additional sets of the plan ordered are available for $45.00 each. Five-set, eight-set, and reproducible packages offer considerable savings.

◆ **Mirror Reverse Plans -** Available for an additional $5.00 per set, these plans are simply a mirror image of the original drawings causing the dimensions and lettering to read backwards. Therefore, when ordering mirror reverse plans, you must purchase at least one set of right reading plans.

◆ **One-Set Study Package -** We offer a one-set plan package so you can study your home in detail. This one set is considered a study set and is marked "not for construction". It is a copyright violation to reproduce blueprints.

*1-Set Study Packages are not available for all plans.
**Available only within 90 days after purchase of plan package or reproducible masters of same plan.

SHIPPING & HANDLING CHARGES

U.S. SHIPPING	1-4 Sets	5-7 Sets	8 Sets or Reproducibles
Regular *(allow 7-10 business days)*	$15.00	$17.50	$25.00
Priority *(allow 3-5 business days)*	$25.00	$30.00	$35.00
Express* *(allow 1-2 business days)*	$35.00	$40.00	$45.00

CANADA SHIPPING (to/from) - Plans with suffix DR & SH

	1-4 Sets	5-7 Sets	8 Sets or Reproducibles
Standard *(allow 8-12 business days)*	$25.00	$30.00	$35.00
Express* *(allow 3-5 business days)*	$40.00	$40.00	$45.00

Overseas Shipping/International - Call, fax, or e-mail (plans@hdainc.com) for shipping costs.

* For express delivery please call us by 11:00 a.m. CST

How To Order
For fastest service, Call Toll-Free
1-877-671-6036
24 HOURS A DAY
Three Easy Ways To Order

1. CALL toll-free 1-877-671-6036 for credit card orders. MasterCard, Visa, Discover and American Express are accepted.

2. FAX your order to 1-314-770-2226.

3. MAIL the Order Form to:

   HDA, Inc.
   4390 Green Ash Drive
   St. Louis, MO 63045

ORDER FORM

Please send me -
PLAN NUMBER   706BT - _____

PRICE CODE _____ (see Plan Index)
(for plans on pgs. 2-309)

Specify Foundation Type - see plan page for availability
☐ Slab   ☐ Crawl space   ☐ Pier
☐ Basement   ☐ Walk-out basement

☐ Reproducible Masters $ _____
☐ Eight-Set Plan Package $ _____
☐ Five-Set Plan Package $ _____
☐ One-Set Study Package (no mirror reverse) $ _____
☐ Additional Plan Sets
   _____ (Qty.) at $45.00 each $ _____
☐ Print in Mirror Reverse
   _____ (Qty.) add $5.00 per set $ _____
☐ Material List $ _____
☐ Legal Kit (see page 14) $ _____
Detail Plan Packages: (see page 14)
   ☐ Framing ☐ Electrical ☐ Plumbing $ _____
                            SUBTOTAL $ _____
SALES TAX (MO residents add 6%) $ _____
☐ Shipping / Handling (see chart at left) $ _____
   TOTAL ENCLOSED (US funds only) $ _____
(Sorry no CODs)

I hereby authorize HDA, Inc. to charge this purchase to my credit card account (check one):

☐ MasterCard   ☐ VISA   ☐ DISCOVER NOVUS   ☐ AMERICAN EXPRESS Cards

Credit Card number _____

Expiration date _____

Signature _____

Name _____
          (Please print or type)

Street Address _____
              (Please **do not** use PO Box)

City _____

State _____   Zip _____

Daytime phone number (_____) - _____

I'm a ☐ Builder/Contractor   I ☐ have
      ☐ Homeowner   ☐ have not
      ☐ Renter   selected my
                             general contractor

Thank you for your order!

15

Home Plans Index

Plan Number	Sq. Ft.	Price Code	Page	Mat. List
706-0102	1,246	A	168	X
706-0105	1,360	A	255	X
706-0112	1,668	C	21	X
706-0162	1,882	D	98	X
706-0171	2,058	C	202	X
706-0173	1,220	A	101	X
706-0174	1,657	B	56	X
706-0190	1,600	C	74	X
706-0191	1,868	D	242	X
706-0200	1,343	A	266	X
706-0201	1,814	D	30	X
706-0203	1,475	B	130	X
706-0213	2,059	C	135	X
706-0214	1,770	B	254	X
706-0217	1,360	A	2	X
706-0218	1,998	D	86	X
706-0221	1,619	B	105	X
706-0225	1,260	A	72	X
706-0226	1,416	A	181	X
706-0227	1,674	B	77	X
706-0228	1,996	C	41	X
706-0229	1,676	B	284	X
706-0230	2,073	D	194	X
706-0234	2,066	C	252	X
706-0244	1,994	D	277	X
706-0249	1,501	B	197	X
706-0255	1,340	A	90	X
706-0270	1,448	A	117	X
706-0274	1,020	AA	236	X
706-0282	1,642	B	161	X
706-0283	1,800	D	274	X
706-0286	1,856	C	228	X
706-0291	1,600	B	190	X
706-0295	1,609	B	263	X
706-0296	1,396	A	261	X
706-0297	1,320	A	257	X
706-0302	1,854	D	111	X
706-0312	1,921	D	42	X
706-0316	1,824	C	251	X
706-0318	2,147	C	238	X
706-0322	2,135	D	281	X
706-0335	1,865	D	39	X
706-0348	2,003	D	243	X
706-0357	1,550	B	113	X
706-0362	1,874	C	210	X
706-0363	2,128	C	174	X
706-0370	1,721	C	99	X
706-0372	1,859	D	46	X
706-0375	1,954	D	249	X
706-0379	1,711	C	225	X
706-0382	1,546	C	83	X
706-0385	1,814	C	167	X
706-0386	2,186	C	85	X
706-0387	1,958	C	239	X
706-0389	1,777	B	241	X
706-0393	1,684	B	180	X
706-0394	1,558	B	187	X
706-0395	1,803	C	87	X
706-0396	1,880	C	232	X
706-0410	1,742	B	172	X
706-0412	2,109	C	237	X
706-0413	2,182	D	10	X
706-0415	1,492	A	69	X
706-0416	1,985	C	115	X
706-0419	1,882	C	206	X
706-0420	1,941	C	220	X
706-0441	1,747	B	235	X
706-0442	1,950	C	164	X
706-0447	1,393	B	44	X
706-0448	1,597	C	8	X
706-0450	1,708	B	223	X
706-0452	2,318	F	293	X
706-0462	1,028	AA	140	X
706-0463	2,986	G	289	X
706-0464	1,992	E	296	X
706-0465	1,704	D	304	X
706-0467	1,904	E	294	X
706-0475	1,711	B	219	X
706-0477	1,140	AA	6	X
706-0478	1,092	AA	157	X
706-0481	2,012	C	156	X
706-0484	1,403	A	231	X
706-0485	1,195	AA	89	X
706-0487	1,189	AA	150	X
706-0488	2,059	C	200	X
706-0489	1,543	B	245	X
706-0490	1,687	B	217	X
706-0491	1,808	C	177	X
706-0494	1,085	AA	233	X
706-0495	987	AA	247	X
706-0496	977	AA	227	X
706-0498	954	AA	211	X
706-0502	864	AAA	79	X
706-0503	1,000	AA	153	X
706-0521	2,050	C	280	X
706-0539	1,769	B	207	X
706-0595	1,536	D	298	X
706-0650	1,020	AA	229	X
706-0652	1,524	B	288	X
706-0656	1,700	B	136	X
706-0657	914	AA	19	X
706-0660	1,321	A	215	X
706-0661	1,712	B	213	X
706-0662	1,516	B	189	X
706-0664	1,776	B	175	X
706-0667	1,560	B	163	X
706-0668	1,617	B	183	X
706-0670	1,170	AA	109	X
706-0671	1,427	A	141	X
706-0672	2,043	D	75	X
706-0674	1,476	B	185	X
706-0676	1,367	B	61	X
706-0678	1,567	C	67	X
706-0680	1,432	B	142	X
706-0681	1,660	C	171	X
706-0685	1,844	C	149	X
706-0686	1,609	B	126	X
706-0690	1,400	B	4	X
706-0692	1,339	A	122	X
706-0694	1,285	A	147	X
706-0702	1,558	B	65	X
706-0711	1,575	B	35	X
706-0712	2,029	C	107	X
706-0717	1,268	B	18	X
706-0718	1,340	A	145	X
706-0723	1,784	B	139	X
706-0724	1,969	C	118	X
706-0726	1,428	A	94	X
706-0731	1,761	B	82	X
706-0732	1,384	B	50	X
706-0733	2,070	C	54	X
706-0739	1,684	B	137	X
706-0740	3,666	H	306	X
706-0741	1,578	B	58	X
706-0747	1,977	C	203	X
706-0755	1,787	B	102	X
706-0759	2,125	C	68	X
706-0762	3,728	H	297	X
706-0768	1,879	C	51	X
706-0774	1,680	B	53	X
706-0776	2,200	C	64	X
706-0786	2,408	F	300	X
706-0789	3,258	H	303	X
706-0794	1,433	A	62	X
706-0796	1,599	B	49	X
706-0798	2,128	C	76	X
706-0799	1,849	C	129	X
706-0806	1,452	A	60	X
706-0807	1,231	A	123	X
706-0808	969	AA	133	X
706-0809	1,084	AA	80	X
706-0813	888	AAA	119	X
706-0822	1,991	C	11	X
706-1101	1,643	B	276	
706-1117	1,440	A	198	
706-1124	1,345	A	193	
706-1205	3,648	H	290	
706-1220	1,540	B	196	
706-1308	2,280	D	287	
706-AMD-1135	1,467	A	88	
706-AMD-2120C	1,893	D	106	
706-AMD-2135	1,902	D	278	
706-AMD-2152B	1,805	D	173	
706-AP-1002	1,050	AA	97	
706-AP-1205	1,296	B	285	
706-AP-1516	1,593	C	52	
706-AP-1717	1,787	B	131	
706-AX-93304	1,860	D	40	
706-AX-93311	1,945	D	282	
706-AX-94341	1,040	B	253	
706-AX-95347	1,709	C	100	
706-BF-1426	1,420	A	166	
706-BF-2107	2,123	E	78	
706-BF-DR1108	1,150	AA	179	
706-BF-DR1109	1,191	AA	244	
706-CHD-11-27	1,123	AA	195	
706-CHD-14-18	1,429	A	275	
706-CHD-20-50	2,080	C	120	
706-CHD-20-51	2,084	C	70	
706-CHD-10002	6,410	H	301	
706-CHD-10004	5,810	H	295	
706-CHP-1332A	1,363	A	269	
706-CHP-1733-A-7	1,737	B	59	
706-CHP-1833-A-13	1,819	C	273	
706-CHP-2132B	2,172	C	114	
706-D-90	1,796	D	305	
706-DBI-1748-19	1,911	C	34	
706-DBI-2619	1,998	C	286	
706-DBI-7603	2,622	G	307	
706-DBI-24038-9P	2,126	C	124	
706-DBI-24045-9P	1,263	A	264	
706-DDI-98-106	1,588	B	138	
706-DDI-100-107	2,068	E	308	
706-DDI-100-215	1,757	B	31	
706-DDI-95220	1,584	B	260	
706-DH-1377	1,377	A	208	
706-DH-1786	1,785	B	24	
706-DH-2005	1,700	B	148	
706-DH-2108	2,156	C	262	
706-DL-16653L1	1,665	B	182	
706-DL-17353L1	1,735	B	93	
706-DL-19603L2	1,960	C	216	
706-DR-2929	1,285	A	192	
706-DR-2939	1,480	A	283	
706-DR-3008	2,172	E	299	
706-DR-3812	2,129	C	84	
706-FB-327	1,281	A	272	
706-FB-894	1,124	AA	212	
706-FB-1076	1,080	AA	20	
706-FB-1132	1,342	A	92	
706-FB-1148	1,491	A	209	
706-FB-1175	1,467	A	134	
706-FB-1217	1,583	B	71	
706-FD8103	1,225	A	265	
706-FDG-4044	1,577	B	25	
706-FDG-7773	1,653	B	169	
706-FDG-9035	1,760	B	178	
706-GH-10785	1,907	C	279	
706-GH-10839	1,738	B	23	
706-GH-24717	1,642	B	230	
706-GH-24724	1,982	C	121	
706-GH-34901	1,763	C	95	
706-GM-1253	1,253	A	22	
706-GM-1333	1,333	A	125	
706-GM-1780	1,780	B	258	
706-GM-1842	1,842	C	176	
706-GM-1849	1,849	C	158	
706-GSD-1023-C	1,890	C	29	
706-GSD-1123	1,734	B	146	
706-GSD-1748	1,496	A	221	
706-HDG-97001	1,872	C	234	
706-HDG-99004	1,231	A	155	
706-HDS-1571	1,571	B	81	
706-HDS-1627	1,627	B	27	
706-HDS-1758	1,783	B	162	
706-HDS-1817	1,817	C	270	
706-HP-C316	1,997	C	43	
706-HP-C460	1,389	A	96	
706-HP-C619	1,771	B	271	
706-HP-C662	1,937	C	165	
706-HP-C681	1,669	B	143	
706-JA-51394	1,508	B	26	
706-JA-59195	1,739	B	152	
706-JA-65996	1,962	C	188	
706-JA-67596	1,919	C	268	
706-JFD-10-1436-1	1,436	A	28	
706-JFD-10-1456-2	1,456	A	240	
706-JFD-10-1875-1	1,875	C	132	
706-JFD-20-2018-1	2,018	C	218	
706-JV-1379	1,379	A	186	
706-JV-1735A	1,735	B	154	
706-JV-1840-A	1,840	C	37	
706-JV-2012-A-SJ	2,012	C	66	
706-LBD-15-2A	1,553	B	45	
706-LBD-17-14A	1,725	B	226	
706-LBD-19-23A	1,932	C	159	
706-MG-02120	2,111	H	204	
706-MG-02236	1,985	G	112	
706-MG-9305	1,606	B	250	
706-MG-9538	1,404	E	128	
706-NDG-108	2,216	D	110	
706-NDG-113-1	1,525	B	38	
706-NDG-148	1,538	B	103	
706-NDG-314	1,934	C	259	
706-NDG-346	1,990	C	73	
706-NDG-405-1	3,419	H	309	
706-NDG-407-1	3,366	H	302	
706-NDG-413	2,502	F	292	
706-NDG-788	2,050	C	205	
706-RDD-1374-9	1,374	A	33	
706-RDD-1753-9	1,753	B	170	
706-RDD-2050-7A	2,050	C	184	
706-RJ-A1079	1,021	AA	214	
706-RJ-A1175	1,192	AA	127	
706-RJ-A1491	1,482	A	256	
706-RJ-A14106	1,497	A	63	
706-RJ-B123	1,270	A	191	
706-RJ-B1416	1,455	A	32	
706-RJ-N17-1	1,713	D	291	
706-SH-SEA-091	1,541	B	108	
706-SH-SEA-182	2,044	C	55	
706-SH-SEA-225	1,230	A	201	
706-SH-SEA-226	1,543	B	199	
706-SH-SEA-242	1,408	A	48	
706-SH-SEA-400	1,568	B	267	
706-SRD-123	1,782	B	36	
706-SRD-142	2,082	C	248	
706-SRD-151	2,157	C	151	
706-SRD-214	1,856	C	91	
706-SRD-244	1,593	B	160	
706-UD-C142	1,698	B	57	
706-UD-C143	1,698	B	224	
706-UD-C161	1,840	C	222	
706-UD-D162	2,198	C	104	
706-VL947	947	AA	47	
706-VL-1458	1,458	A	144	
706-VL-1594	1,594	B	246	
706-VL2069	2,069	C	116	

QUICK AND EASY CUSTOMIZING
MAKE CHANGES TO YOUR HOME PLAN IN 4 STEPS

HERE'S AN **AFFORDABLE** AND **EFFICIENT** WAY TO MAKE CHANGES TO YOUR PLAN.

1 **Select the house plan that most closely meets your needs.** Purchase of a reproducible master is necessary in order to make changes to a plan.

2 **Call 1-877-671-6036 to place your order.** Tell the sales representative you're interested in customizing a plan. A $50 refundable consultation fee will be charged. You will then be instructed to complete a customization checklist indicating all the changes you wish to make to your plan. You may attach sketches if necessary. If you proceed with the custom changes the $50 will be credited to the total amount charged.

3 **FAX the completed customization checklist** to our design consultant at 1-866-477-5173 or e-mail custom@drummonddesigns.com. Within *24-48 business hours you will be provided with a written cost estimate to modify your plan. Our design consultant will contact you by phone if you wish to discuss any of your changes in greater detail.

4 **Once you approve the estimate,** a 75% retainer fee is collected and customization work gets underway. Preliminary drawings can usually be completed within *5-10 business days. Following approval of the preliminary drawings your design changes are completed within *5-10 business days. Your remaining 25% balance due is collected prior to shipment of your completed drawings. You will be shipped five sets of revised blueprints or a reproducible master, plus a customized materials list if required.

*Terms are subject to change without notice.

BEFORE
Plan 2829

Customized Version of Plan 2829

AFTER

MODIFICATION PRICING GUIDE

CATEGORIES	Average Cost from… to
Adding or removing living space (square footage)	Quote required
Adding or removing a garage	$400 $680
Garage: Front entry to side load or vice versa	Starting at $300
Adding a screened porch	$280 $600
Adding a bonus room in the attic	$450 $780
Changing full basement to crawl space or vice versa	Starting at $220
Changing full basement to slab or vice versa	Starting at $260
Changing exterior building material	Starting at $200
Changing roof lines	$360 $630
Adjusting ceiling height	$280 $500
Adding, moving or removing an exterior opening	$55 per opening
Adding or removing a fireplace	$90 $200
Modifying a non-bearing wall or room	$55 per room
Changing exterior walls from 2"x4" to 2"x6"	Starting at $200
Redesigning a bathroom or a kitchen	$120 $280
Reverse plan right reading	Quote required
Adapting plans for local building code requirements	Quote required
Engineering stamping only	Quote required
Any other engineering services	Quote required
Adjust plan for handicapped accessibility	Quote required
Interactive illustrations (choices of exterior materials)	Quote required
Metric conversion of home plan	$400

Note: Any home plan can be customized to accommodate your desired changes. The average prices specified above are provided only as examples for the most commonly requested changes, and are subject to change without notice. Prices for changes will vary according to the number of modifications requested, plan size, style, and method of design used by the original designer. To obtain a detailed cost estimate, please contact us.

Distinguished Styling For A Small Lot

1,268 total square feet of living area

Price Code B

Special features

- Multiple gables, large porch and arched windows create classy exterior
- Innovative design provides openness in great room, kitchen and breakfast room
- Secondary bedrooms have private hall with bath
- 3 bedrooms, 2 baths, 2-car garage
- Basement foundation

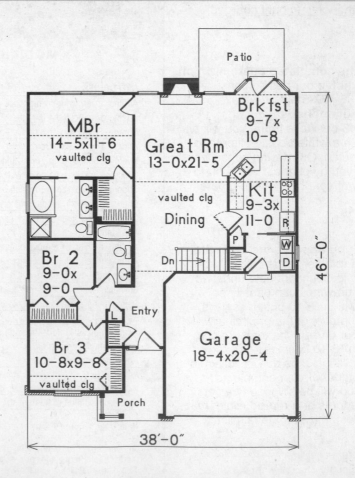

Small Home Is Remarkably Spacious

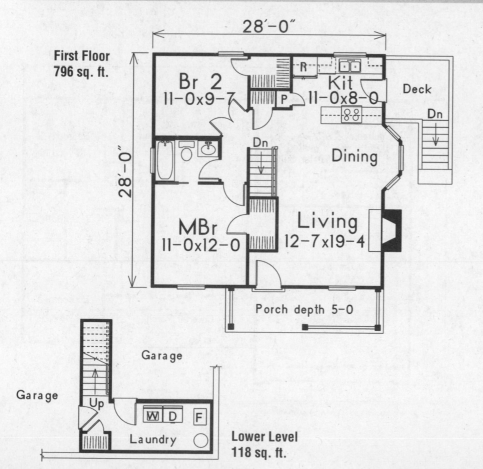

914 total square feet of living area

Price Code AA

First Floor
796 sq. ft.

28'-0"

28'-0"

Br 2
11-0x9-7

Kit
11-0x8-0

Deck

R

P

Dn

Dn

Dining

MBr
11-0x12-0

Living
12-7x19-4

Porch depth 5-0

Garage

Garage

Up

W D F

Laundry

Lower Level
118 sq. ft.

Special features

- Large porch for leisure evenings
- Dining area with bay window, open stair and pass-through kitchen creates openness
- Basement includes generous garage space, storage area, finished laundry and mechanical room
- 2 bedrooms, 1 bath, 2-car drive under garage
- Basement foundation

TO ORDER BLUEPRINTS USE THE FORM ON PAGE 15 OR CALL TOLL-FREE 1-877-671-6036
View thousands more home plans online at www.familyhandyman.com/homeplans

19

Luxurious Master Suite

1,080 total square feet of living area   **Price Code AA**

Special features

- Secondary bedrooms separate from master suite allowing privacy
- Compact kitchen is well-organized
- Conveniently located laundry closet
- 3 bedrooms, 2 baths, 2-car garage
- Walk-out basement or crawl space foundation, please specify when ordering

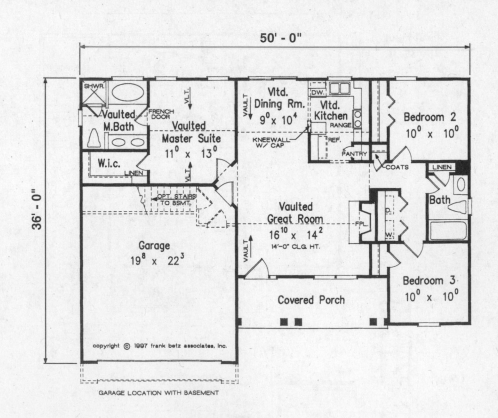

copyright © 1997 frank betz associates, inc.

GARAGE LOCATION WITH BASEMENT

20

TO ORDER BLUEPRINTS USE THE FORM ON PAGE 15 OR CALL TOLL-FREE 1-877-671-6036
View thousands more home plans online at www.familyhandyman.com/homeplans

Bay Window Graces Master Bedroom

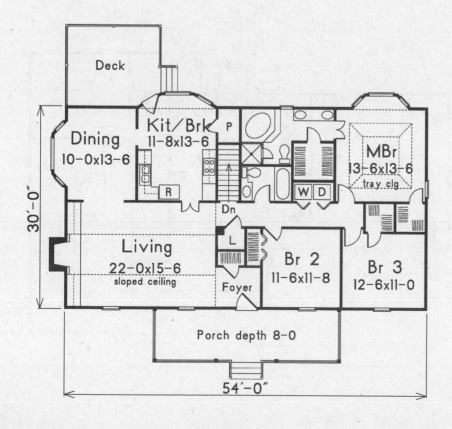

1,668 total square feet of living area

Price Code C

Special features

- Large bay windows in breakfast area, master bedroom and dining room
- Extensive walk-in closets and storage spaces throughout the home
- Handy covered entry porch
- Large living room has fireplace, built-in bookshelves and sloped ceiling
- 3 bedrooms, 2 baths, 2-car drive under garage
- Basement foundation

TO ORDER BLUEPRINTS USE THE FORM ON PAGE 15 OR CALL TOLL-FREE 1-877-671-6036
View thousands more home plans online at www.familyhandyman.com/homeplans

21

Covered Rear Porch

1,253 total square feet of living area

Price Code A

Special features

- Sloped ceiling and fireplace in family room adds drama
- U-shaped kitchen is efficiently designed
- Large walk-in closets are found in all the bedrooms
- 3 bedrooms, 2 baths, 2-car garage
- Crawl space or slab foundation, please specify when ordering

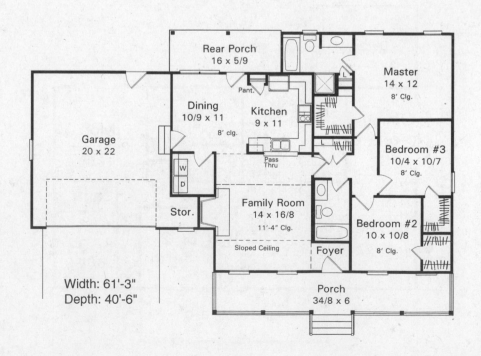

Width: 61'-3"
Depth: 40'-6"

Garage 20 x 22

Rear Porch 16 x 5/9

Dining 10/9 x 11 8' clg.

Kitchen 9 x 11

Pant.

Pass Thru

W D

Stor.

Family Room 14 x 16/8 11'-4" Clg.

Sloped Ceiling

Foyer

Porch 34/8 x 6

Master 14 x 12 8' Clg.

Bedroom #3 10/4 x 10/7 8' Clg.

Bedroom #2 10 x 10/8 8' Clg.

TO ORDER BLUEPRINTS USE THE FORM ON PAGE 15 OR CALL TOLL-FREE 1-877-671-6036
View thousands more home plans online at www.familyhandyman.com/homeplans

Perfect Compact Ranch

1,738 total square feet of living area

Price Code B

Rear View

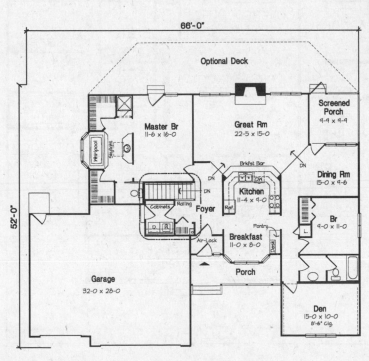

Special features

- A den in the front of the home can easily be converted to a third bedroom

- Kitchen includes an eating nook for family gatherings

- Master bedroom has an unforgettable bath with a super skylight

- Large sunken great room centralized with a cozy fireplace

- 2 bedrooms, 2 baths, 3-car garage

- Basement, crawl space or slab foundation, please specify when ordering

Traditional Southern Style Home

1,785 total square feet of living area

Price Code B

Special features

- 9' ceilings throughout home
- Luxurious master bath includes whirlpool tub and separate shower
- Cozy breakfast area is convenient to kitchen
- 3 bedrooms, 3 baths, 2-car detached garage
- Basement, crawl space or slab foundation, please specify when ordering

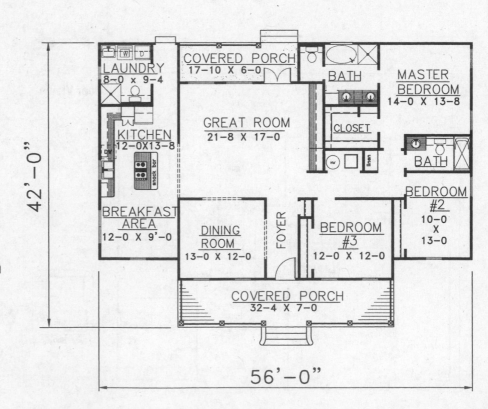

Alpine Style Creates Cozy Cabin Feel

1,577 total square feet of living area

Price Code B

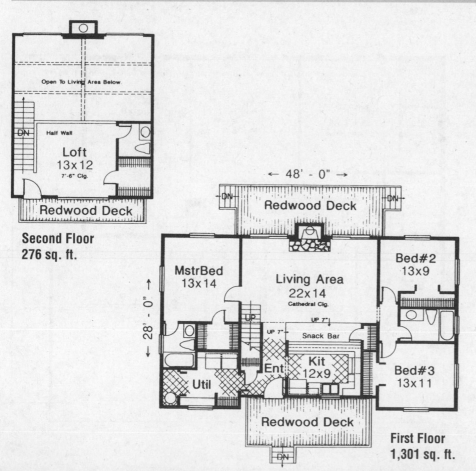

Loft
13x12
7'-6" Clg.

Open To Living Area Below.

Half Wall

DN

Redwood Deck

Second Floor
276 sq. ft.

← 48' - 0" →

DN — **Redwood Deck** — DN

MstrBed
13x14

Living Area
22x14
Cathedral Clg.

Bed#2
13x9

UP

UP 7"

UP 7"

Snack Bar

28' - 0"

Ent

Kit
12x9

Bed#3
13x11

Util

Redwood Deck

DN

First Floor
1,301 sq. ft.

Special features

- Large living area is a great gathering place with enormous stone fireplace, cathedral ceiling and kitchen with snack bar nearby
- Second floor loft has half-wall creating an open atmosphere
- 3 bedrooms, 2 1/2 baths
- Crawl space foundation

Vaulted Ceiling And Lots Of Windows In Living Room

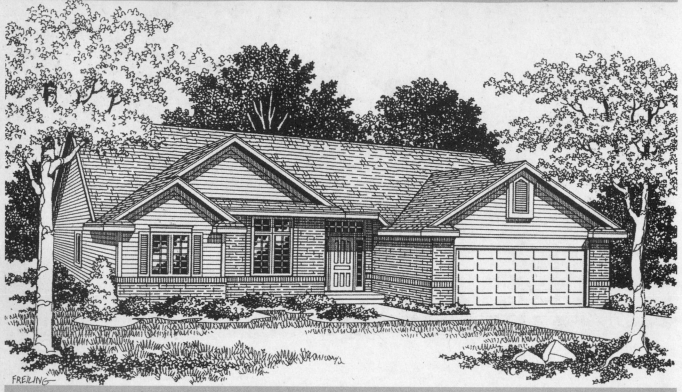

1,508 total square feet of living area

Price Code B

Special features

- A spacious kitchen layout makes food preparation easy
- A vaulted entry is inviting
- Varied ceiling heights through-out
- 3 bedrooms, 2 baths, 2-car garage
- Basement foundation

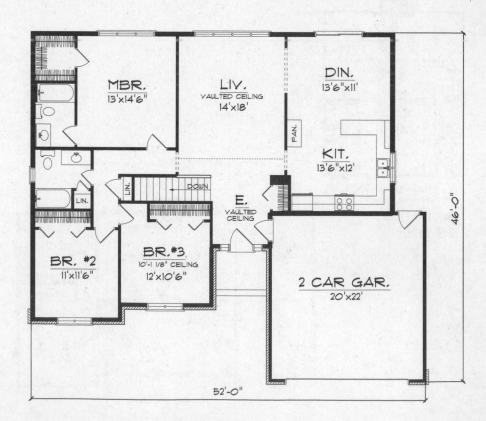

MBR.
13'x14'6"

LIV.
VAULTED CEILING
14'x18'

DIN.
13'6"x11'

PAN.

KIT.
13'6"x12'

LIN.

DOWN

E.
VAULTED CEILING

BR. #2
11'x11'6"

BR. #3
10'-1 1/8" CEILING
12'x10'6"

2 CAR GAR.
20'x22'

46'-0"

52'-0"

Ranch Design With All The Luxuries

© HOME DESIGN SERVICES, INC.

1,627 total square feet of living area

Price Code B

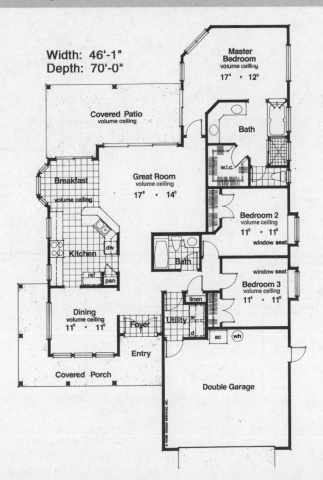

Width: 46'-1"
Depth: 70'-0"

Covered Patio
volume ceiling

Master Bedroom
volume ceiling
17⁴ • 12⁰

Bath

w.l.c.

Breakfast
volume ceiling

Great Room
volume ceiling
17⁸ • 14⁰

Bedroom 2
volume ceiling
11⁰ • 11⁰
window seat

Kitchen

dw

Bath

window seat

ref   pan

Bedroom 3
volume ceiling
11⁴ • 11⁰

Dining
volume ceiling
11⁰ • 11⁰

Foyer

Utility

linen

w

d

Entry

ac   wh

Covered Porch

Double Garage

Special features

- Bay-shaped breakfast room is sunny and bright
- Angled window wall and volume ceiling in master bedroom adds interest
- Box bay windows are featured in secondary bedrooms
- 3 bedrooms, 2 baths, 2-car garage
- Slab foundation

TO ORDER BLUEPRINTS USE THE FORM ON PAGE 15 OR CALL TOLL-FREE 1-877-671-6036
View thousands more home plans online at www.familyhandyman.com/homeplans

27

Dramatic Cathedral Ceilings

1,436 total square feet of living area

Price Code A

Special features

- Covered entry is inviting
- Kitchen has handy breakfast bar which overlooks great room and dining room
- Private master suite with bath and walk-in closet is separate from other bedrooms
- 3 bedrooms, 2 baths, 2-car garage
- Basement foundation

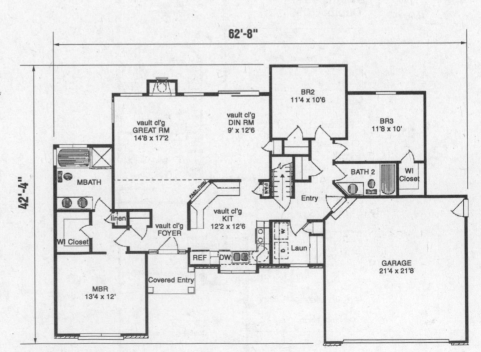

Formal Living And Dining Rooms

1,890 total square feet of living area

Price Code C

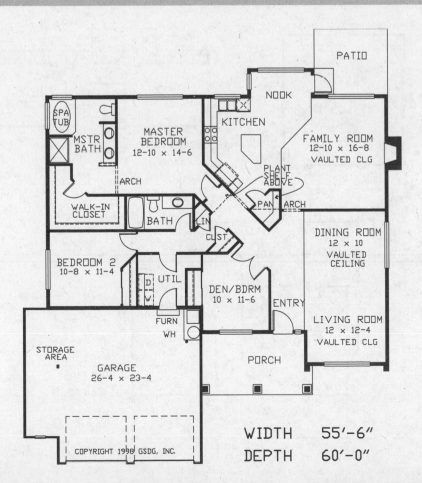

WIDTH   55'-6"
DEPTH   60'-0"

COPYRIGHT 1998 GSDG, INC.

Special features

- Inviting covered porch
- Vaulted ceilings in living, dining and family rooms
- Kitchen is open to family room and nook
- Large walk-in pantry in kitchen
- Arch accented master bath has spa tub, dual sinks and walk-in closet
- 3 bedrooms, 2 baths, 2-car garage
- Crawl space foundation

TO ORDER BLUEPRINTS USE THE FORM ON PAGE 15 OR CALL TOLL-FREE 1-877-671-6036
View thousands more home plans online at www.familyhandyman.com/homeplans

29

Two-Story Foyer Adds Spacious Feeling

1,814 total square feet of living area

Price Code D

Special features

- Large master suite includes a spacious bath with garden tub, separate shower and large walk-in closet

- Spacious kitchen and dining area brightened by large windows and patio access

- Detached two-car garage with walkway leading to house adds charm to this country home

- Large front porch

- 3 bedrooms, 2 1/2 baths, 2-car detached side entry garage

- Crawl space foundation, drawings also include slab foundation

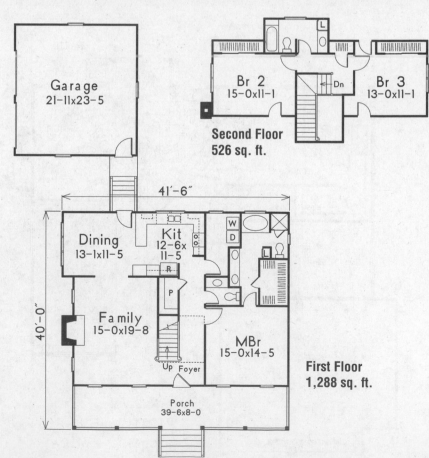

Garage
21-11x23-5

Second Floor
526 sq. ft.

Br 2
15-0x11-1

Br 3
13-0x11-1

Dn

41'-6"

40'-0"

Dining
13-1x11-5

Kit
12-6x 11-5

W D

R

P

Family
15-0x19-8

MBr
15-0x14-5

Up Foyer

Porch
39-6x8-0

First Floor
1,288 sq. ft.

30

TO ORDER BLUEPRINTS USE THE FORM ON PAGE 15 OR CALL TOLL-FREE 1-877-671-6036
View thousands more home plans online at www.familyhandyman.com/homeplans

Inviting Country Home

1,757 total square feet of living area

Price Code B

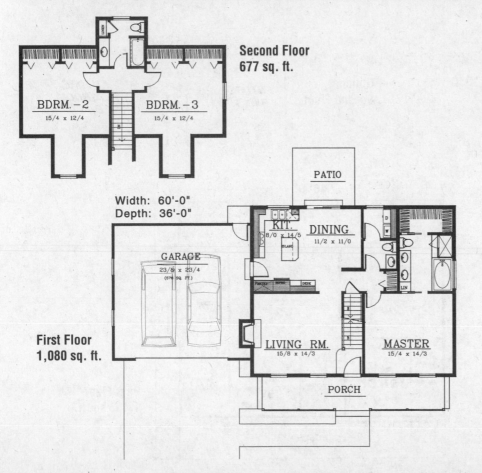

Second Floor
677 sq. ft.

BDRM. – 2
15/4 x 12/4

BDRM. – 3
15/4 x 12/4

Width: 60'-0"
Depth: 36'-0"

PATIO

GARAGE
23/8 x 23/4
(576 SQ. FT.)

KIT.
8/0 x 14/5

DINING
11/2 x 11/0

LIVING RM.
15/8 x 14/3

MASTER
15/4 x 14/3

First Floor
1,080 sq. ft.

PORCH

Special features

- Energy efficient home with 2" x 6" exterior walls

- First floor master bedroom has privacy as well as its own bath and walk-in closet

- Cozy living room includes fireplace for warmth

- 3 bedrooms, 2 1/2 baths, 2-car garage

- Crawl space or slab foundation, please specify when ordering

TO ORDER BLUEPRINTS USE THE FORM ON PAGE 15 OR CALL TOLL-FREE 1-877-671-6036
View thousands more home plans online at www.familyhandyman.com/homeplans

31

Decorative Accents Featured On Front Porch

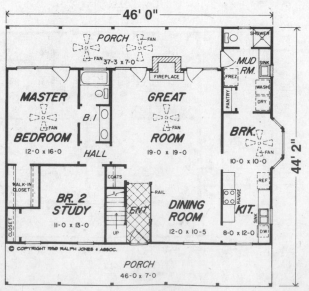

1,455 total square feet of living area

Price Code A

Special features

- Spacious mud room has a large pantry, space for a freezer, sink/counter area and bath with shower

- Bedroom #2 can easily be converted to a study or office area

- Optional second floor bedroom and playroom have an additional 744 square feet of living area

- 2 bedrooms, 2 baths

- Slab or crawl space foundation, please specify when ordering

Optional Second Floor

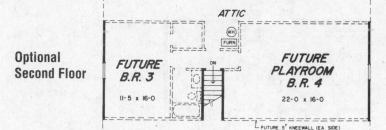

ATTIC

FUTURE B.R. 3
11-5 x 16-0

FUTURE PLAYROOM B.R. 4
22-0 x 16-0

FUTURE 5' KNEEWALL (EA. SIDE)

46' 0"

PORCH
37-3 x 7-0

FIREPLACE

MUD RM.

MASTER BEDROOM
12-0 x 16-0

B.1

HALL

GREAT ROOM
19-0 x 19-0

BRK.
10-0 x 10-0

PANTRY

FREZ

WASH

DRY

SHOWER

SINK

44' 2"

WALK-IN CLOSET

BR. 2 STUDY
11-0 x 13-0

COATS

ENT

RAIL

DINING ROOM
12-0 x 10-5

KIT.
8-0 x 12-0

REF

RANGE

SINK

DW

CLOSET

UP

© COPYRIGHT 1998 RALPH JONES & ASSOC.

First Floor 1,455 sq. ft.

PORCH
46-0 x 7-0

Scalloped Front Porch

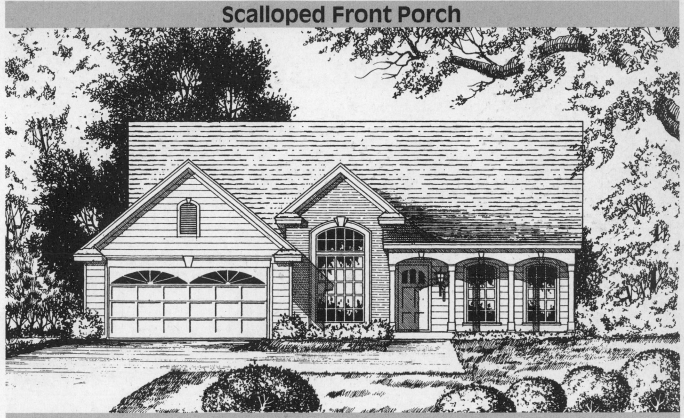

1,374 total square feet of living area   **Price Code A**

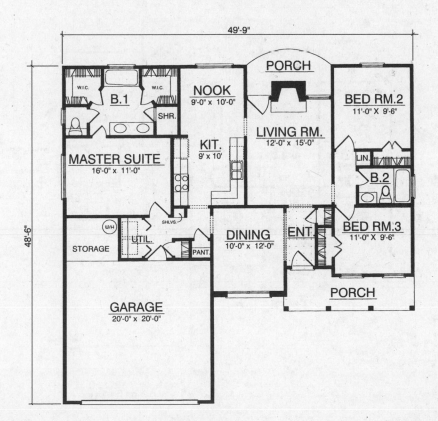

Special features

■ Garage has extra storage space

■ Spacious living room has fireplace

■ Well-designed kitchen with adjacent breakfast nook

■ Separated master suite maintains privacy

■ 3 bedrooms, 2 baths, 2-car garage

■ Slab or crawl space foundation, please specify when ordering

Whirlpool With Skylight Above

1,911 total square feet of living area

Price Code C

Special features

- Large entry opens into beautiful great room with angled see-through fireplace

- Terrific design includes kitchen and breakfast area with adjacent sunny bayed hearth room

- Luxury master suite has privacy from other bedrooms

- 3 bedrooms, 2 baths, 2-car garage

- Basement foundation

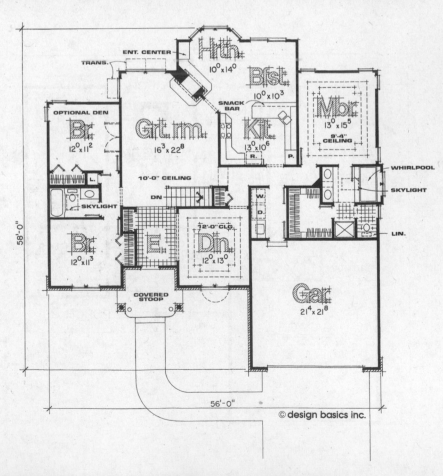

© design basics inc.

34

TO ORDER BLUEPRINTS USE THE FORM ON PAGE 15 OR CALL TOLL-FREE 1-877-671-6036
View thousands more home plans online at www.familyhandyman.com/homeplans

Stylish Living For A Narrow Lot

1,575 total square feet of living area

Price Code B

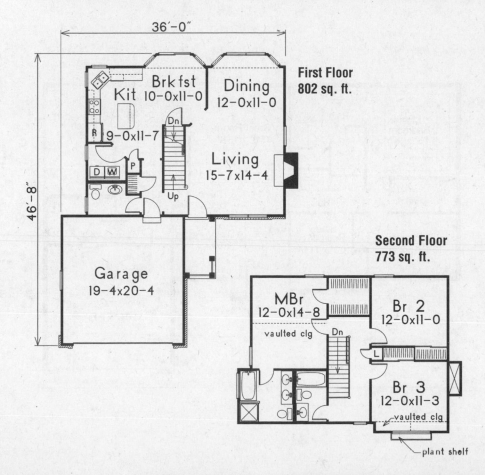

36'-0"

46'-8"

First Floor
802 sq. ft.

Kit 9-0x11-7

Brkfst 10-0x11-0

Dining 12-0x11-0

Dn

Living 15-7x14-4

Up

D W P

R

Garage 19-4x20-4

Second Floor
773 sq. ft.

MBr 12-0x14-8
vaulted clg

Br 2 12-0x11-0

Dn

L

Br 3 12-0x11-3
vaulted clg

plant shelf

Special features

- Inviting porch leads to spacious living and dining rooms
- Kitchen with corner windows features an island snack bar, attractive breakfast room bay, convenient laundry and built-in pantry
- A luxury bath and walk-in closet adorn master bedroom suite
- 3 bedrooms, 2 1/2 baths, 2-car garage
- Basement foundation

TO ORDER BLUEPRINTS USE THE FORM ON PAGE 15 OR CALL TOLL-FREE 1-877-671-6036
View thousands more home plans online at www.familyhandyman.com/homeplans

35

Sloped Ceilings Throughout

1,782 total square feet of living area　　　　　**Price Code B**

Special features

- Outstanding breakfast area accesses the outdoors through French doors
- Generous counter space and cabinets combine to create an ideal kitchen
- The master bedroom is enhanced with a beautiful bath featuring a whirlpool tub and double-bowl vanity
- 3 bedrooms, 2 baths, 2-car garage
- Basement foundation

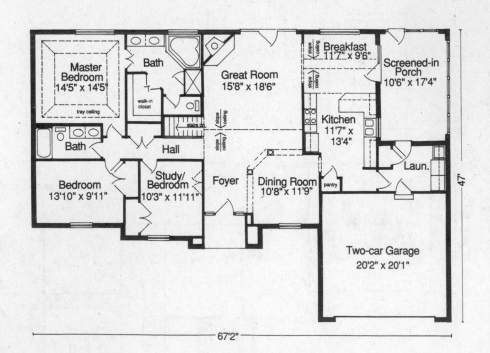

Charming Design

1,840 total square feet of living area

Price Code C

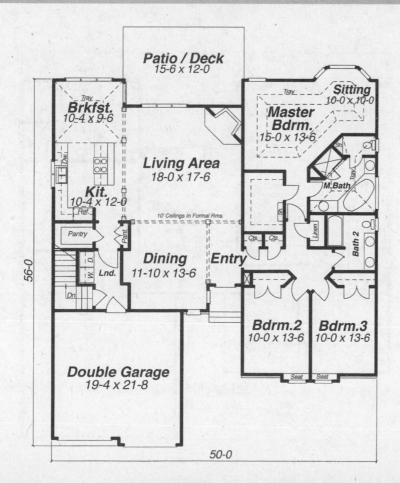

Patio / Deck
15-6 x 12-0

Tray
Brkfst.
10-4 x 9-6

Tray
Sitting
10-0 x 10-0

Master Bdrm.
15-0 x 13-6

Living Area
18-0 x 17-6

M. Bath

Kit.
10-4 x 12-0

Ref.

Pantry

10' Ceilings In Formal Rms.

Linen

Bath 2

Cts. Cts.

Dining
11-10 x 13-6

Entry

W. D.

Lnd.

Dn

Bdrm.2
10-0 x 13-6

Bdrm.3
10-0 x 13-6

Seat Seat

56-0

Double Garage
19-4 x 21-8

50-0

Special features

- Master suite has a private sitting area with large bay window
- Sunny breakfast room has wall of windows and easy access to kitchen
- Formal dining area has decorative columns separating it from spacious living area
- 3 bedrooms, 2 1/2 baths, 2-car garage
- Walk-out basement, slab or crawl space foundation, please specify when ordering

TO ORDER BLUEPRINTS USE THE FORM ON PAGE 15 OR CALL TOLL-FREE 1-877-671-6036
View thousands more home plans online at www.familyhandyman.com/homeplans

37

Built-In Computer Desk

1,525 total square feet of living area

Price Code B

Special features

- Corner fireplace highlighted in great room

- Unique glass block window over whirlpool tub in master bath

- Open bar overlooks both the kitchen and great room

- Breakfast room leads to an outdoor grilling and covered porch

- 3 bedrooms, 2 baths, 2-car garage

- Basement, walk-out basement, crawl space or slab foundation, please specify when ordering

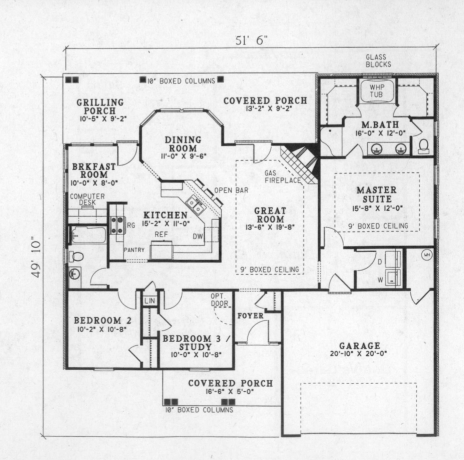

Plan #706-0335

Wonderful Great Room

1,865 total square feet of living area

Price Code D

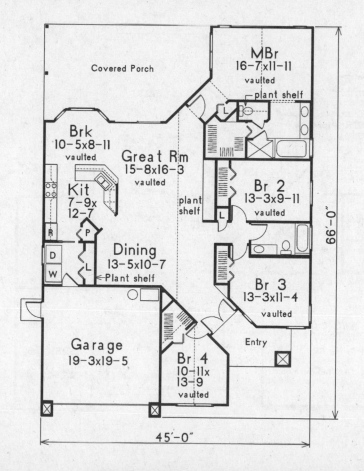

Special features

- Large foyer opens into expansive dining area and great room
- Home features vaulted ceilings throughout
- Master suite features bath with double-bowl vanity, shower, tub and toilet in separate room for privacy
- 4 bedrooms, 2 baths, 2-car garage
- Slab foundation, drawings also include crawl space foundation

TO ORDER BLUEPRINTS USE THE FORM ON PAGE 15 OR CALL TOLL-FREE 1-877-671-6036
View thousands more home plans online at www.familyhandyman.com/homeplans

39

Distinctive Ranch Home With A Columned Porch

1,860 total square feet of living area

Price Code D

Special features

- Dining room has an 11' stepped ceiling with a bay window creating a pleasant dining experience

- Breakfast room has a 12' sloped ceiling with French doors leading to a covered porch

- Great room has a columned arched entrance, a built-in media center and a fireplace

- 3 bedrooms, 2 baths, 2-car side entry garage

- Basement, crawl space or slab foundation, please specify when ordering

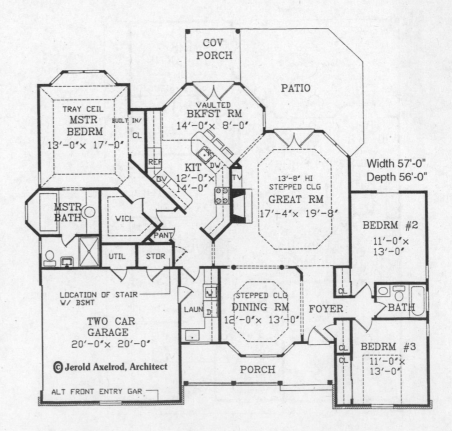

COV PORCH

PATIO

TRAY CEIL
MSTR
BEDRM
13'-0" x 17'-0"

BUILT IN/
CL

VAULTED
BKFST RM
14'-0" x 8'-0"

Width 57'-0"
Depth 56'-0"

KIT
12'-0" x
14'-0"

REF

DV

DW

TV

13'-8' HI
STEPPED CLG
GREAT RM
17'-4" x 19'-8"

BEDRM #2
11'-0" x
13'-0"

MSTR
BATH

WICL

PANT

UTIL

STOR

LOCATION OF STAIR
W/ BSMT

LAUN

D

STEPPED CLG
DINING RM
12'-0" x 13'-0"

FOYER

BATH

TWO CAR
GARAGE
20'-0" x 20'-0"

© Jerold Axelrod, Architect

PORCH

BEDRM #3
11'-0" x
13'-0"

CL

CL

ALT FRONT ENTRY GAR

Blends Open And Private Living Areas

1,996 total square feet of living area

Price Code C

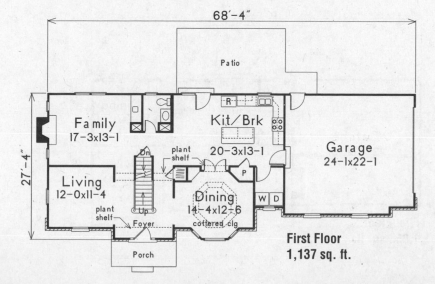

Br 3
11-4x10-10

Br 2
12-0x11-3

MBr
14-4x16-5
coffered clg

Second Floor
859 sq. ft.

Dn
open to below
skylt
skylt

68'-4"

27'-4"

Patio

Family
17-3x13-1

Kit/Brk
20-3x13-1

Garage
24-1x22-1

Living
12-0x11-4

Dining
14-4x12-6
coffered clg

plant shelf
plant shelf
Dn
Up
Foyer
Porch
W D
R
P

First Floor
1,137 sq. ft.

Special features

- Dining area features octagon-shaped coffered ceiling and built-in china cabinet

- Both the master bath and second floor bath have cheerful skylights

- Family room includes wet bar and fireplace flanked by attractive quarter round windows

- 9' ceilings throughout first floor with plant shelving in foyer and dining area

- 3 bedrooms, 2 1/2 baths, 2-car side entry garage

- Basement foundation, drawings also include crawl space and slab foundations

TO ORDER BLUEPRINTS USE THE FORM ON PAGE 15 OR CALL TOLL-FREE 1-877-671-6036
View thousands more home plans online at www.familyhandyman.com/homeplans

41

Country Classic With Modern Floor Plan

1,921 total square feet of living area

Price Code D

Special features

- Energy efficient home with 2" x 6" exterior walls

- Sunken family room includes a built-in entertainment center and coffered ceiling

- Sunken formal living room features a coffered ceiling

- Dressing area has double sinks, spa tub, shower and French door to private deck

- Large front porch adds to home's appeal

- 3 bedrooms, 2 1/2 baths, 2-car garage

- Basement foundation

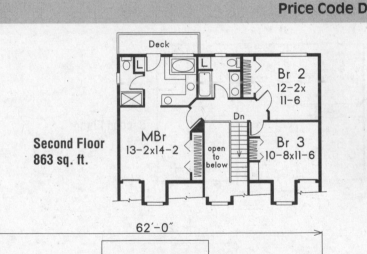

Deck

Second Floor 863 sq. ft.

Br 2
12-2x 11-6

MBr
13-2x14-2

Dn

open to below

Br 3
10-8x11-6

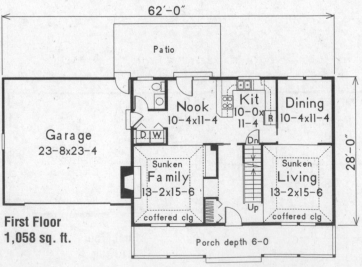

62'-0"

Patio

Garage
23-8x23-4

Nook
10-4x11-4

Kit
10-0x 11-4

Dining
10-4x11-4

D W

Dn

28'-0"

Sunken
Family
13-2x15-6
coffered clg

Up

Sunken
Living
13-2x15-6
coffered clg

First Floor 1,058 sq. ft.

Porch depth 6-0

42

TO ORDER BLUEPRINTS USE THE FORM ON PAGE 15 OR CALL TOLL-FREE 1-877-671-6036
View thousands more home plans online at www.familyhandyman.com/homeplans

Plan #706-HP-C316

A Charming Home Loaded With Extras

1,997 total square feet of living area

Price Code C

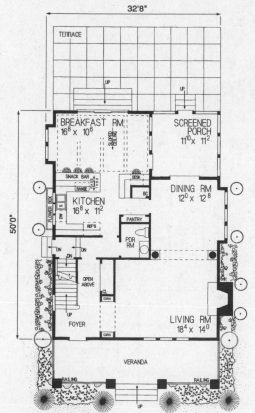

First Floor
1,111 sq. ft.

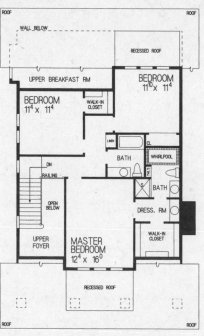

Second Floor
886 sq. ft.

Special features

- Screened porch leads to a rear terrace with access to the breakfast room
- Living and dining rooms combine adding spaciousness to the floor plan
- Other welcome amenities include boxed windows in breakfast and dining rooms, a fireplace in living room and a pass-through snack bar in the kitchen
- 3 bedrooms, 2 1/2 baths
- Basement foundation

TO ORDER BLUEPRINTS USE THE FORM ON PAGE 15 OR CALL TOLL-FREE 1-877-671-6036
View thousands more home plans online at www.familyhandyman.com/homeplans

43

Cozy Front Porch Welcomes Guests

1,393 total square feet of living area

Price Code B

Special features

- L-shaped kitchen features walk-in pantry, island cooktop and is convenient to laundry room and dining area

- Master bedroom features large walk-in closet and private bath with separate tub and shower

- Convenient storage/coat closet in hall

- View to the patio from the dining area

- 3 bedrooms, 2 baths, 2-car detached garage

- Crawl space foundation, drawings also include slab foundation

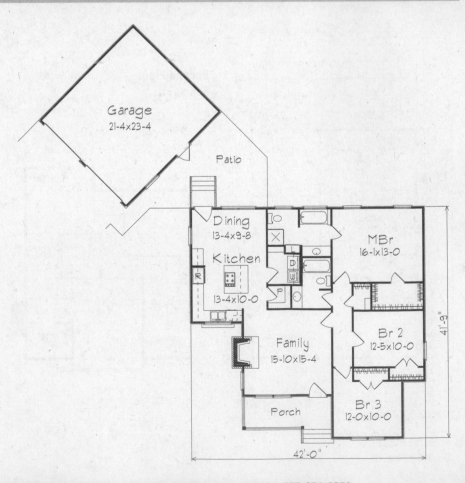

Handsome Double Brick Gables

1,553 total square feet of living area | Price Code B

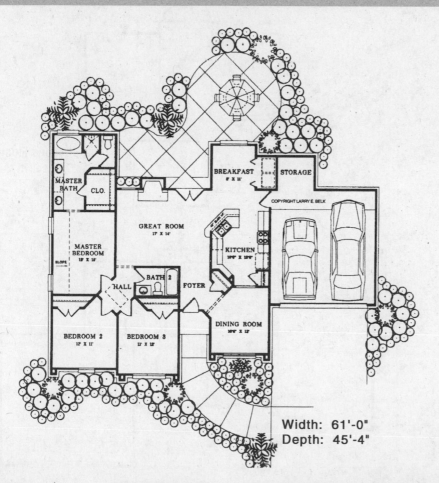

Width: 61'-0"
Depth: 45'-4"

Special features

- Kitchen counter extends into great room with space for dining
- Extra storage provided in garage
- Sloped ceiling in master bedroom adds a dramatic feel
- 3 bedrooms, 2 baths, 2-car garage
- Crawl space or slab foundation, please specify when ordering

TO ORDER BLUEPRINTS USE THE FORM ON PAGE 15 OR CALL TOLL-FREE 1-877-671-6036
View thousands more home plans online at www.familyhandyman.com/homeplans

45

Striking, Covered Arched Entry

1,859 total square feet of living area

Price Code D

Special features

- Fireplace highlights vaulted great room
- Master suite includes large closet and private bath
- Kitchen adjoins breakfast room providing easy access to the outdoors
- 3 bedrooms, 2 1/2 baths, 2-car garage
- Basement foundation

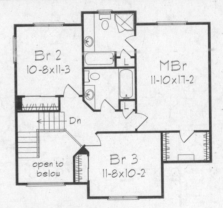

Br 2
10-8x11-3

MBr
11-10x17-2

Dn

Br 3
11-8x10-2

open to below

Second Floor 789 sq. ft.

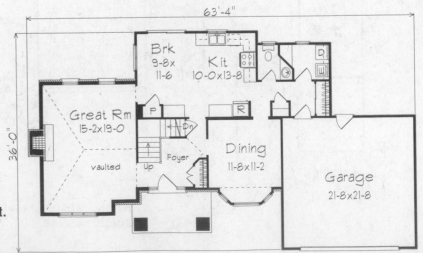

63'-4"

36'-0"

Brk
9-8x
11-6

Kit
10-0x13-8

Great Rm
15-2x19-0

vaulted

P

Dn

Up

Foyer

Dining
11-8x11-2

Garage
21-8x21-8

R

First Floor 1,070 sq. ft.

Inviting Victorian Details

947 total square feet of living area

Price Code AA

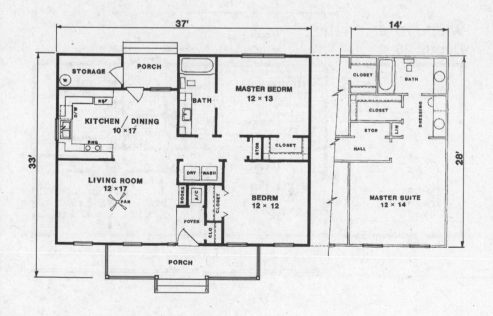

Special features

- Efficiently designed kitchen/ dining area accesses the outdoors onto a rear porch
- Future expansion plans included which allow the home to become 392 square feet larger with 3 bedrooms and 2 baths
- 2 bedrooms, 1 bath
- Crawl space or slab foundation, please specify when ordering

TO ORDER BLUEPRINTS USE THE FORM ON PAGE 15 OR CALL TOLL-FREE 1-877-671-6036
View thousands more home plans online at www.familyhandyman.com/homeplans

47

Vaulted Ceilings Add A Sense Of Spaciousness

1,408 total square feet of living area

Price Code A

Special features

- A bright country kitchen boasts an abundance of counterspace and cupboards
- The front entry is sheltered by a broad verandah
- A spa tub is brightened by a box bay window in the master bath
- 3 bedrooms, 2 baths, 2-car side entry garage
- Basement or crawl space foundation, please specify when ordering

Width: 70'-0"
Depth: 28'-0"

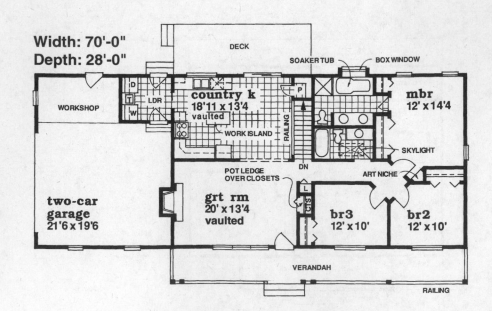

48

TO ORDER BLUEPRINTS USE THE FORM ON PAGE 15 OR CALL TOLL-FREE 1-877-671-6036
View thousands more home plans online at www.familyhandyman.com/homeplans

Colossal Great Room

1,599 total square feet of living area   **Price Code B**

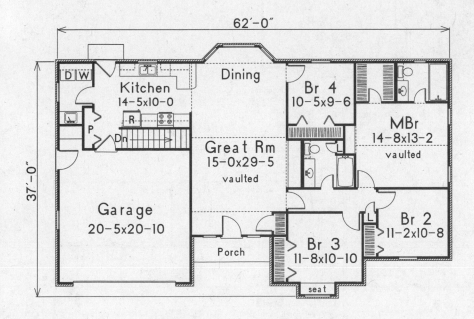

Special features

- Efficiently designed kitchen with large pantry and easy access to laundry room
- Bedroom #3 has a charming window seat
- Master bedroom has a full bath and large walk-in closet
- 4 bedrooms, 2 baths, 2-car garage
- Basement foundation, drawings also include crawl space and slab foundations

TO ORDER BLUEPRINTS USE THE FORM ON PAGE 15 OR CALL TOLL-FREE 1-877-671-6036
View thousands more home plans online at www.familyhandyman.com/homeplans

49

Tranquility Of An Atrium Cottage

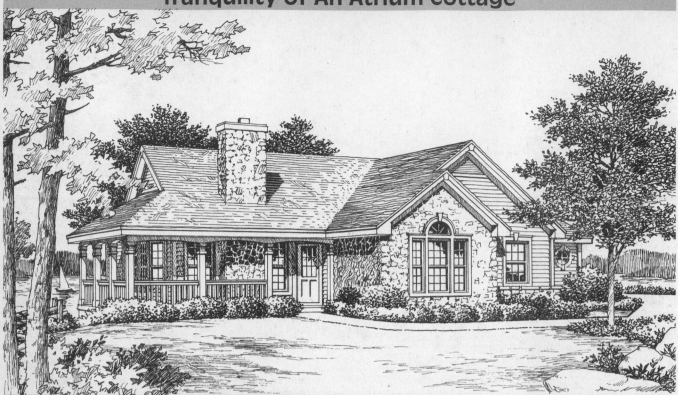

1,384 total square feet of living area

Price Code B

Rear View

Special features

- Wrap-around country porch for peaceful evenings

- Vaulted great room enjoys a large bay window, stone fireplace, pass-through kitchen and awesome rear views through atrium window wall

- Master suite features double entry doors, walk-in closet and a fabulous bath

- Atrium open to 611 square feet of optional living area below

- 2 bedrooms, 2 baths, 1-car side entry garage

- Walk-out basement foundation

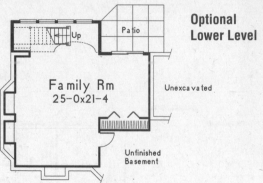

Optional Lower Level

Patio

Family Rm
25-0x21-4

Unexcavated

Unfinished Basement

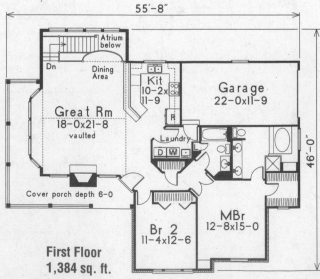

55'-8"

Up

Dn

Atrium below

Dining Area

Kit
10-2x11-9

Garage
22-0x11-9

Great Rm
18-0x21-8
vaulted

Laundry

DW

46'-0"

Cover porch depth 6-0

Br 2
11-4x12-6

MBr
12-8x15-0

First Floor
1,384 sq. ft.

TO ORDER BLUEPRINTS USE THE FORM ON PAGE 15 OR CALL TOLL-FREE 1-877-671-6036
View thousands more home plans online at www.familyhandyman.com/homeplans

50

Charming Wrap-Around Porch

1,879 total square feet of living area

Price Code C

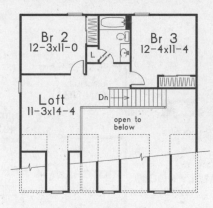

**Second Floor
565 sq. ft.**

Br 2
12-3x11-0

Br 3
12-4x11-4

Loft
11-3x14-4

Dn

open to below

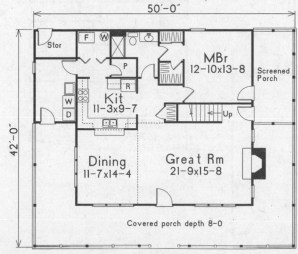

50'-0"

Stor

F W

MBr
12-10x13-8

Screened Porch

P

R

Kit
11-3x9-7

W
D

42'-0"

Dining
11-7x14-4

Great Rm
21-9x15-8

Up

**First Floor
1,314 sq. ft.**

Covered porch depth 8-0

Special features

- Open floor plan on both floors makes home appear larger
- Loft area overlooks great room or can become an optional fourth bedroom
- Large walk-in pantry in kitchen and large storage in rear of home with access from exterior
- 3 bedrooms, 2 baths
- Crawl space foundation

Covered Rear Porch Is A Nice Dining Place

1,593 total square feet of living area

Price Code C

Special features

- Large sitting area is enjoyed by the master bedroom which also features a walk-in closet and bath

- Centrally located kitchen accesses the family, dining and breakfast rooms with ease

- Storage/mechanical area is ideal for seasonal storage or hobby supplies

- 3 bedrooms, 2 baths, 2-car garage

- Basement, crawl space or slab foundation, please specify when ordering

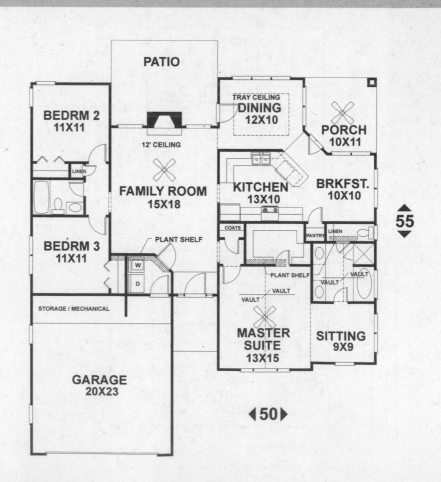

PATIO

BEDRM 2
11X11

TRAY CEILING
DINING
12X10

PORCH
10X11

12' CEILING

LINEN

FAMILY ROOM
15X18

KITCHEN
13X10

BRKFST.
10X10

55

PLANT SHELF

COATS

PANTRY LINEN

BEDRM 3
11X11

W
D

PLANT SHELF

VAULT VAULT

VAULT

STORAGE / MECHANICAL

VAULT

MASTER SUITE
13X15

SITTING
9X9

GARAGE
20X23

◄50►

Open Floor Plan With Extra Amenities

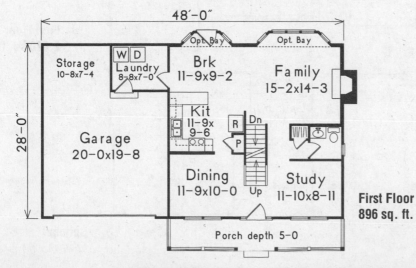

1,680 total square feet of living area

Price Code B

Second Floor
784 sq. ft.

Br 2
11-8x10-9

L

Dn

Br 3
11-8x10-9

MBr
11-10x15-0

Special features

- Compact and efficient layout in an affordable package
- Second floor has three bedrooms all with oversized closets
- All bedrooms on second floor for privacy
- 3 bedrooms, 2 1/2 baths, 2-car garage
- Basement foundation

48´-0"

28´-0"

Storage
10-8x7-4

W D
Laundry
8-8x7-0

Opt. Bay

Brk
11-9x9-2

Opt. Bay

Family
15-2x14-3

Garage
20-0x19-8

Kit
11-9x
9-6

R

Dn

P

Up

Dining
11-9x10-0

Study
11-10x8-11

First Floor
896 sq. ft.

Porch depth 5-0

TO ORDER BLUEPRINTS USE THE FORM ON PAGE 15 OR CALL TOLL-FREE 1-877-671-6036
View thousands more home plans online at www.familyhandyman.com/homeplans

53

Exciting Atrium

Rear View

2,070 total square feet of living area

Price Code C

Special features

- Great room has fireplace, wet bar and rear views through two-story vaulted atrium

- Dining area near U-shaped kitchen, walk-in pantry, computer center and breakfast balcony with atrium overlook

- Master bath has Roman whirlpool, TV alcove, separate shower/toilet area and closet

- Atrium open to 1,062 square feet of optional living area below

- 3 bedrooms, 2 baths, 2-car drive-under garage with storage area

- Walk-out basement foundation

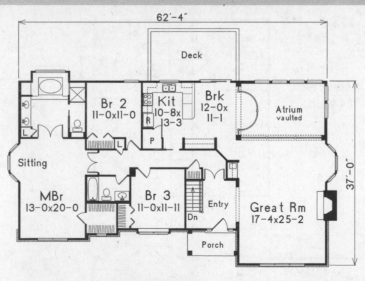

62'-4"

Deck

Br 2
11-0x11-0

Kit
10-8x
3-3

Brk
12-0x
11-1

Atrium
vaulted

Sitting

MBr
13-0x20-0

Br 3
11-0x11-11

Entry

Dn

Great Rm
17-4x25-2

Porch

37'-0"

**First Floor
2,070 sq. ft.**

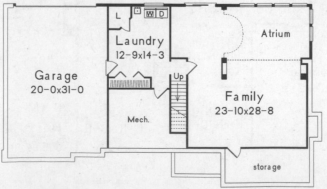

Laundry
12-9x14-3

Atrium

Garage
20-0x31-0

Up

Family
23-10x28-8

Mech.

storage

**Optional
Lower Level**

TO ORDER BLUEPRINTS USE THE FORM ON PAGE 15 OR CALL TOLL-FREE 1-877-671-6036
View thousands more home plans online at www.familyhandyman.com/homeplans

Dormers Grace This Cozy Country Home

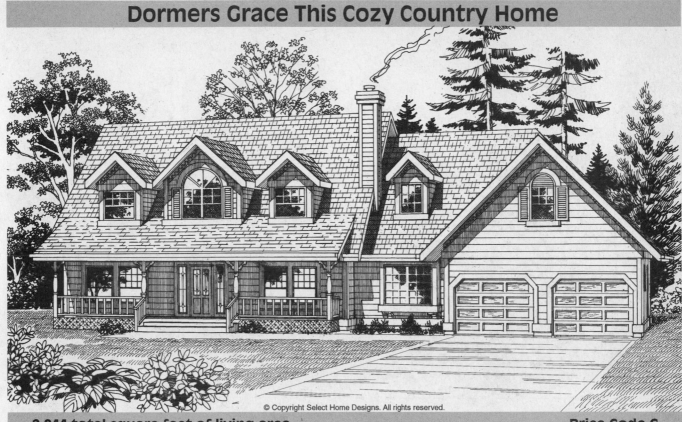

2,044 total square feet of living area

Price Code C

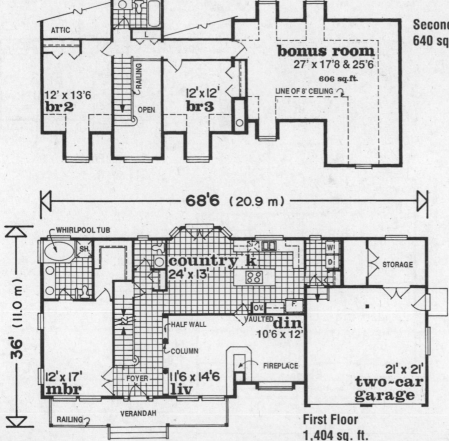

Second Floor
640 sq. ft.

ATTIC

bonus room
27' x 17'8 & 25'6
606 sq.ft.
LINE OF 8' CEILING

12' x 13'6
br 2

RAILING

OPEN

12' x 12'
br 3

68'6 (20.9 m)

36' (11.0 m)

WHIRLPOOL TUB
SH

country k
24' x 13'

STORAGE

W

HALF WALL
COLUMN

VAULTED din
10'6 x 12'

OV.
F.

FIREPLACE

12' x 17'
mbr

FOYER

11'6 x 14'6
liv

21' x 21'
two-car
garage

RAILING
VERANDAH

First Floor
1,404 sq. ft.

Special features

- Bonus room on the second floor has an additional 606 square feet of living area

- Country kitchen is oversized for large family gatherings

- 3 bedrooms, 2 1/2 baths, 2-car garage

- Basement or crawl space foundation, please specify when ordering

Quaint Exterior, Full Front Porch

1,657 total square feet of living area

Price Code B

Special features

- Stylish pass-through between living and dining areas
- Master bedroom is secluded from living area for privacy
- Large windows in breakfast and dining areas
- 3 bedrooms, 2 1/2 baths, 2-car drive under garage
- Basement foundation

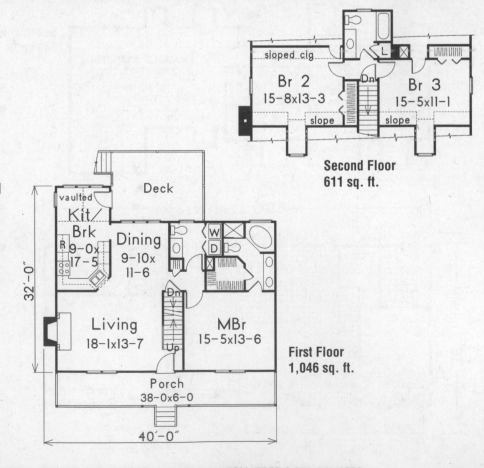

Second Floor
611 sq. ft.

Br 2
15-8x13-3

Br 3
15-5x11-1

sloped clg

slope

slope

Dn

First Floor
1,046 sq. ft.

Deck

vaulted

Kit/ Brk
9-0x 17-5

Dining
9-10x 11-6

W D

Living
18-1x13-7

MBr
15-5x13-6

Dn

Up

32'-0"

40'-0"

Porch
38-0x6-0

Stunning Triple Dormers And Arches

1,698 total square feet of living area

Price Code B

GARAGE
21'-0"x22'-0"
(CARPORT OR NO
GARAGE OPTIONAL)

16' OVERHEAD DOOR

WORK BENCH/STORAGE

PATIO
20'-0"x12'-0"

WALK-IN
CLOSET

PANTRY

KITCHEN
13'-0"x10'-0"

DINING
11'-0"x10'-0"

BEDROOM #3
13'-0"x11'-10"

HALL

MSTR
BATH

PWDR

COLUMNS

OPTIONAL PRIVACY DOOR
(POCKET)

BATH

LINEN

SITTING
AREA

8' CLG

BUILT-IN

GREAT ROOM
24'-0"x20'-0"
(10' CLG)

FP

BUILT-IN

RIDGE OF VAULT

MASTER BEDROOM
15'-5"x16'-0"
(VAULTED CLG)

BEDROOM #2
13'-0"x11'-10"

OPTIONAL
ROOM DIVIDER

Width 59'-0"
Depth 61'-0"

COVERED PORCH
25'-0"x8'-0"
(10' CLG)

Special features

- Vaulted master bedroom has a private bath and a walk-in closet
- Decorative columns flank the entrance to the dining room
- Open great room is perfect for gathering family together
- 3 bedrooms, 2 1/2 baths, 2-car side entry garage with storage
- Basement, crawl space or slab foundation, please specify when ordering

TO ORDER BLUEPRINTS USE THE FORM ON PAGE 15 OR CALL TOLL-FREE 1-877-671-6036
View thousands more home plans online at www.familyhandyman.com/homeplans

57

Designed For Handicap Access

1,578 total square feet of living area

Price Code B

Special features

- Plenty of closet, linen and storage space
- Covered porches in the front and rear of the home add charm to this design
- Open floor plan has unique angled layout
- 3 bedrooms, 2 baths, 2-car garage
- Basement foundation

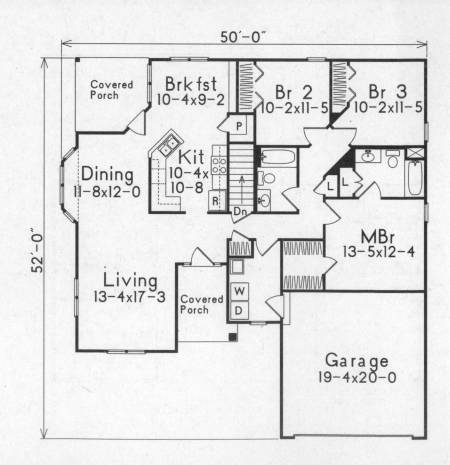

50'-0"

52'-0"

Covered Porch

Brk fst
10-4x9-2

Br 2
10-2x11-5

Br 3
10-2x11-5

P

Kit
10-4x
10-8

R

Dn

L L

Dining
11-8x12-0

MBr
13-5x12-4

Living
13-4x17-3

Covered Porch

W
D

Garage
19-4x20-0

58

TO ORDER BLUEPRINTS USE THE FORM ON PAGE 15 OR CALL TOLL-FREE 1-877-671-6036
View thousands more home plans online at www.familyhandyman.com/homeplans

Quaint Country Home

1,737 total square feet of living area

Price Code B

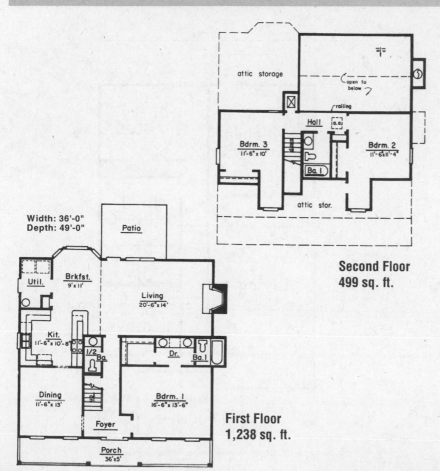

Width: 36'-0"
Depth: 49'-0"

Patio

Util.

Brkfst.
9' x 11'

Living
20'-6" x 14'

Kit.
11'-6" x 10'-8"

1/2 Ba.

Dr.

Ba. I

Dining
11'-6" x 13'

Bdrm. I
16'-6" x 13'-6"

Foyer

Porch
36' x 5'

First Floor
1,238 sq. ft.

attic storage

open to below

railing

Hall

Bdrm. 3
11'-6" x 10'

Bdrm. 2
11'-6" x 11'-4"

Ba. I

attic stor.

Second Floor
499 sq. ft.

Special features

- U-shaped kitchen, sunny bayed breakfast room and living area become one large gathering area
- Living area has sloped ceilings and a balcony overlook from second floor
- Second floor includes lots of storage area
- 3 bedrooms, 2 1/2 baths
- Slab or crawl space foundation, please specify when ordering

TO ORDER BLUEPRINTS USE THE FORM ON PAGE 15 OR CALL TOLL-FREE 1-877-671-6036
View thousands more home plans online at www.familyhandyman.com/homeplans

59

Four Bedroom Living For A Narrow Lot

1,452 total square feet of living area

Price Code A

Special features

- Large living room features cozy corner fireplace, bayed dining area and access from entry with guest closet

- Forward master bedroom suite enjoys having its own bath and linen closet

- Three additional bedrooms share a bath with double-bowl vanity

- 4 bedrooms, 2 baths

- Basement foundation

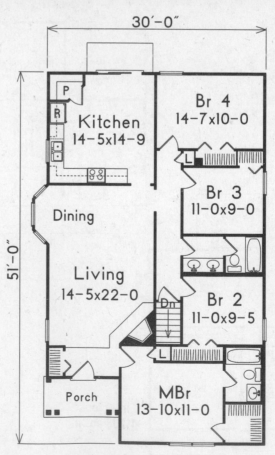

30'-0"

51'-0"

P
R
Kitchen
14-5x14-9

Br 4
14-7x10-0

L

Dining

Br 3
11-0x9-0

Living
14-5x22-0

Dn

Br 2
11-0x9-5

L

Porch

MBr
13-10x11-0

Comfortable One-Story Country Home

1,367 total square feet of living area

Price Code B

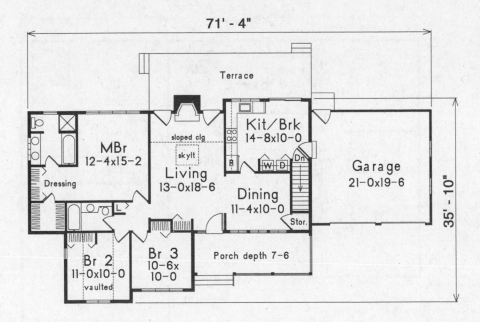

71' - 4"

Terrace

MBr
12-4x15-2

Dressing

sloped clg

skylt

Living
13-0x18-6

Kit/Brk
14-8x10-0

R

W D

Dn

Dining
11-4x10-0

Garage
21-0x19-6

35' - 10"

Stor.

Br 2
11-0x10-0
vaulted

Br 3
10-6x
10-0

Porch depth 7-6

Special features

- Neat front porch shelters the entrance
- Dining room has full wall of windows and a convenient storage area
- Breakfast area leads to the rear terrace through sliding doors
- Large living room with high ceiling, skylight and fireplace
- 3 bedrooms, 2 baths, 2-car garage
- Basement foundation, drawings also include slab foundation

Spacious Living In This Ranch

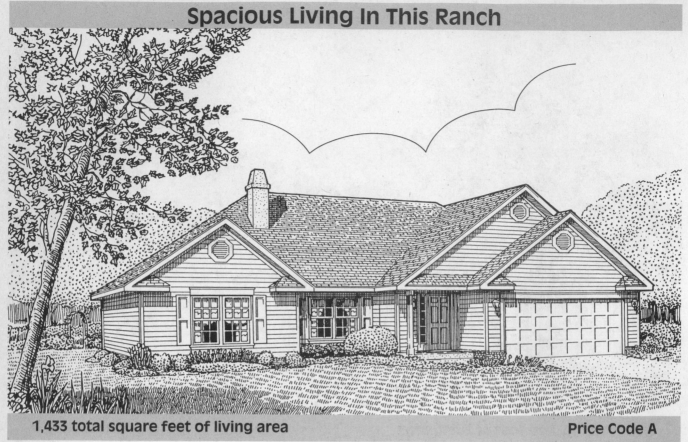

1,433 total square feet of living area

Price Code A

Special features

- Vaulted living room includes cozy fireplace and an oversized entertainment center

- Bedrooms #2 and #3 share a full bath

- Master bedroom has a full bath and large walk-in closet

- 3 bedrooms, 2 baths, 2-car garage

- Basement foundation, drawings also include crawl space and slab foundations

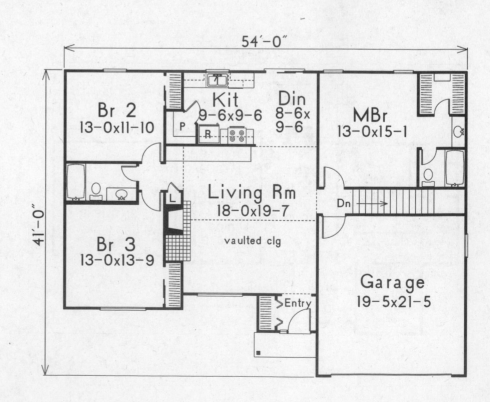

Double Gables Accent Facade

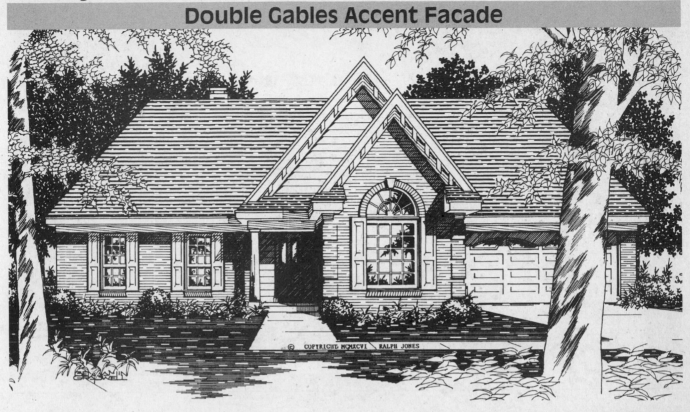

1,497 total square feet of living area   **Price Code A**

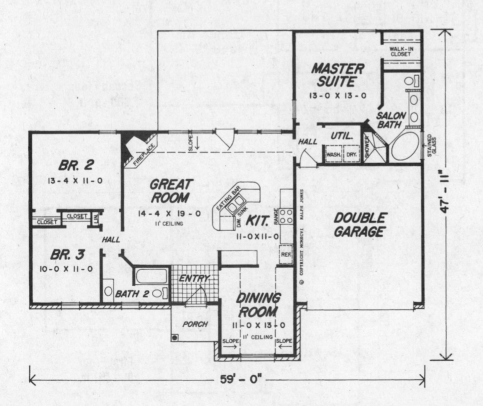

Special features

- Open living area with kitchen counter overlooking a cozy great room with fireplace
- Sloped ceiling accents dining room
- Master suite has privacy from other bedrooms
- 3 bedrooms, 2 baths, 2-car garage
- Slab foundation

TO ORDER BLUEPRINTS USE THE FORM ON PAGE 15 OR CALL TOLL-FREE 1-877-671-6036
View thousands more home plans online at www.familyhandyman.com/homeplans

63

Double Gables Create Appealing Facade

2,200 total square feet of living area

Price Code D

Special features

- Open first floor features convenient access to laundry area
- Second floor captures space above garage for large recreation area or future bedrooms
- Oversized country kitchen has plenty of space for entertaining
- 3 bedrooms, 2 1/2 baths, 2-car garage
- Basement foundation

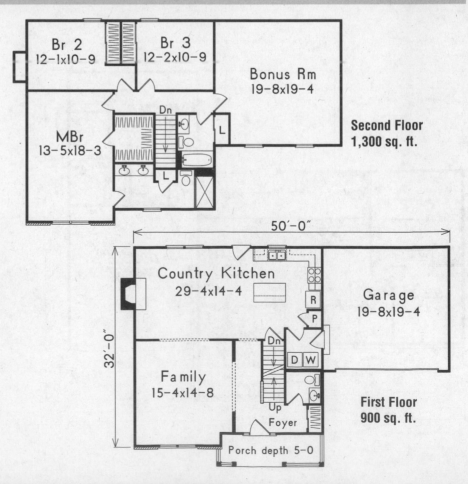

Br 2
12-1x10-9

Br 3
12-2x10-9

Bonus Rm
19-8x19-4

Dn

L

MBr
13-5x18-3

L

**Second Floor
1,300 sq. ft.**

50'-0"

Country Kitchen
29-4x14-4

R

P

Garage
19-8x19-4

32'-0"

Dn

D W

Family
15-4x14-8

Up

Foyer

**First Floor
900 sq. ft.**

Porch depth 5-0

64

TO ORDER BLUEPRINTS USE THE FORM ON PAGE 15 OR CALL TOLL-FREE 1-877-671-6036
View thousands more home plans online at www.familyhandyman.com/homeplans

Lovely, Spacious Floor Plan

1,558 total square feet of living area

Price Code B

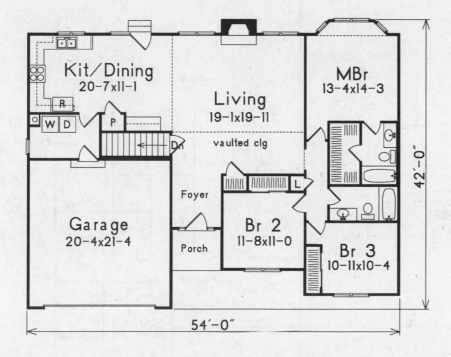

Special features

- Spacious utility room located conveniently between garage and kitchen/dining area
- Private bedrooms separated off main living area by hallway
- Enormous living area with fireplace and vaulted ceiling opens to kitchen and dining area
- Master suite enhanced with large bay window, walk-in closet and private bath
- 3 bedrooms, 2 baths, 2-car garage
- Basement foundation

Classy Master Bedroom

2,012 total square feet of living area

Price Code C

Special features

- Kitchen with eat-in breakfast bar overlooks breakfast room
- Sunny living room is open and airy with vaulted ceiling
- Secondary bedrooms with convenient vanities skillfully share bath
- 3 bedrooms, 2 1/2 baths, 2-car side entry garage
- Basement foundation

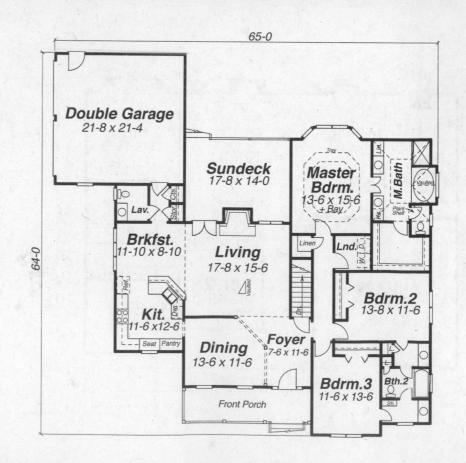

65-0

64-0

Double Garage
21-8 x 21-4

Sundeck
17-8 x 14-0

Master Bdrm.
13-6 x 15-6
+ Bay

M. Bath

Lav.

Stor. Cts.

Brkfst.
11-10 x 8-10

Living
17-8 x 15-6

Linen

Lnd.

Bdrm.2
13-8 x 11-6

Ref.

Kit.
11-6 x12-6

Seat Pantry

Dining
13-6 x 11-6

Foyer
7-6 x 11-6

Bth.2

Bdrm.3
11-6 x 13-6

Front Porch

Pillared Front Porch Generates Charm And Warmth

1,567 total square feet of living area

Price Code C

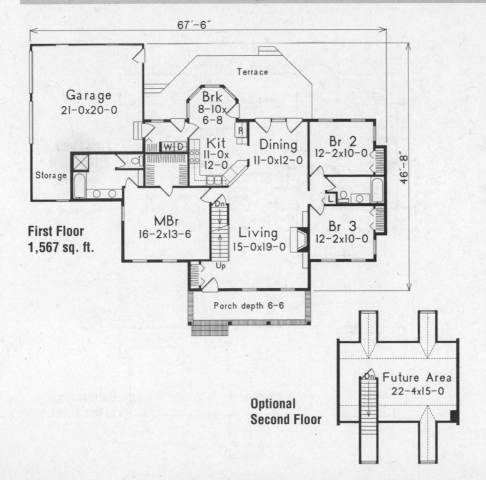

67'-6"

Terrace

Garage
21-0x20-0

Brk
8-10x
6-8

Kit
11-0x
12-0

W D

Dining
11-0x12-0

R

Br 2
12-2x10-0

Storage

46'-8"

MBr
16-2x13-6

Dn

Living
15-0x19-0

Br 3
12-2x10-0

Up

**First Floor
1,567 sq. ft.**

Porch depth 6-6

Dn

Future Area
22-4x15-0

**Optional
Second Floor**

Special features

- Living room flows into dining room shaped by an angled pass-through into the kitchen
- Cheerful, windowed dining area
- Future area available on the second floor has an additional 338 square feet of living area
- Master suite separated from other bedrooms for privacy
- 3 bedrooms, 2 baths, 2-car side entry garage
- Basement foundation, drawings also include slab foundation

TO ORDER BLUEPRINTS USE THE FORM ON PAGE 15 OR CALL TOLL-FREE 1-877-671-6036
View thousands more home plans online at www.familyhandyman.com/homeplans

67

Duo Atrium For Fantastic Views

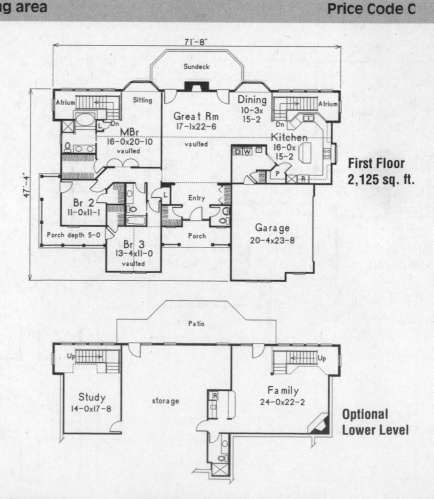

2,125 total square feet of living area

Price Code C

Special features

- A cozy porch leads to the vaulted great room with fireplace through the entry which has a walk-in closet and bath

- Large and well-arranged kitchen offers spectacular views from its cantilevered sink cabinetry through a two-story atrium window wall

- Master bedroom boasts a sitting room, large walk-in closet and bath with garden tub overhanging a brightly lit atrium

- 1,047 square feet of optional living area on the lower level featuring a study and family room with walk-in bar and full bath below the kitchen

- 3 bedrooms, 2 1/2 baths, 2-car side entry garage

- Walk-out basement foundation

**First Floor
2,125 sq. ft.**

71'-8"

Sundeck

Atrium
Sitting

Dining
10-3x
15-2

Atrium

Great Rm
17-1x22-6
vaulted

MBr
16-0x20-10
vaulted

Kitchen
16-0x
15-2

DW

47'-4"

Br 2
11-0x11-1

Entry

P   R

Porch depth 5-0

Garage
20-4x23-8

Br 3
13-4x11-0
vaulted

Porch

**Optional
Lower Level**

Patio

Up

Up

Study
14-0x17-8

storage

R

Family
24-0x22-2

TO ORDER BLUEPRINTS USE THE FORM ON PAGE 15 OR CALL TOLL-FREE 1-877-671-6036
View thousands more home plans online at www.familyhandyman.com/homeplans

Home For Narrow Lot Offers Wide Open Spaces

I.N. HANSEN S.D.G.

1,492 total square feet of living area   **Price Code A**

Second Floor
732 sq. ft.

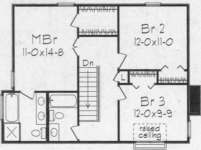

MBr
11-0x14-8

Br 2
12-0x11-0

Dn

Br 3
12-0x9-9

raised ceiling

Special features

- Cleverly angled entry spills into living and dining rooms which share warmth of fireplace flanked by arched windows

- Master suite includes double-door entry, huge walk-in closet, shower and bath with picture window

- Stucco and dutch hipped roofs add warmth and charm to facade

- 3 bedrooms, 2 1/2 baths, 2-car garage

- Basement foundation

35'-0"

Deck

Brk
9-0x
11-0

Dining
12-0x9-4

Kit
10-9x14-6

Dn

Living
15-8x14-0

47'-8"

Up

Porch

Garage
19-4x21-4

First Floor
760 sq. ft.

TO ORDER BLUEPRINTS USE THE FORM ON PAGE 15 OR CALL TOLL-FREE 1-877-671-6036
View thousands more home plans online at www.familyhandyman.com/homeplans

69

Victorian Styled Gazebo Enhances Front Porch

2,084 total square feet of living area

Price Code C

Special features

- Charming bay window in master suite allows sunlight in as well as style

- Great room accesses front covered porch extending the living area to the outdoors

- Large playroom on second floor is ideal for family living

- 3 bedrooms, 2 1/2 baths, 2-car side entry garage

- Slab, crawl space or basement foundation, please specify when ordering

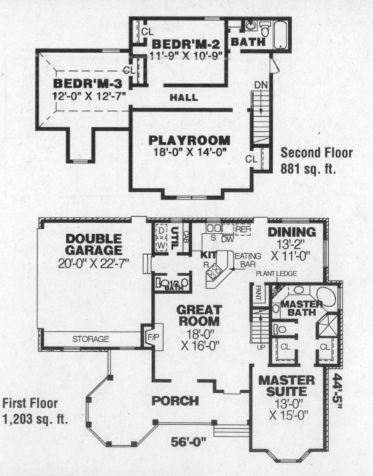

Second Floor
881 sq. ft.

BEDR'M-2
11'-9" X 10'-9"

BATH

CL

BEDR'M-3
12'-0" X 12'-7"

CL

HALL

DN

PLAYROOM
18'-0" X 14'-0"

CL

DOUBLE GARAGE
20'-0" X 22'-7"

UTL

CAB

DINING
13'-2" X 11'-0"

REF

S   DW

KIT

EATING BAR

PLANT LEDGE

BATH

STORAGE

F/P

GREAT ROOM
18'-0" X 16'-0"

PANT

MASTER BATH

CL   CL

UP

First Floor
1,203 sq. ft.

PORCH

MASTER SUITE
13'-0" X 15'-0"

44'-5"

56'-0"

Cozy Covered Front Porch

1,583 total square feet of living area   **Price Code B**

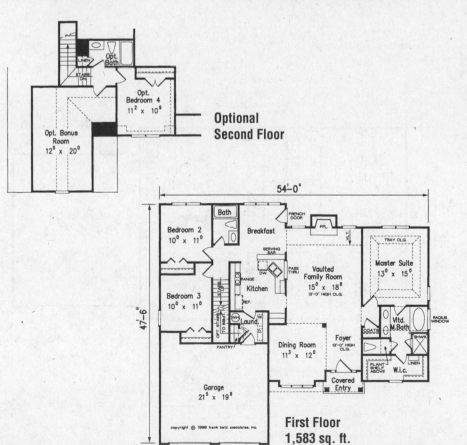

Optional Second Floor

LINEN
Opt. Bath
STAIRS DN.
Opt. Bedroom 4
11² x 10⁹
Opt. Bonus Room
12⁰ x 20⁰

54'-0"

47'-6"

Bedroom 2
10⁰ x 11⁰

Bath

Breakfast

FRENCH DOOR

FPL

VLT.

TRAY CLG.

Master Suite
13⁰ x 15⁰

SERVING BAR

RANGE

DW.

PASS THRU

Kitchen

REF.

Vaulted Family Room
15⁰ x 18⁸
13'-0" HIGH CLG.

Bedroom 3
10⁰ x 11⁰

OPT. STAIRS TO BSMT.

W/H

Laund.

RADIUS WINDOW

Vltd. M.Bath

COATS

PANTRY

Dining Room
11³ x 12⁰

Foyer
13'-0" HIGH CLG.

PLANT SHELF ABOVE

LINEN

W.i.c.

Garage
21⁵ x 19⁹

Covered Entry

copyright © 1998 frank betz associates, inc.

**First Floor
1,583 sq. ft.**

Special features

■ 9' ceilings throughout this home

■ Optional second floor has an additional 532 square feet of living area

■ Additional bedrooms are located away from master bedroom for privacy

■ 3 bedrooms, 2 baths, 2-car garage

■ Walk-out basement or crawl space, please specify when ordering

TO ORDER BLUEPRINTS USE THE FORM ON PAGE 15 OR CALL TOLL-FREE 1-877-671-6036
View thousands more home plans online at www.familyhandyman.com/homeplans

71

Central Fireplace Brightens Family Living

1,260 total square feet of living area

Price Code A

Special features

- Spacious kitchen and dining area features large pantry, storage area, easy access to garage and laundry room

- Pleasant covered front porch adds a practical touch

- Master bedroom with a private bath adjoins two other bedrooms, all with plenty of closet space

- 3 bedrooms, 2 baths, 2-car garage

- Basement foundation, drawings also include crawl space and slab foundations

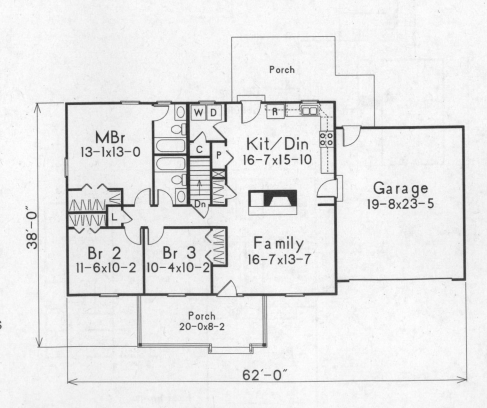

Porch

MBr
13-1x13-0

Kit/Din
16-7x15-10

W D

C

P

R

Garage
19-8x23-5

38'-0"

L

Dn

Family
16-7x13-7

Br 2
11-6x10-2

Br 3
10-4x10-2

Porch
20-0x8-2

62'-0"

Charming Entry Is Focal Point

1,990 total square feet of living area

Price Code C

Second Floor 475 sq. ft.

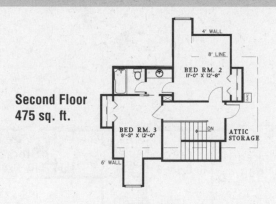

Special features

- A media wall is conveniently located next to the fireplace in the great room
- Creatively designed glass blocks behind the whirlpool tub in the master bath allow in light while maintaining privacy
- Extra counterspace dining available in the kitchen
- 3 bedrooms, 2 1/2 baths, 2-car garage
- Walk-out basement, basement, crawl space or slab foundation, please specify when ordering

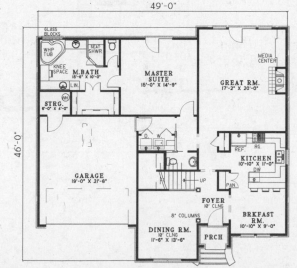

First Floor 1,515 sq. ft.

Charming Country Styling In This Ranch

1,600 total square feet of living area

Price Code C

Special features

- Energy efficient home with 2" x 6" exterior walls

- Impressive sunken living room has massive stone fireplace and 16' vaulted ceilings

- Dining room conveniently located next to kitchen and divided for privacy

- Special amenities include sewing room, glass shelves in kitchen and master bath and a large utility area

- Sunken master bedroom features a distinctive sitting room

- 3 bedrooms, 2 baths, 2-car side entry garage

- Slab foundation, drawings also include crawl space and basement foundations

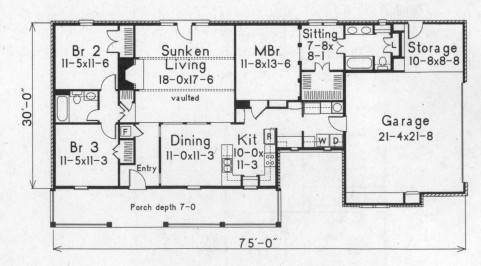

Welcoming Front Porch, A Country Touch

2,043 total square feet of living area

Price Code D

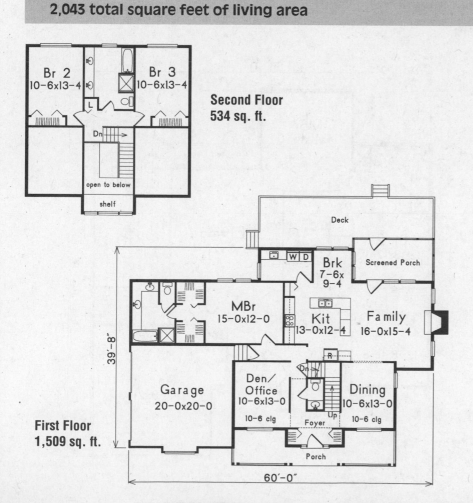

Second Floor
534 sq. ft.

Br 2
10-6x13-4

Br 3
10-6x13-4

Dn

open to below

shelf

First Floor
1,509 sq. ft.

Deck

Brk
7-6x
9-4

Screened Porch

W D

MBr
15-0x12-0

Kit
13-0x12-4

Family
16-0x15-4

Garage
20-0x20-0

Den/
Office
10-6x13-0

10-6 clg

Dn

R

Up

Dining
10-6x13-0

10-6 clg

Foyer

Porch

39'-8"

60'-0"

Special features

- Energy efficient home with 2" x 6" exterior walls
- Two-story central foyer includes two coat closets
- Large combined space provided by the kitchen, family and breakfast rooms
- Breakfast nook for informal dining looks out to the deck and screened porch
- 3 bedrooms, 2 1/2 baths, 2-car side entry garage
- Basement foundation, drawings also include slab foundation

TO ORDER BLUEPRINTS USE THE FORM ON PAGE 15 OR CALL TOLL-FREE 1-877-671-6036
View thousands more home plans online at www.familyhandyman.com/homeplans

75

Inviting Gabled Entry

2,128 total square feet of living area

Price Code C

Special features

- Versatile kitchen has plenty of space for entertaining with large dining area and counter seating

- Luxurious master bedroom has double-door entry and private bath with jacuzzi tub, double sinks and large walk-in closet

- Secondary bedrooms include spacious walk-in closets

- Coat closet in front entry is a nice added feature

- 4 bedrooms, 2 baths, 2-car garage

- Slab foundation, drawings also include crawl space foundation

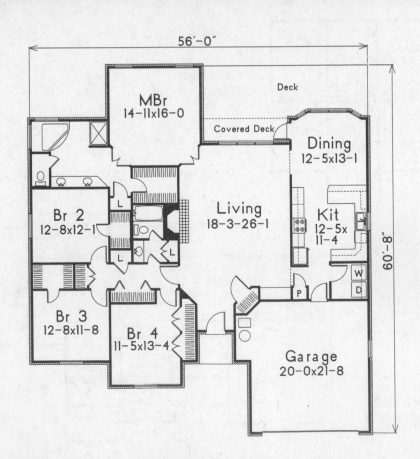

Sculptured Roof Line And Facade Add Charm

1,674 total square feet of living area

Price Code B

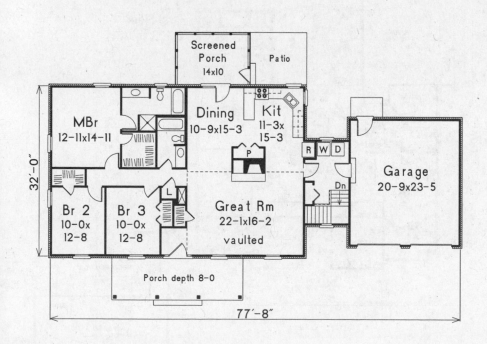

Special features

- Great room, dining area and kitchen, surrounded with vaulted ceiling, central fireplace and log bin

- Convenient laundry/mud room located between garage and family area with handy stairs to basement

- Easily expandable screened porch and adjacent patio with access from dining area

- Master bedroom features full bath with tub, separate shower and walk-in closet

- 3 bedrooms, 2 baths, 2-car garage

- Basement foundation, drawings also include crawl space and slab foundations

Expansive Counter Space

2,123 total square feet of living area

Price Code E

Special features

- Energy efficient home with 2" x 6" exterior walls

- Living room has wood burning fireplace, built-in bookshelves and a wet bar

- Skylights make sun porch bright and comfortable

- 3 bedrooms, 2 1/2 baths, 2-car side entry garage

- Crawl space, slab or basement foundation, please specify when ordering

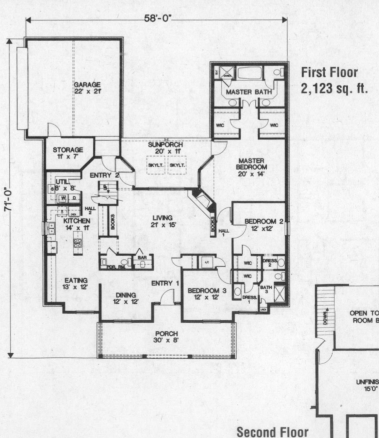

First Floor 2,123 sq. ft.

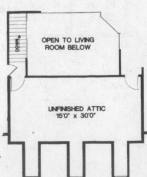

Second Floor 450 sq. ft.

Perfect Home For A Small Family

864 total square feet of living area

Price Code AAA

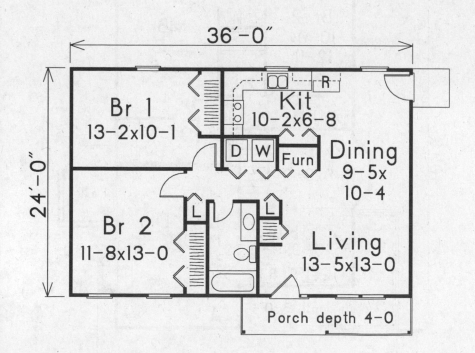

36'-0"

24'-0"

Br 1
13-2x10-1

Kit
10-2x6-8

R

D W Furn

Dining
9-5x 10-4

Br 2
11-8x13-0

L L

Living
13-5x13-0

Porch depth 4-0

Special features

- L-shaped kitchen with convenient pantry is adjacent to dining area
- Easy access to laundry area, linen closet and storage closet
- Both bedrooms include ample closet space
- 2 bedrooms, 1 bath
- Crawl space foundation, drawings also include basement and slab foundations

TO ORDER BLUEPRINTS USE THE FORM ON PAGE 15 OR CALL TOLL-FREE 1-877-671-6036
View thousands more home plans online at www.familyhandyman.com/homeplans

79

Stylish Retreat For A Narrow Lot

1,084 total square feet of living area

Price Code AA

Special features

- Delightful country porch for quiet evenings
- Living room has a front feature window which invites the sun and includes a fireplace and dining area with private patio
- The U-shaped kitchen features lots of cabinets and bayed breakfast room with built-in pantry
- Both bedrooms have walk-in closets and access to their own bath
- 2 bedrooms, 2 baths
- Basement foundation

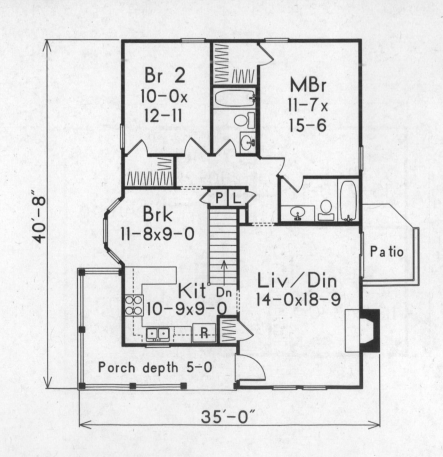

Br 2
10-0x
12-11

MBr
11-7 x
15-6

P L

Brk
11-8x9-0

Patio

Kit
10-9x9-0

Dn

Liv/Din
14-0x18-9

R

Porch depth 5-0

40'-8"

35'-0"

Whirlpool Tub In Master Bath

1,571 total square feet of living area

Price Code B

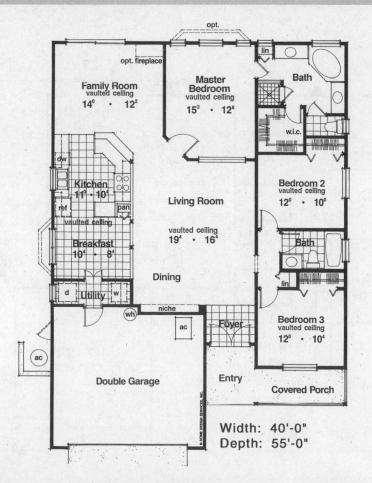

Width: 40'-0"
Depth: 55'-0"

Special features

- Bedrooms #2 and #3 share a bath in their own private hall
- Kitchen counter overlooks family room
- Open living area adds appeal with vaulted ceiling and display niche
- 3 bedrooms, 2 baths, 2-car garage
- Slab foundation

TO ORDER BLUEPRINTS USE THE FORM ON PAGE 15 OR CALL TOLL-FREE 1-877-671-6036
View thousands more home plans online at www.familyhandyman.com/homeplans

81

Small Ranch For A Perfect Country Haven

1,761 total square feet of living area

Price Code B

Special features

- Exterior window dressing, roof dormers and planter boxes provide visual warmth and charm

- Great room boasts a vaulted ceiling, fireplace and opens to a pass-through kitchen

- Master bedroom is vaulted with luxury bath and walk-in closet

- Home features eight separate closets with an abundance of storage

- 4 bedrooms, 2 baths, 2-car side entry garage

- Basement foundation

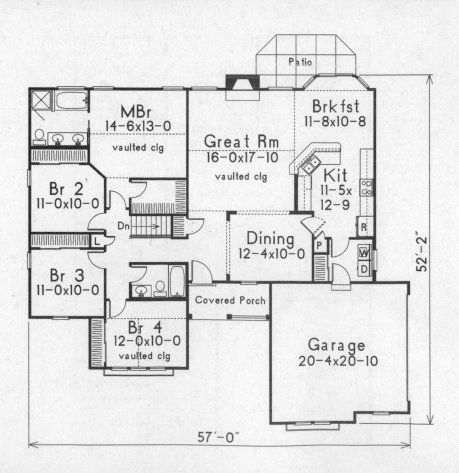

TO ORDER BLUEPRINTS USE THE FORM ON PAGE 15 OR CALL TOLL-FREE 1-877-671-6036

View thousands more home plans online at www.familyhandyman.com/homeplans

1,546 total square feet of living area

Price Code C

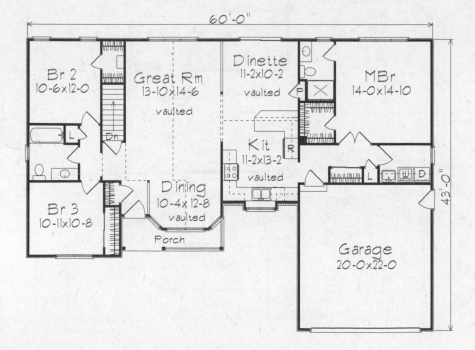

60'-0"

43'-0"

Br 2
10-6x12-0

Great Rm
13-10x14-6
vaulted

Dinette
11-2x10-2
vaulted

MBr
14-0x14-10

Kit
11-2x13-2
vaulted

Dn

Dining
10-4x12-8
vaulted

Br 3
10-11x10-8

Porch

Garage
20-0x22-0

Special features

- Spacious, open rooms create a casual atmosphere
- Master suite secluded for privacy
- Dining room features large bay window
- Kitchen and dinette combine for added space and include access to the outdoors
- Large laundry room includes convenient sink
- 3 bedrooms, 2 baths, 2-car garage
- Basement foundation

TO ORDER BLUEPRINTS USE THE FORM ON PAGE 15 OR CALL TOLL-FREE 1-877-671-6036
View thousands more home plans online at www.familyhandyman.com/homeplans

83

Perfect Farmhouse For Family Living

2,129 total square feet of living area

Price Code C

Special features

- Energy efficient home with 2" x 6" exterior walls

- Home office has a double-door entry and is secluded from other living areas

- Corner fireplace in living area is a nice focal point

- Bonus room above the garage has an additional 407 square feet of living area

- 3 bedrooms, 2 1/2 baths, 2-car side entry garage

- Basement foundation

Second Floor
993 sq. ft.

First Floor
1,136 sq. ft.

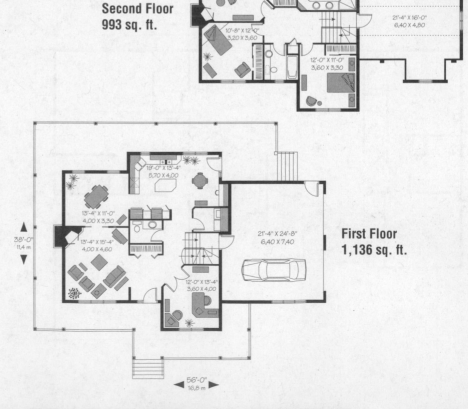

TO ORDER BLUEPRINTS USE THE FORM ON PAGE 15 OR CALL TOLL-FREE 1-877-671-6036
View thousands more home plans online at www.familyhandyman.com/homeplans

Centralized Living Area Is Functional And Appealing

2,186 total square feet of living area

Price Code C

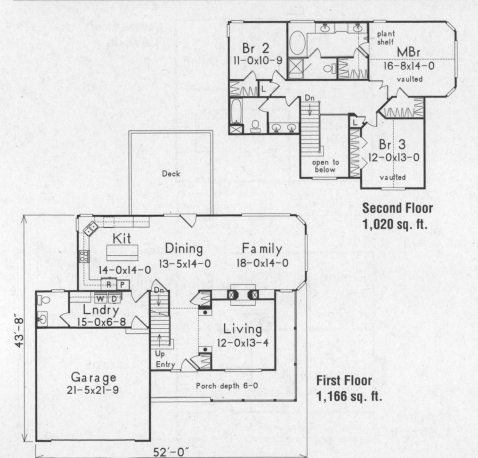

Br 2
11-0x10-9

plant shelf

MBr
16-8x14-0
vaulted

Dn

L

open to below

Br 3
12-0x13-0
vaulted

Second Floor
1,020 sq. ft.

Deck

Kit
14-0x14-0

Dining
13-5x14-0

Family
18-0x14-0

R P

W D

Lndry
15-0x6-8

Dn

Living
12-0x13-4

Up
Entry

Garage
21-5x21-9

Porch depth 6-0

43'-8"

52'-0"

First Floor
1,166 sq. ft.

Special features

- See-through fireplace is a focal point in family and living areas
- Columns grace the entrance into the living room
- Large laundry room with adjoining half bath
- Ideal second floor bath includes separate vanity with double sinks
- 3 bedrooms, 2 1/2 baths, 2-car garage
- Basement foundation

Two-Story Country Home Features Large Living Areas

1,998 total square feet of living area

Price Code D

Special features

- Large family room features fireplace and access to kitchen and dining area

- Skylights add daylight to second floor baths

- Utility room conveniently located near garage and kitchen

- Kitchen/breakfast area includes pantry, island work space and easy access to the patio

- 3 bedrooms, 2 1/2 baths, 2-car side entry garage

- Basement foundation, drawings also include crawl space and slab foundations

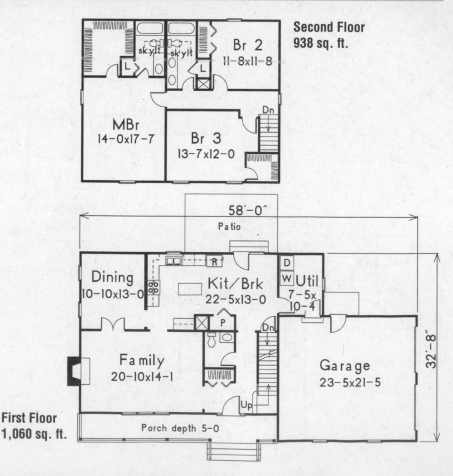

Second Floor
938 sq. ft.

Br 2
11-8x11-8

MBr
14-0x17-7

Br 3
13-7x12-0

Dn

58'-0"

Patio

Dining
10-10x13-0

Kit/Brk
22-5x13-0

Util
7-5x
10-4

Family
20-10x14-1

Garage
23-5x21-5

Up

Dn

32'-8"

First Floor
1,060 sq. ft.

Porch depth 5-0

Split Entry With Lots Of Room For Future Growth

1,803 total square feet of living area

Price Code C

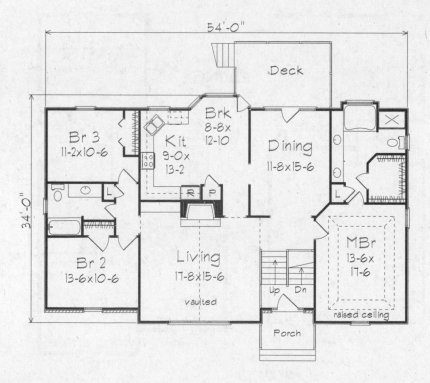

54'-0"

34'-0"

Deck

Br 3
11-2x10-6

Kit
9-0x
13-2

Brk
8-8x
12-10

Dining
11-8x15-6

Br 2
13-6x10-6

Living
17-8x15-6
vaulted

Up   Dn

MBr
13-6x
17-6

raised ceiling

Porch

Special features

- Master bedroom features raised ceiling and private bath with walk-in closet, large double-bowl vanity and separate tub and shower

- U-shaped kitchen includes corner sink and convenient pantry

- Vaulted living room complete with fireplace and built-in cabinet

- 3 bedrooms, 2 baths, 3-car drive under garage

- Basement foundation

TO ORDER BLUEPRINTS USE THE FORM ON PAGE 15 OR CALL TOLL-FREE 1-877-671-6036
View thousands more home plans online at www.familyhandyman.com/homeplans

87

Striking Plant Shelf

1,467 total square feet of living area

Price Code C

Special features

- Vaulted ceilings, an open floor plan and a wealth of windows create an inviting atmosphere
- Efficiently arranged kitchen has an island with built-in cooktop and a snack counter
- Plentiful storage and closet space throughout this home
- 3 bedrooms, 2 baths, 2-car garage
- Crawl space foundation

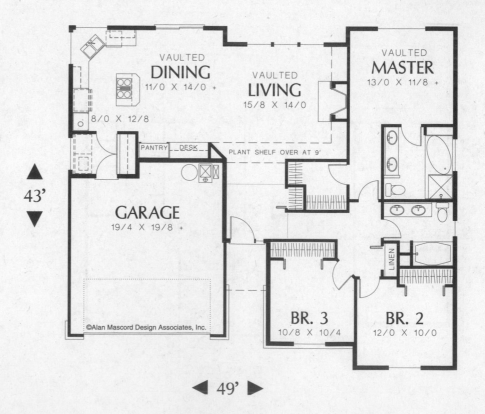

VAULTED **DINING** 11/0 X 14/0 +

8/0 X 12/8

VAULTED **LIVING** 15/8 X 14/0

VAULTED **MASTER** 13/0 X 11/8 +

PANTRY DESK

PLANT SHELF OVER AT 9'

GARAGE 19/4 X 19/8 +

©Alan Mascord Design Associates, Inc.

BR. 3 10/8 X 10/4

LINEN

BR. 2 12/0 X 10/0

43'

49'

Vaulted Ceiling Frames Circle-Top Window

1,195 total square feet of living area

Price Code AA

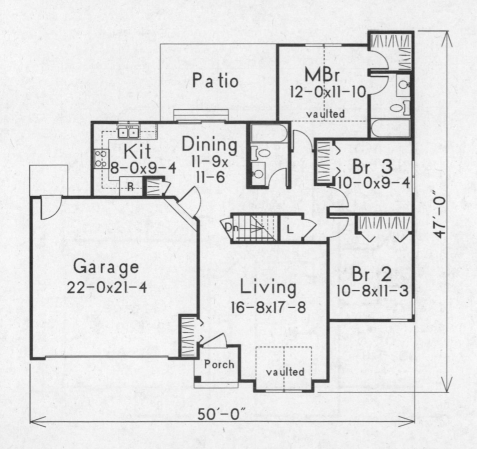

Special features

- Dining room opens onto the patio
- Master bedroom features vaulted ceiling, private bath and walk-in closet
- Coat closets located by both the entrances
- Convenient secondary entrance at the back of the garage
- 3 bedrooms, 2 baths, 2-car garage
- Basement foundation

TO ORDER BLUEPRINTS USE THE FORM ON PAGE 15 OR CALL TOLL-FREE 1-877-671-6036
View thousands more home plans online at www.familyhandyman.com/HOMEPLANS

89

Open Living Area Adds Drama To Home

1,340 total square feet of living area

Price Code A

Special features

- Master bedroom has private bath and walk-in closet

- Recessed entry leads to vaulted family room with see-through fireplace to dining area

- Garage includes handy storage area

- Convenient laundry closet in the kitchen

- 3 bedrooms, 2 baths, 2-car side entry garage

- Slab foundation, drawings also include crawl space foundation

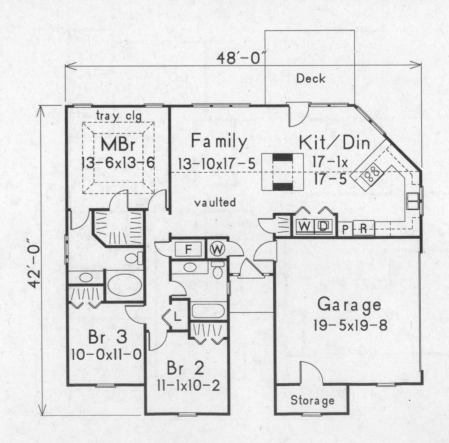

A Functional Floor Plan For Family Living

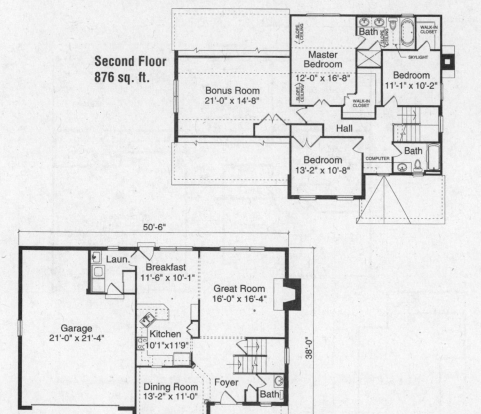

1,856 total square feet of living area

Price Code C

Second Floor 876 sq. ft.

Bonus Room 21'-0" x 14'-8"

Master Bedroom 12'-0" x 16'-8"

SLOPE CEILING

WALK-IN CLOSET

Bath

SLOPE CEILING

SKYLIGHT

Bedroom 11'-1" x 10'-2"

WALK-IN CLOSET

Hall

Bedroom 13'-2" x 10'-8"

COMPUTER

Bath

50'-6"

Laun.

Breakfast 11'-6" x 10'-1"

Great Room 16'-0" x 16'-4"

Garage 21'-0" x 21'-4"

Kitchen 10'1"x11'9"

38'-0"

Dining Room 13'-2" x 11'-0"

Foyer

Bath

Porch

First Floor 980 sq. ft.

Special features

- The roomy kitchen offers an abundance of cabinets and counter space as well as a convenient pantry

- Master bedroom includes a sloped ceiling and deluxe bath

- Bonus room on the second floor has an additional 325 square feet of living area

- 3 bedrooms, 2 1/2 baths, 2-car garage

- Walk-out basement or basement foundation, please specify when ordering

TO ORDER BLUEPRINTS USE THE FORM ON PAGE 15 OR CALL TOLL-FREE 1-877-671-6036
View thousands more home plans online at www.familyhandyman.com/homeplans

91

Ranch Style With Many Extras

1,342 total square feet of living area   **Price Code A**

Special features

- 9' ceilings throughout this home
- Master suite has tray ceiling and wall of windows that overlook backyard
- Dining room includes serving bar connecting it to the kitchen and sliding glass doors that lead outdoors
- 3 bedrooms, 2 baths, 2-car garage
- Optional second floor has an additional 350 square feet of living area
- Slab, walk-out basement or crawl space foundation, please specify when ordering

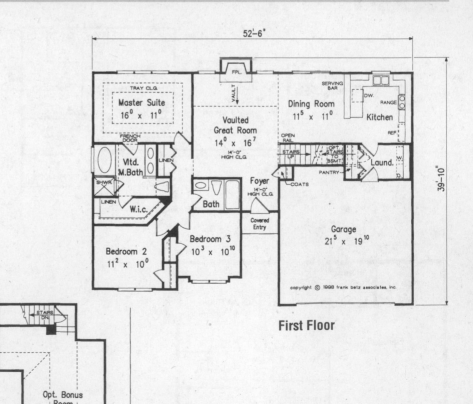

First Floor

Optional Second Floor

Sunny Dining Room

1,735 total square feet of living area

Price Code B

Width: 50'-0"
Depth: 55'-0"

Special features

- Luxurious master bath has spa tub, shower, double vanity and large walk-in closet
- Peninsula in kitchen has sink and dishwasher
- Massive master bedroom has step up ceiling and private location
- 3 bedrooms, 2 baths, 2-car garage
- Slab foundation

Surrounding Porch For Country Views

1,428 total square feet of living area   Price Code A

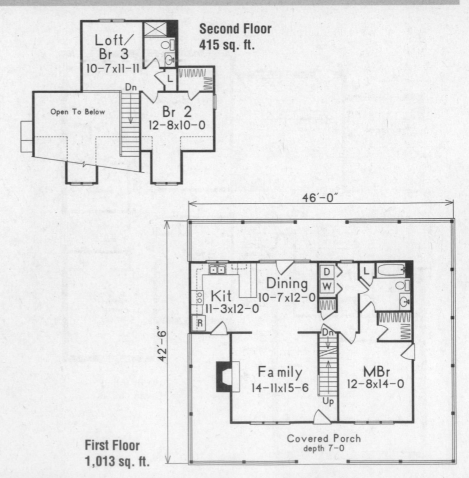

Second Floor
415 sq. ft.

Loft/
Br 3
10-7x11-11

Open To Below

Dn

Br 2
12-8x10-0

Special features

- Large vaulted family room opens to dining area and kitchen with breakfast bar and access to surrounding porch

- First floor master suite offers large bath, walk-in closet and nearby laundry facilities

- A spacious loft/bedroom #3 overlooking family room and an additional bedroom and bath conclude the second floor

- 3 bedrooms, 2 baths

- Basement foundation

46'-0"

42'-6"

Kit
11-3x12-0

Dining
10-7x12-0

Family
14-11x15-6

MBr
12-8x14-0

Up   Dn

Covered Porch
depth 7-0

First Floor
1,013 sq. ft.

Unique, Traditional Style, Farmhouse Flavor

Rear View

1,763 total square feet of living area

Price Code C

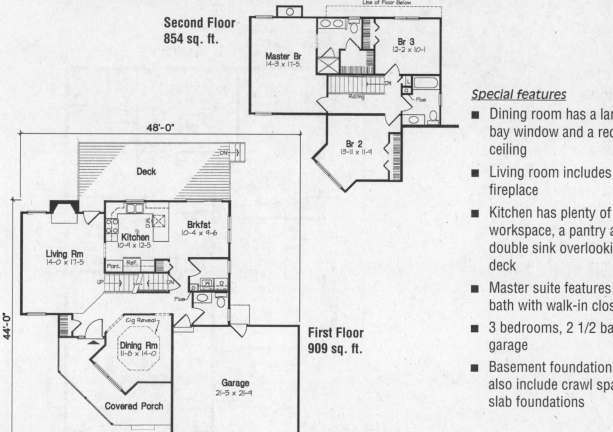

Second Floor
854 sq. ft.

Line of Floor Below

Master Br
14-3 x 17-5

Br 3
12-2 x 10-1

Railing

DN

Flue

Br 2
13-11 x 11-9

48'-0"

44'-0"

Deck

DN

Kitchen
10-9 x 12-5

Brkfst
10-4 x 9-6

Living Rm
14-0 x 17-5

Pant. Ref.

UP DN

Flue

Clg Reveal

Dining Rm
11-8 x 14-0

Garage
21-5 x 21-9

Covered Porch

First Floor
909 sq. ft.

Special features

- Dining room has a large box bay window and a recessed ceiling

- Living room includes a large fireplace

- Kitchen has plenty of workspace, a pantry and a double sink overlooking the deck

- Master suite features a large bath with walk-in closet

- 3 bedrooms, 2 1/2 baths, 2-car garage

- Basement foundation, drawings also include crawl space and slab foundations

TO ORDER BLUEPRINTS USE THE FORM ON PAGE 15 OR CALL TOLL-FREE 1-877-671-6036
View thousands more home plans online at www.familyhandyman.com/homeplans

95

Simple Rooflines And Inviting Porch

1,389 total square feet of living area

Price Code A

Special features

- Formal living room has warming fireplace and a delightful bay window
- U-shaped kitchen shares a snack bar with the bayed family room
- Lovely master suite has its own private bath
- 3 bedrooms, 2 baths, 2-car garage
- Slab foundation

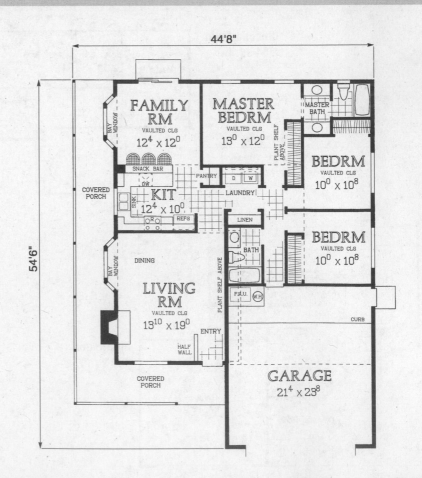

Open Living Spaces

1,050 total square feet of living area

Price Code AA

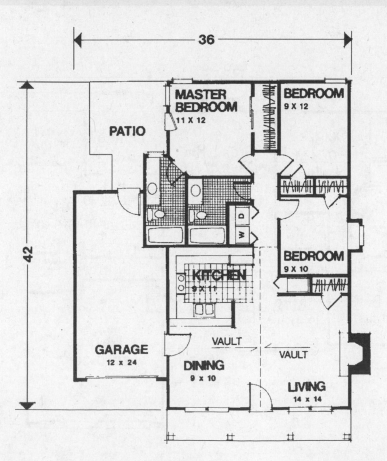

Special features

- Master bedroom features a private bath and access outdoors onto a private patio
- A vaulted ceiling in the living and dining areas creates a feeling of spaciousness
- Laundry closet is convenient to all bedrooms
- Efficient U-shaped kitchen
- 3 bedrooms, 2 baths, 1-car garage
- Basement or slab foundation, please specify when ordering

Traditional Exterior, Handsome Accents

1,882 total square feet of living area

Price Code D

Special features

- Wide, handsome entrance opens to the vaulted great room with fireplace

- Living and dining areas are conveniently joined but still allow privacy

- Private covered porch extends breakfast area

- Practical passageway runs through laundry and mud room from garage to kitchen

- Vaulted ceiling in master bedroom

- 3 bedrooms, 2 baths, 2-car garage

- Basement foundation

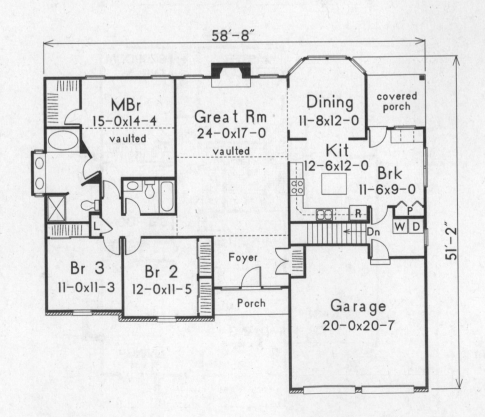

58'-8"

51'-2"

MBr 15-0x14-4 vaulted

Great Rm 24-0x17-0 vaulted

Dining 11-8x12-0

covered porch

Kit 12-6x12-0

Brk 11-6x9-0

Br 3 11-0x11-3

Br 2 12-0x11-5

Foyer

Porch

Garage 20-0x20-7

98

TO ORDER BLUEPRINTS USE THE FORM ON PAGE 15 OR CALL TOLL-FREE 1-877-671-6036
View thousands more home plans online at www.familyhandyman.com/homeplans

Atrium's Dramatic Ambiance, Compliments Of Windows

1,721 total square feet of living area

Price Code C

Rear View

Special features

- Roof dormers add great curb appeal
- Vaulted dining and great rooms immersed in light from atrium window wall
- Breakfast room opens onto covered porch
- Functionally designed kitchen
- 3 bedrooms, 2 baths, 3-car garage
- Walk-out basement foundation, drawings also include crawl space and slab foundations

83'-0"

42'-0"

Atrium Below

Covered Porch

Brk 11-5x12-0

Great Rm 16-0x16-10 vaulted

MBr 16-0x14-0 vaulted

Kit 11-5x 12-0

Garage 29-4x21-4

Dining 11-0x11-6 vaulted

Br 3 11-1x13-3

Br 2 11-0x12-9

Porch 27-8x5-0

TO ORDER BLUEPRINTS USE THE FORM ON PAGE 15 OR CALL TOLL-FREE 1-877-671-6036
View thousands more home plans online at www.familyhandyman.com/homeplans

99

Angled Ranch Suited To Fit Any Lot

1,709 total square feet of living area

Price Code C

Special features

- The fireplace is flanked by a media center for convenient relaxation

- Dining room features a beautiful built-in cabinet to hold fine collectibles and china

- Centrally located kitchen is a great gethering place

- 3 bedrooms, 2 1/2 baths, 2-car side entry garage

- Basement, crawl space or slab foundation, please specify when ordering

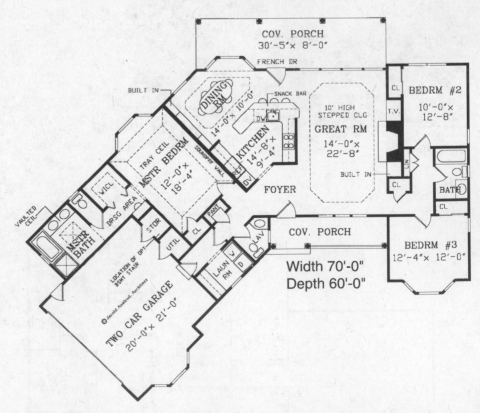

100

TO ORDER BLUEPRINTS USE THE FORM ON PAGE 15 OR CALL TOLL-FREE 1-877-671-6036
View thousands more home plans online at www.familyhandyman.com/homeplans

Compact Home For Functional Living

1,220 total square feet of living area

Price Code A

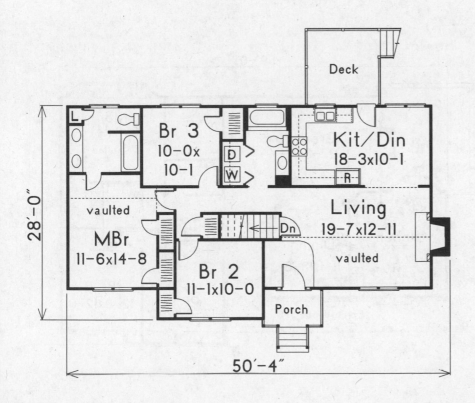

Deck

Br 3
10-0x
10-1

D
W

Kit/Din
18-3x10-1

R

vaulted

MBr
11-6x14-8

Living
19-7x12-11

vaulted

Dn

Br 2
11-1x10-0

Porch

28'-0"

50'-4"

Special features

- Vaulted ceilings add luxury to living room and master suite
- Spacious living room accented with a large fireplace and hearth
- Gracious dining area is adjacent to the convenient wrap-around kitchen
- Washer and dryer handy to the bedrooms
- Covered porch entry adds appeal
- Rear sun deck adjoins dining area
- 3 bedrooms, 2 baths, 2-car drive under garage
- Basement foundation

TO ORDER BLUEPRINTS USE THE FORM ON PAGE 15 OR CALL TOLL-FREE 1-877-671-6036
View thousands more home plans online at www.familyhandyman.com/homeplans

101

Ranch Offers Country Elegance

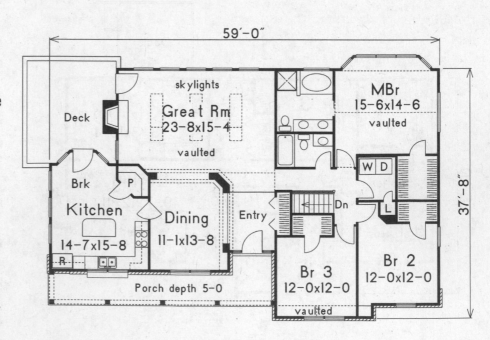

1,787 total square feet of living area

Price Code B

Special features

- Large great room with fireplace and vaulted ceiling features three large skylights and windows galore

- Cooking is sure to be a pleasure in this L-shaped well-appointed kitchen which includes bayed breakfast area with access to rear deck

- Every bedroom offers a spacious walk-in closet with a convenient laundry room just steps away

- 415 square feet of optional living area on the lower level

- 3 bedrooms, 2 baths, 2-car rear entry garage

- Walk-out basement foundation

102

TO ORDER BLUEPRINTS USE THE FORM ON PAGE 15 OR CALL TOLL-FREE 1-877-671-6036
View thousands more home plans online at www.familyhandyman.com/homeplans

Bayed Dining Room

1,538 total square feet of living area

Price Code B

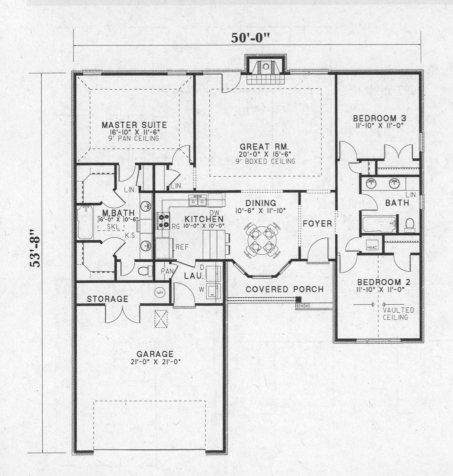

Special features

- Dining and great rooms highlighted in this design
- Master suite has many amenities
- kitchen and laundry are accessible from any room in the house
- 3 bedrooms, 2 baths, 2-car garage
- Basement, walk-out basement, crawl space or slab foundation, please specify when ordering

Wrap-Around Porch Adds Outdoor Style

2,198 total square feet of living area

Price Code C

Special features

- Great room features a warm fireplace flanked by bookshelves for storage
- Double French doors connect the formal dining room to the kitchen
- An oversized laundry room has extra counterspace
- 4 bedrooms, 2 1/2 baths, 2-car side entry garage with shop/storage
- Basement, crawl space or slab foundation, please specify when ordering

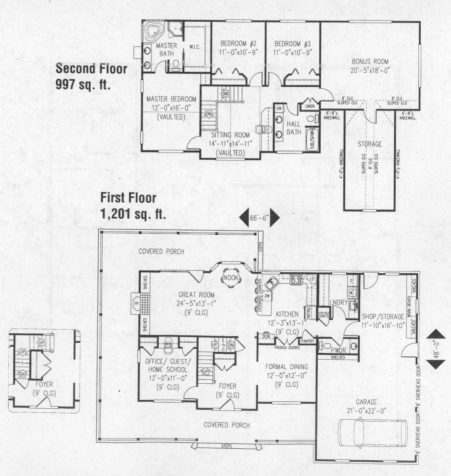

Second Floor
997 sq. ft.

First Floor
1,201 sq. ft.

Wrap-Around Porch Adds Country Charm

1,619 total square feet of living area

Price Code B

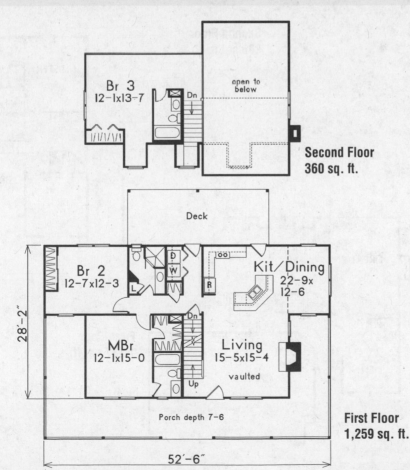

Br 3
12-1x13-7

open to below

Dn

Second Floor
360 sq. ft.

Deck

Br 2
12-7x12-3

D
W

L

R

Kit/Dining
22-9x 12-6

MBr
12-1x15-0

Dn

Up

Living
15-5x15-4

vaulted

28'-2"

Porch depth 7-6

52'-6"

First Floor
1,259 sq. ft.

Special features

- Private second floor bedroom and bath
- Kitchen features a snack bar and adjacent dining area
- Master bedroom has a private bath
- Centrally located washer and dryer
- 3 bedrooms, 3 baths
- Basement foundation, drawings also include crawl space and slab foundations

TO ORDER BLUEPRINTS USE THE FORM ON PAGE 15 OR CALL TOLL-FREE 1-877-671-6036
View thousands more home plans online at www.familyhandyman.com/homeplans

105

Towering Stone Entry

1,893 total square feet of living area

Price Code D

Special features

- Two-story home delivers comfort and beauty
- Handsome open staircase adds interest
- Master suite includes walk-in closet and a private bath with twin sinks, oversized tub and a shower
- 3 bedrooms, 2 1/2 baths, 3-car garage
- Crawl space foundation

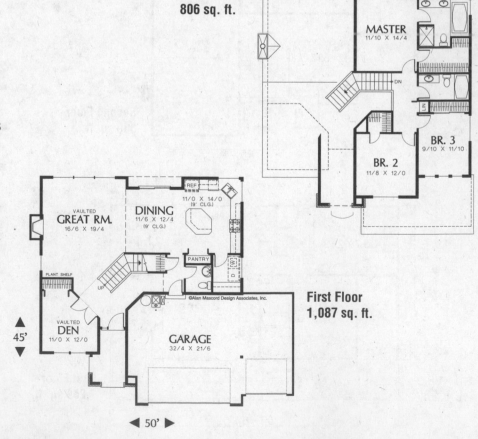

Second Floor 806 sq. ft.

MASTER 11/10 X 14/4

BR. 3 9/10 X 11/10

BR. 2 11/8 X 12/0

First Floor 1,087 sq. ft.

VAULTED GREAT RM. 16/6 X 19/4

DINING 11/6 X 12/4 (9' CLG.)

11/0 X 14/0 (9' CLG.)

REF.

PANTRY

PLANT SHELF

UP

VAULTED DEN 11/0 X 12/0

GARAGE 32/4 X 21/6

©Alan Mascord Design Associates, Inc.

45'

50'

TO ORDER BLUEPRINTS USE THE FORM ON PAGE 15 OR CALL TOLL-FREE 1-877-671-6036
View thousands more home plans online at www.familyhandyman.com/homeplans

106

Country Home With Front Orientation

2,029 total square feet of living area

Price Code C

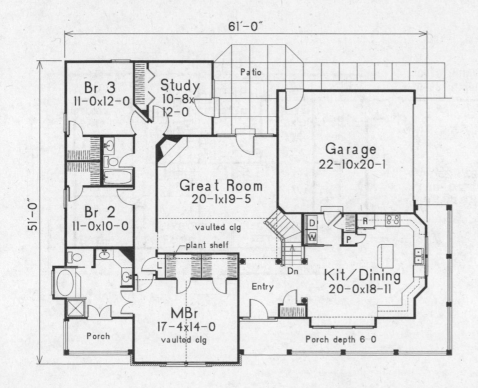

Special features

- Stonework, gables, roof dormer and double porches create a country flavor
- Kitchen enjoys extravagant cabinetry and counterspace in a bay, island snack bar, built-in pantry and cheery dining area with multiple tall windows
- Angled stair descends from large entry with wood columns and is open to vaulted great room with corner fireplace
- Master bedroom boasts his and hers walk-in closets, double-doors leading to an opulent master bath and private porch
- 4 bedrooms, 2 baths, 2-car side entry garage
- Basement foundation

Country Ranch With Spacious Wrap-Around Porch

1,541 total square feet of living area

Price Code B

Special features

- Dining area offers access to a screened porch for outdoor dining and entertaining

- Country kitchen features a center island and a breakfast bay for casual meals

- Great room is warmed by a woodstove

- 3 bedrooms, 2 baths, 2-car garage

- Basement or crawl space foundation, please specify when ordering

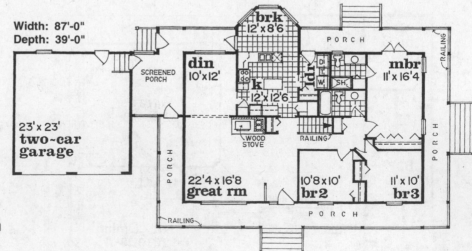

Width: 87'-0"
Depth: 39'-0"

SCREENED PORCH

23' x 23' two-car garage

PORCH

brk 12'x8'6

din 10'x12'

k 12'x12'6

ldr

mbr 11'x16'4

WOOD STOVE

RAILING

22'4 x 16'8 great rm

10'8 x 10' br2

11' x 10' br3

PORCH

RAILING

108

TO ORDER BLUEPRINTS USE THE FORM ON PAGE 15 OR CALL TOLL-FREE 1-877-671-6036
View thousands more home plans online at www.familyhandyman.com/homeplans

Brick And Siding Enhance This Traditional Home

1,170 total square feet of living area

Price Code AA

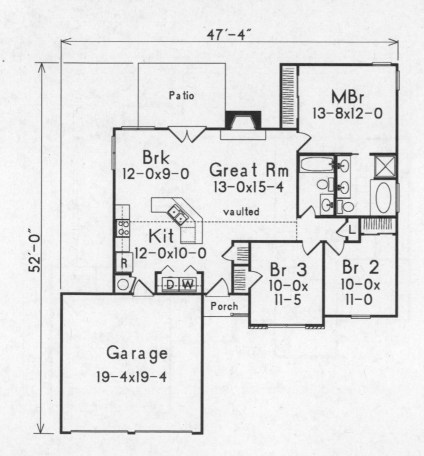

Special features

- Master bedroom enjoys privacy at the rear of this home
- Kitchen has angled bar that overlooks great room and breakfast area
- Living areas combine to create a greater sense of spaciousness
- Great room has a cozy fireplace
- 3 bedrooms, 2 baths, 2-car garage
- Slab foundation

TO ORDER BLUEPRINTS USE THE FORM ON PAGE 15 OR CALL TOLL-FREE 1-877-671-6036
View thousands more home plans online at www.familyhandyman.com/homeplans

109

Fireplace Warms Breakfast And Hearth Rooms

2,216 total square feet of living area

Price Code D

Special features

- Grilling porch is a lovely addition to the breakfast room and adds convenience

- Extra storage in garage

- Gallery foyer adds a dramatic feel to the great room

- 3 bedrooms, 2 1/2 baths, 2-car garage

- Crawl space or slab foundation, please specify when ordering

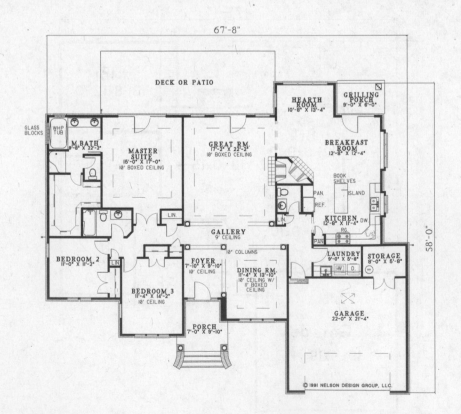

Stucco And Stone Add Charm To Facade

1,854 total square feet of living area

Price Code D

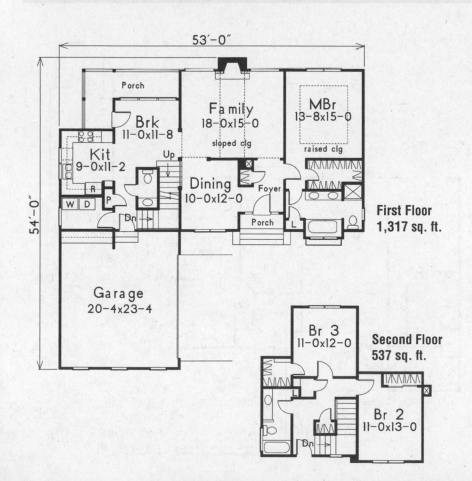

53'-0"

Porch

Brk
11-0x11-8

Kit
9-0x11-2

W D P R

Dn

Up

Family
18-0x15-0
sloped clg

Dining
10-0x12-0

Foyer

Porch

MBr
13-8x15-0
raised clg

First Floor
1,317 sq. ft.

54'-0"

Garage
20-4x23-4

Br 3
11-0x12-0

Second Floor
537 sq. ft.

Br 2
11-0x13-0

Dn

Special features

- Front entrance enhanced by arched transom windows and rustic stone

- Isolated master bedroom with dressing area and walk-in closet

- Family room features high, sloped ceilings and large fireplace

- Breakfast area accesses covered rear porch

- 3 bedrooms, 2 1/2 baths, 2-car side entry garage

- Basement foundation

TO ORDER BLUEPRINTS USE THE FORM ON PAGE 15 OR CALL TOLL-FREE 1-877-671-6036
View thousands more home plans online at www.familyhandyman.com/homeplans

111

Ranch With Traditional Feel

© 2003, Garrell Associates, Inc.

1,985 total square feet of living area

Price Code G

Special features

- 9' ceilings throughout home
- Master suite has direct access into sunroom
- Sunny breakfast room features bay window
- Bonus room on the second floor has an additional 191 square feet of living area
- 3 bedrooms, 3 baths, 2-car side entry garage
- Slab foundation

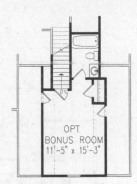

Optional Second Floor

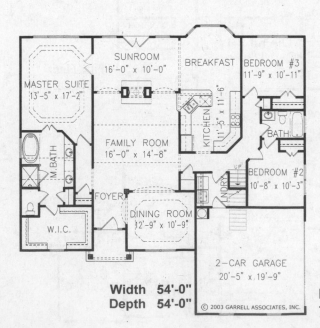

Width 54'-0"
Depth 54'-0"

© 2003 GARRELL ASSOCIATES, INC.

First Floor
1,985 sq. ft.

TO ORDER BLUEPRINTS USE THE FORM ON PAGE 15 OR CALL TOLL-FREE 1-877-671-6036
View thousands more home plans online at www.familyhandyman.com/homeplans

Vaulted Ceilings Add Dimension

1,550 total square feet of living area   **Price Code B**

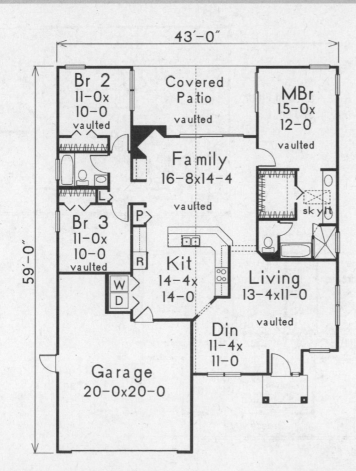

43'-0"

59'-0"

Br 2
11-0x
10-0
vaulted

Covered
Patio
vaulted

MBr
15-0x
12-0
vaulted

Family
16-8x14-4
vaulted

Br 3
11-0x
10-0
vaulted

P
R
W
D

Kit
14-4x
14-0

sky lt

Living
13-4x11-0

Din
11-4x
11-0

vaulted

Garage
20-0x20-0

Special features

- Cozy corner fireplace provides focal point in family room
- Master bedroom features large walk-in closet, skylight and separate tub and shower
- Convenient laundry closet
- Kitchen with pantry and breakfast bar connects to family room
- Family room and master bedroom access covered patio
- 3 bedrooms, 2 baths, 2-car garage
- Slab foundation

Southern Beachfront Styling

2,172 total square feet of living area

Price Code C

Special features

- 10' ceilings throughout the first floor

- 9' ceilings throughout the second floor

- Unique second floor loft makes great space for office or quiet space

- Unbelievable two floor breeze-way surrounds home so every angle has access to a nice view

- 3 bedrooms, 2 baths, 2-car garage

- Slab, pier or crawl space foundation, please specify when ordering

Second Floor 920 sq. ft.

WIC
Loft 11'x 12'
Open To Below
1/2 Bath
Master Bath
Master Bedroom 25'4"x 15'6"
Wood Deck
Breezeway

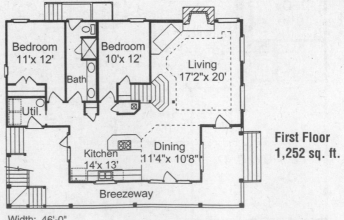

First Floor 1,252 sq. ft.

Bedroom 11'x 12'
Bedroom 10'x 12'
Living 17'2"x 20'
Bath
Util.
Kitchen 14'x 13'
Dining 11'4"x 10'8"
Breezeway

Width: 46'-0"
Depth: 40'-6"

Great Room's Symmetry Steals The Show

1,985 total square feet of living area

Price Code C

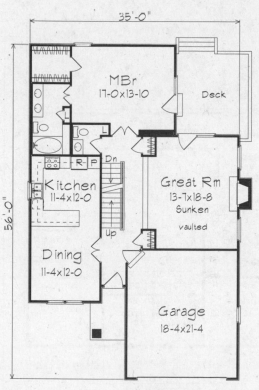

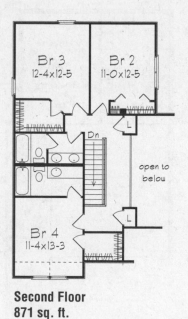

First Floor
1,114 sq. ft.

MBr
17-0x13-10

Deck

Kitchen
11-4x12-0

Great Rm
13-7x18-8
Sunken
vaulted

Dining
11-4x12-0

Garage
18-4x21-4

Dn

Up

35'-0"

56'-0"

Second Floor
871 sq. ft.

Br 3
12-4x12-5

Br 2
11-0x12-5

Br 4
11-4x13-3

Dn

open to below

Special features

- Charming design for narrow lot
- Dramatic sunken great room features vaulted ceiling, large double-hung windows and transomed patio doors
- Grand master suite includes double entry doors, large closet, elegant bath and patio access
- 4 bedrooms, 3 1/2 baths, 2-car garage
- Basement foundation

TO ORDER BLUEPRINTS USE THE FORM ON PAGE 15 OR CALL TOLL-FREE 1-877-671-6036
View thousands more home plans online at www.familyhandyman.com/homeplans

115

Covered Porch Adds Charm

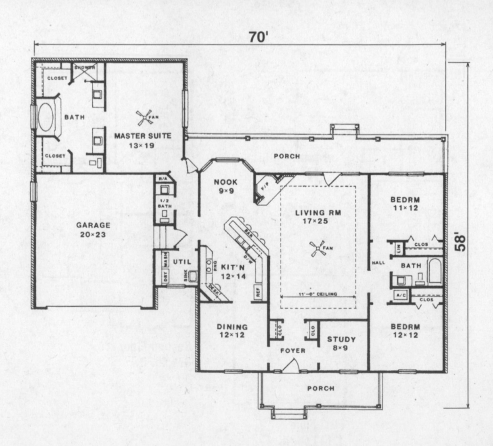

2,069 total square feet of living area

Price Code C

Special features

- 9' ceilings throughout this home
- Kitchen has many amenities including a snack bar
- Large front and rear porches
- 3 bedrooms, 2 1/2 baths, 2-car garage
- Slab or crawl space foundation, please specify when ordering

Vaulted Living Area With Corner Fireplace

1,448 total square feet of living area

Price Code A

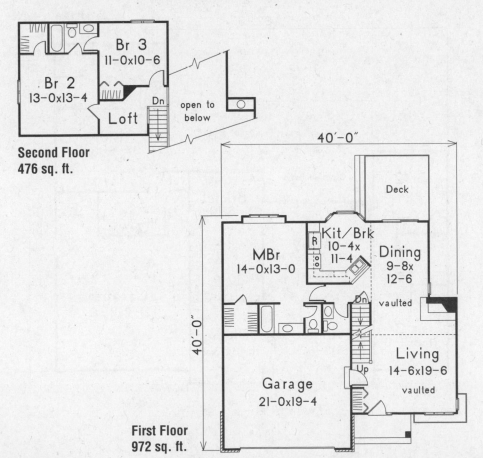

Second Floor
476 sq. ft.

Br 3
11-0x10-6

Br 2
13-0x13-4

Loft

Dn

open to below

40'-0"

40'-0"

Deck

MBr
14-0x13-0

Kit/Brk
10-4x
11-4

Dining
9-8x
12-6

vaulted

Dn

Up

Garage
21-0x19-4

Living
14-6x19-6

vaulted

First Floor
972 sq. ft.

Special features

- Dining room conveniently adjoins kitchen and accesses rear deck
- Private first floor master bedroom
- Secondary bedrooms share a bath and cozy loft area
- 3 bedrooms, 2 1/2 baths, 2-car garage
- Basement foundation

TO ORDER BLUEPRINTS USE THE FORM ON PAGE 15 OR CALL TOLL-FREE 1-877-671-6036
View thousands more home plans online at www.familyhandyman.com/homeplans

117

Plan #706-0724

Upscale Ranch With Formal And Informal Areas

1,969 total square feet of living area

Price Code C

Special features

- Master suite boasts luxurious bath with double sinks, two walk-in closets and an over-sized tub

- Corner fireplace warms a conveniently located family area

- Formal living and dining areas in the front of the home lend a touch of privacy when entertaining

- Spacious utility room has counter space and a sink

- 3 bedrooms, 2 baths, 2-car garage

- Crawl space foundation, drawings also include slab foundation

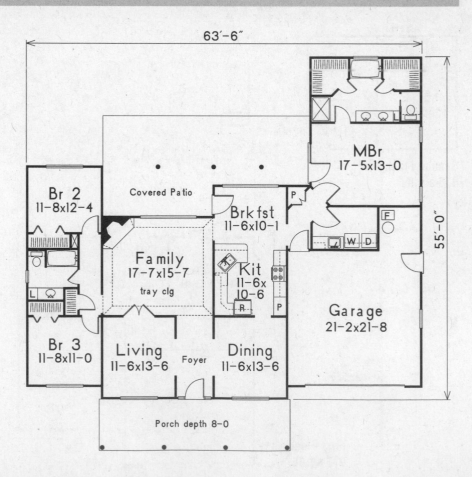

TO ORDER BLUEPRINTS USE THE FORM ON PAGE 15 OR CALL TOLL-FREE 1-877-671-6036
View thousands more home plans online at www.familyhandyman.com/homeplans

Elegance In A Starter Or Retirement Home

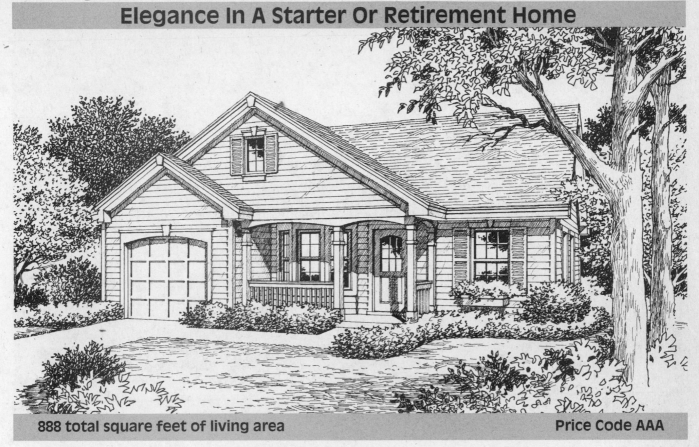

888 total square feet of living area

Price Code AAA

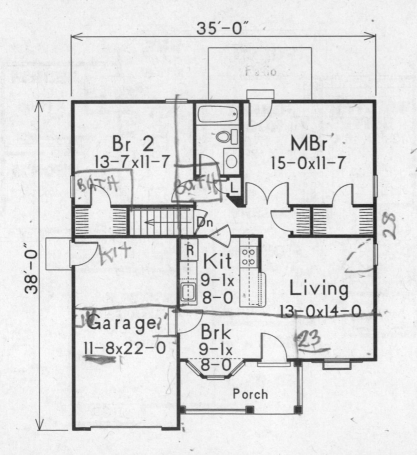

Special features

- Home features an eye-catching exterior and includes a spacious porch

- The breakfast room with bay window is open to living room and adjoins kitchen with pass-through snack bar

- The bedrooms are quite roomy and feature walk-in closets and the master bedroom has double entry doors and access to rear patio

- The master bedroom has double entry doors and access to rear patio

- 2 bedrooms, 1 bath, 1-car garage

- Basement foundation

Lattice Is Uncommon Touch

2,080 total square feet of living area

Price Code C

Special features

- Gallery hall creates a grand entrance into the great room
- Computer nook located in breakfast room is a functional living area near the center of activity
- A window seat in one of the secondary bedrooms adds enjoyment
- Built-in entertainment center and bookshelves make relaxing a breeze in the great room
- 3 bedrooms, 2 baths, 2-car side entry garage
- Basement, crawl space or slab foundation, please specify when ordering

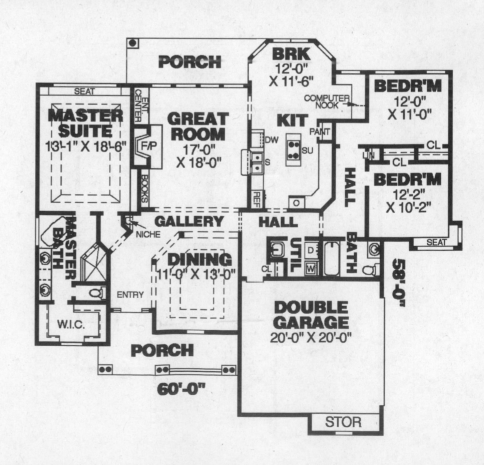

Plan #706-GH-24724

Two-Story With Victorian Feel

1,982 total square feet of living area

Price Code C

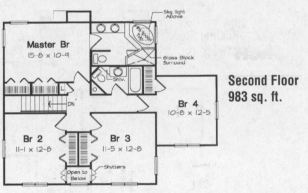

Master Br
15-8 x 10-9

Sky light Above

Glass Block Surround

Shlv.

DN

Second Floor
983 sq. ft.

Br 4
10-8 x 12-5

Br 2
11-1 x 12-8

Br 3
11-5 x 12-8

Open to Below

Shutters

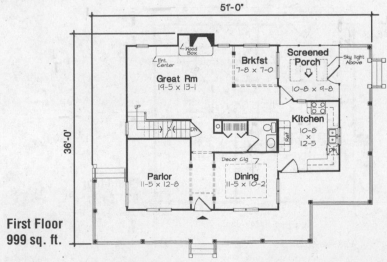

51'-0"

36'-0"

Wood Box

Ent. Center

Great Rm
19-5 x 13-1

Brkfst
7-8 x 7-0

Screened Porch
10-8 x 9-8

Sky light Above

UP

DN

Kitchen
10-8 x 12-5

Ref.

Decor Clg

Parlor
11-5 x 12-8

Dining
11-5 x 10-2

First Floor
999 sq. ft.

Special features

- Spacious master bedroom has bath with corner whirlpool tub and sunny skylight above
- Breakfast area overlooks into great room
- Screened porch with skylight above extends the home outdoors and allows for entertainment area
- 4 bedrooms, 2 1/2 baths
- Crawl space or slab foundation, please specify when ordering

Year-Round Or Weekend Getaway Home

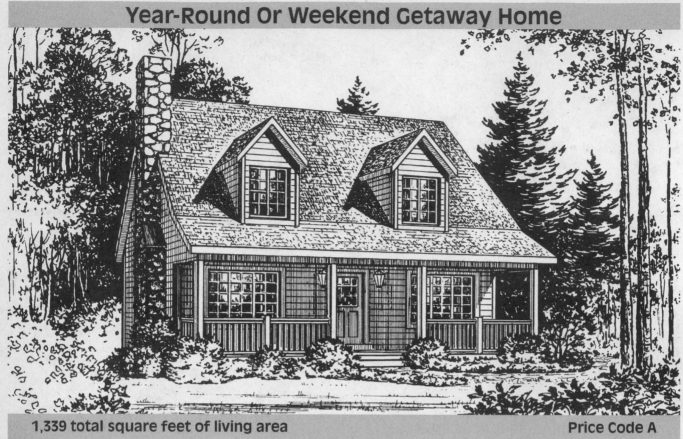

1,339 total square feet of living area

Price Code A

Special features

- Full-length covered porch enhances front facade
- Vaulted ceiling and stone fireplace add drama to family room
- Walk-in closets in bedrooms provide ample storage space
- Combined kitchen/dining area adjoins family room for perfect entertaining space
- 3 bedrooms, 2 1/2 baths
- Crawl space foundation

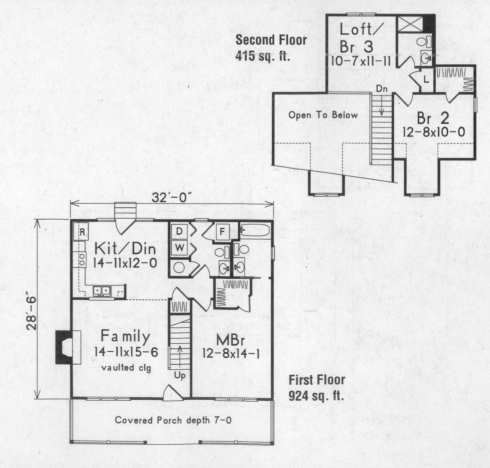

Second Floor 415 sq. ft.

Loft/ Br 3
10-7x11-11

Open To Below

Dn

Br 2
12-8x10-0

32'-0"

Kit/Din
14-11x12-0

R

D W F

28'-6"

Family
14-11x15-6
vaulted clg

Up

MBr
12-8x14-1

First Floor 924 sq. ft.

Covered Porch depth 7-0

Atrium Living For Views On A Narrow Lot

1,231 total square feet of living area

Price Code A

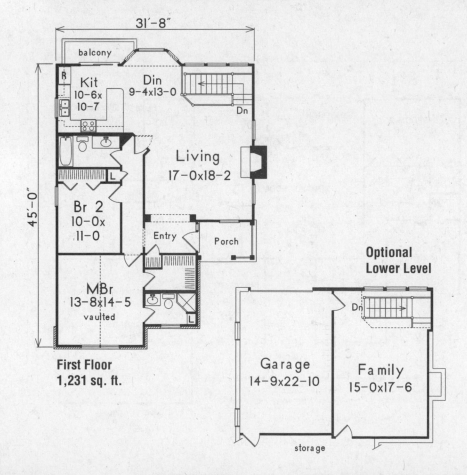

First Floor
1,231 sq. ft.

Optional Lower Level

Special features

- Dutch gables and stone accents provide an enchanting appearance for a small cottage
- The spacious living room offers a masonry fireplace, atrium with window wall and is open to a dining area with bay window
- A breakfast counter, lots of cabinet space and glass sliding doors to a walk-out balcony create a sensational kitchen
- 380 square feet of optional living area available on the lower level
- 2 bedrooms, 2 baths, 1-car drive under garage
- Walk-out basement foundation

TO ORDER BLUEPRINTS USE THE FORM ON PAGE 15 OR CALL TOLL-FREE 1-877-671-6036
View thousands more home plans online at www.familyhandyman.com/homeplans

123

Unique Three-Way Fireplace

2,126 total square feet of living area

Price Code C

Special features

- Elegant bay windows in master bedroom welcome the sun
- Double vanities in master bath separated by large whirlpool tub
- 3 bedrooms, 2 baths, 2-car side entry garage
- Slab foundation

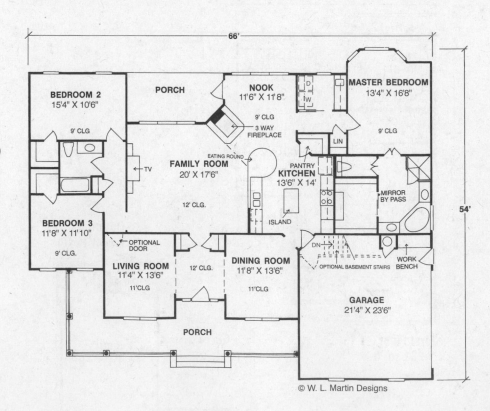

© W. L. Martin Designs

Carport With Storage

1,333 total square feet of living area

Price Code A

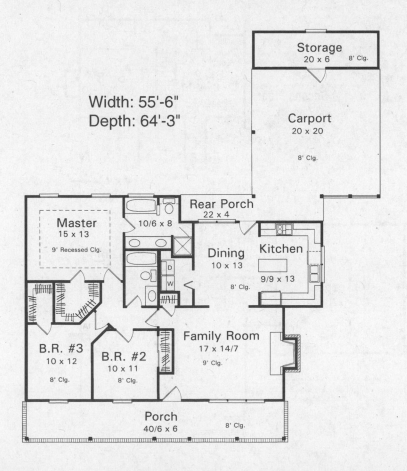

Width: 55'-6"
Depth: 64'-3"

Storage
20 x 6   8' Clg.

Carport
20 x 20

8' Clg.

Rear Porch
22 x 4

Master
15 x 13
9' Recessed Clg.

10/6 x 8

Dining
10 x 13
8' Clg.

Kitchen
9/9 x 13

D
W

B.R. #3
10 x 12
8' Clg.

B.R. #2
10 x 11
8' Clg.

Family Room
17 x 14/7
9' Clg.

Porch
40/6 x 6   8' Clg.

Special features

- Country charm with covered front porch
- Dining area looks into family room with fireplace
- Master suite has walk-in closet and private bath
- 3 bedrooms, 2 baths, 2-car attached carport
- Slab or crawl space foundation, please specify when ordering

Plan #706-0686

Charming Home Arranged For Open Living

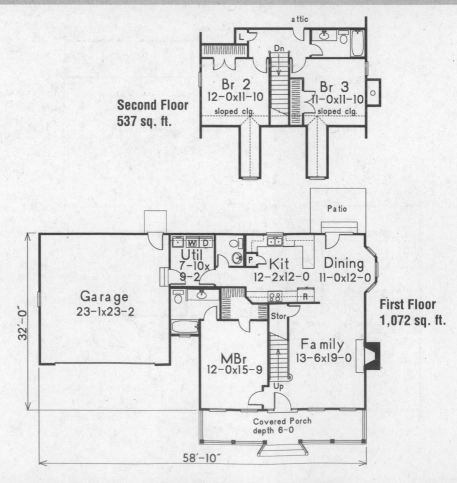

1,609 total square feet of living area

Price Code B

Special features

- Kitchen captures full use of space with pantry, ample cabinets and workspace

- Master bedroom is well-secluded with walk-in closet and private bath

- Large utility room includes sink and extra storage

- Attractive bay window in dining area provides light

- 3 bedrooms, 2 1/2 baths, 2-car garage

- Slab foundation

Second Floor
537 sq. ft.

attic

Br 2
12-0x11-10
sloped clg.

Dn

Br 3
11-0x11-10
sloped clg.

Patio

Util
7-10x
9-2

W D

Kit
12-2x12-0

Dining
11-0x12-0

Garage
23-1x23-2

32'-0"

Stor

MBr
12-0x15-9

Up

Family
13-6x19-0

First Floor
1,072 sq. ft.

Covered Porch
depth 6-0

58'-10"

© COPYRIGHT 1990
RALPH JONES

1,192 total square feet of living area

Price Code AA

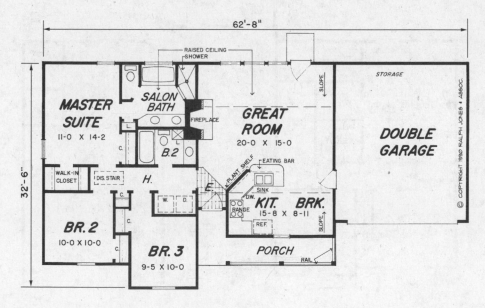

62'-8"

RAISED CEILING
SHOWER

STORAGE

SLOPE

MASTER
SUITE
11-0 X 14-2

SALON
BATH

FIREPLACE

GREAT
ROOM
20-0 X 15-0

DOUBLE
GARAGE

32'-6"

B.2

C.

WALK-IN
CLOSET

DIS. STAIR

H.

PLANT SHELF

EATING BAR

W. D.

SINK

© COPYRIGHT 1990 RALPH JONES & ASSOC.

BR. 2
10-0 X 10-0

C.

C.

DW.

KIT.
15-8 X 8-11

BRK.
8-11

RANGE

SLOPE

BR. 3
9-5 X 10-0

REF.

PORCH

RAIL

Special features

- Kitchen eating bar overlooks well-designed great room
- Private bath in master suite
- Extra storage space in garage
- 3 bedrooms, 2 baths, 2-car garage
- Slab or crawl space foundation, please specify when ordering

Comfortable Colonial Ranch

Christine Canova 03/02
© 2003, Garrell Associates, Inc.

1,404 total square feet of living area

Price Code E

Special features

- Dining area and kitchen connect allowing for convenience and ease
- Well-located laundry area is within steps of bedrooms and baths
- Vaulted grand room creates a feeling of spaciousness for this gathering area
- 3 bedrooms, 2 1/2 baths, 2-car garage
- Slab foundation

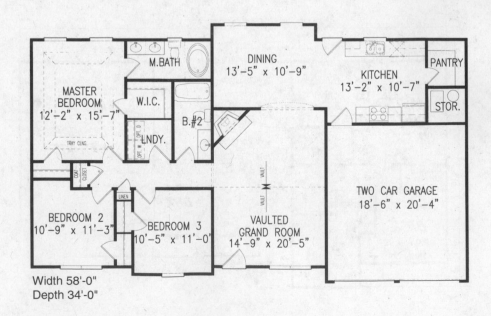

M.BATH

MASTER BEDROOM
12'-2" x 15'-7"

W.I.C.

LNDY.

B.#2

TRAY CLNG.

COAT CLOSET

LINEN

BEDROOM 2
10'-9" x 11'-3"

BEDROOM 3
10'-5" x 11'-0"

DINING
13'-5" x 10'-9"

KITCHEN
13'-2" x 10'-7"

PANTRY

STOR.

VAULT

VAULT

VAULTED GRAND ROOM
14'-9" x 20'-5"

TWO CAR GARAGE
18'-6" x 20'-4"

Width 58'-0"
Depth 34'-0"

Bedrooms Separate From Rest Of Home

1,849 total square feet of living area

Price Code C

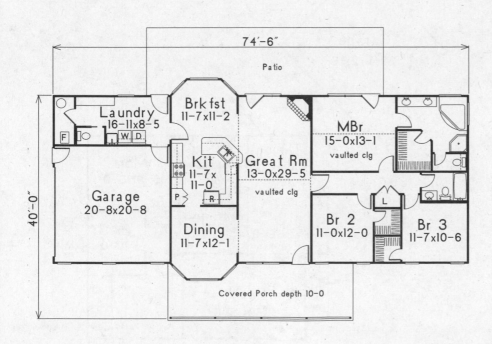

Special features

- Enormous laundry/mud room has many extras including storage area and half bath

- Lavish master bath has corner jacuzzi tub, double sinks, separate shower and walk-in closet

- Secondary bedrooms include walk-in closets

- Kitchen has wrap-around eating counter and is positioned between formal dining area and breakfast room for convenience

- 3 bedrooms, 2 1/2 baths, 2-car side entry garage

- Slab foundation, drawings also include crawl space foundation

TO ORDER BLUEPRINTS USE THE FORM ON PAGE 15 OR CALL TOLL-FREE 1-877-671-6036
View thousands more home plans online at www.familyhandyman.com/homeplans

129

Rambling Country Bungalow

1,475 total square feet of living area

Price Code B

Special features

- Family room features a high ceiling and prominent corner fireplace

- Kitchen with island counter and garden window makes a convenient connection between the family and dining rooms

- Hallway leads to three bedrooms all with large walk-in closets

- Covered breezeway joins main house and garage

- Full-width covered porch entry lends a country touch

- 3 bedrooms, 2 baths, 2-car side entry garage

- Slab foundation, drawings also include crawl space foundation

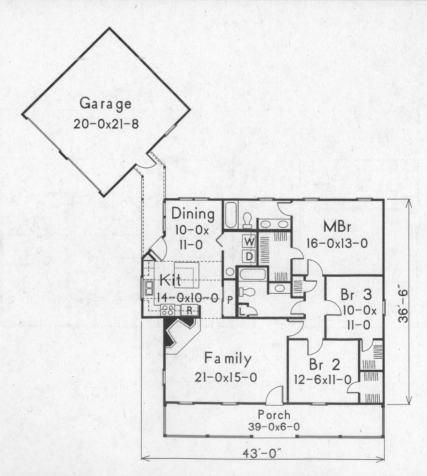

Garage
20-0x21-8

Dining
10-0x
11-0

MBr
16-0x13-0

Kit
14-0x10-0

Br 3
10-0x
11-0

Family
21-0x15-0

Br 2
12-6x11-0

Porch
39-0x6-0

36'-6"

43'-0"

TO ORDER BLUEPRINTS USE THE FORM ON PAGE 15 OR CALL TOLL-FREE 1-877-671-6036
View thousands more home plans online at www.familyhandyman.com/homeplans

Uncommon Style With This Ranch

1,787 total square feet of living area

Price Code B

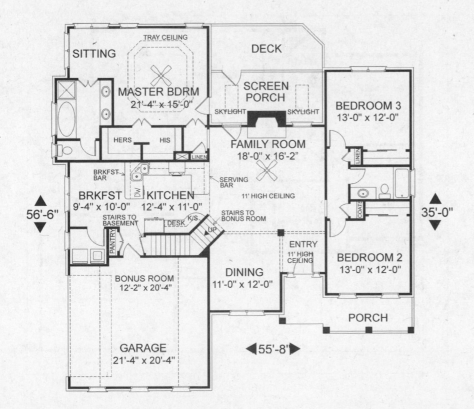

SITTING

TRAY CEILING

MASTER BDRM
21'-4" x 15'-0"

DECK

SCREEN PORCH

SKYLIGHT   SKYLIGHT

BEDROOM 3
13'-0" x 12'-0"

HERS   HIS

LINEN

FAMILY ROOM
18'-0" x 16'-2"

SERVING BAR

11' HIGH CEILING

LINEN

BRKFST BAR

COATS

56'-6"

BRKFST
9'-4" x 10'-0"

KITCHEN
12'-4" x 11'-0"

DW

STAIRS TO BONUS ROOM

DESK   K/S

STAIRS TO BASEMENT

UP

35'-0"

BEDROOM 2
13'-0" x 12'-0"

PANTRY

ENTRY
11' HIGH CEILING

BONUS ROOM
12'-2" x 20'-4"

DINING
11'-0" x 12'-0"

GARAGE
21'-4" x 20'-4"

55'-8"

PORCH

Special features

- Skylights brighten screened porch which connects to family room and deck outdoors

- Master bedroom features a comfortable sitting area, large private bath and direct access to screened porch

- Kitchen has serving bar which extends dining into family room

- 3 bedrooms, 2 baths, 2-car side entry garage

- Basement, crawl space or slab foundation, please specify when ordering

TO ORDER BLUEPRINTS USE THE FORM ON PAGE 15 OR CALL TOLL-FREE 1-877-671-6036
View thousands more home plans online at www.familyhandyman.com/homeplans

131

Open Feeling In This Ranch

1,875 total square feet of living area

Price Code C

Special features

- Peninsula separating kitchen and dining room has sink, dishwasher and eating area
- Tall ceilings throughout living area create spaciousness
- Columned foyer adds style
- 3 bedrooms, 2 1/2 baths, 2-car garage
- Basement foundation

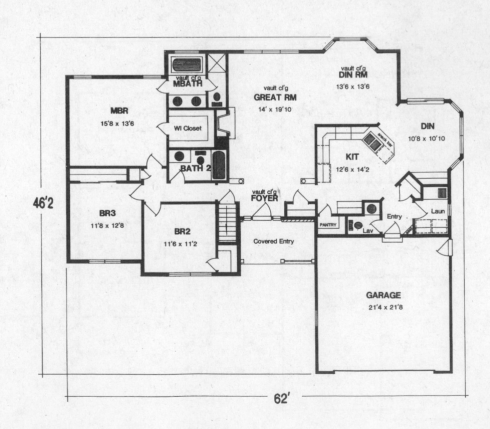

Cottage With Atrium

969 total square feet of living area

Price Code AA

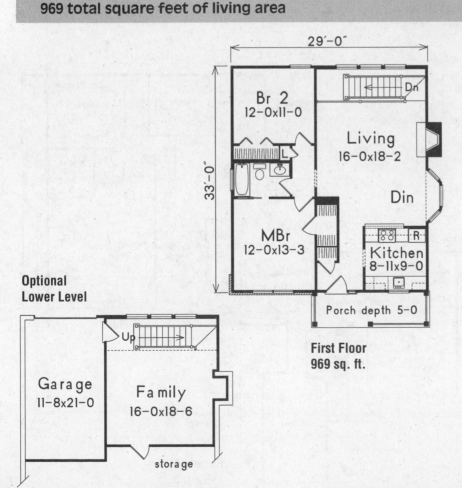

Optional Lower Level

Garage
11-8x21-0

Family
16-0x18-6

storage

Up

29'-0"

Br 2
12-0x11-0

Living
16-0x18-2

Dn

33'-0"

MBr
12-0x13-3

Din

Kitchen
8-11x9-0

R

Porch depth 5-0

**First Floor
969 sq. ft.**

Special features

- Eye-pleasing facade enjoys stone accents with country porch for quiet evenings
- A bayed dining area, cozy fireplace and atrium with sunny two-story windows are the many features of the living room
- Step-saver kitchen includes a pass-through snack bar
- 325 square feet of optional living area available on the lower level
- 2 bedrooms, 1 bath, 1-car rear entry garage
- Walk-out basement foundation

The Family Handyman

Plan #706-FB-1175

Exterior Accents Make This A Standout

1,467 total square feet of living area

Price Code A

Special features

- 9' ceilings throughout this home
- Two-story family and dining rooms are open and airy
- Bonus room above the garage has an additional 292 square feet of living area
- 3 bedrooms, 2 1/2 baths, 2-car garage
- Walk-out basement or crawl space foundation, please specify when ordering

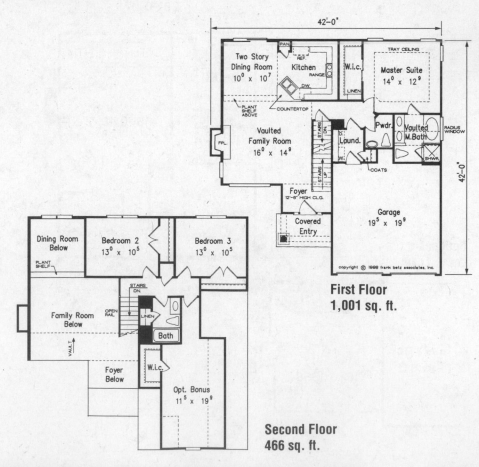

First Floor
1,001 sq. ft.

Second Floor
466 sq. ft.

TO ORDER BLUEPRINTS USE THE FORM ON PAGE 15 OR CALL TOLL-FREE 1-877-671-6036
View thousands more home plans online at www.familyhandyman.com/homeplans

Country Charm Wrapped In A Veranda

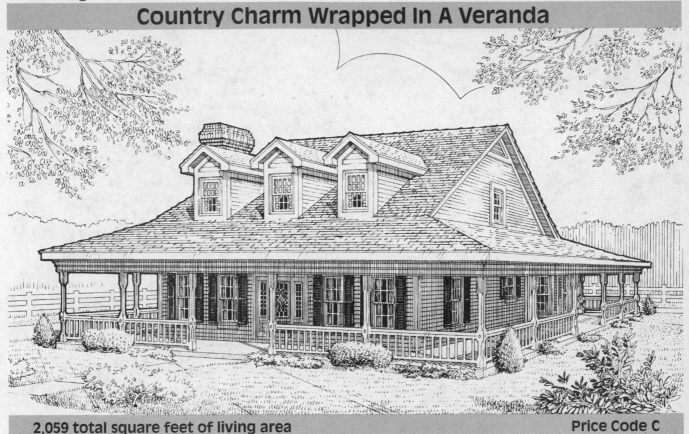

2,059 total square feet of living area

Price Code C

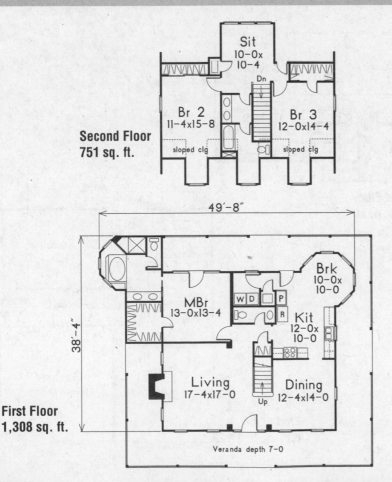

Second Floor 751 sq. ft.

Sit
10-0x
10-4

Dn

Br 2
11-4x15-8
sloped clg

Br 3
12-0x14-4
sloped clg

First Floor 1,308 sq. ft.

49'-8"

38'-4"

Brk
10-0x
10-0

MBr
13-0x13-4

W D P
R

Kit
12-0x
10-0

Living
17-4x17-0

Dining
12-4x14-0

Up.

Veranda depth 7-0

Special features

■ Octagon-shaped breakfast room offers plenty of windows and creates a view to the veranda

■ First floor master bedroom has large walk-in closet and deluxe bath

■ 9' ceilings throughout the home

■ Secondary bedrooms and bath feature dormers and are adjacent to cozy sitting area

■ 3 bedrooms, 2 1/2 baths, 2-car detached garage

■ Slab foundation, drawings also include basement and crawl space foundations

Smaller Home Offers Stylish Exterior

1,700 total square feet of living area

Price Code B

Special features

- Two-story entry with T-stair is illuminated with decorative oval window

- Skillfully designed U-shaped kitchen has a built-in pantry

- All bedrooms have generous closet storage and are common to spacious hall with walk-in cedar closet

- 4 bedrooms, 2 1/2 baths, 2-car side entry garage

- Basement foundation

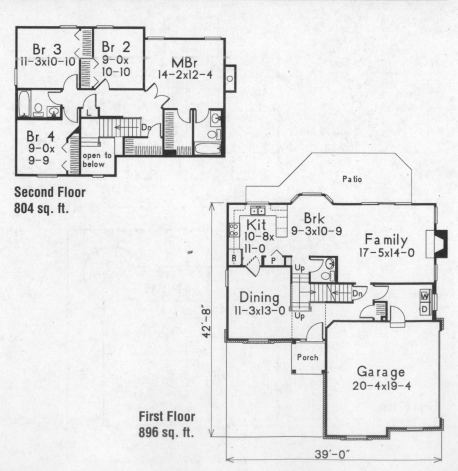

Second Floor
804 sq. ft.

Br 3
11-3x10-10

Br 2
9-0x 10-10

MBr
14-2x12-4

Br 4
9-0x 9-9

open to below

L

Dn

First Floor
896 sq. ft.

Patio

Kit
10-8x 11-0

Brk
9-3x10-9

Family
17-5x14-0

Dining
11-3x13-0

Up

Up

Dn

R

P

W D

Porch

Garage
20-4x19-4

42'-8"

39'-0"

A Special Home For Views

1,684 total square feet of living area

Price Code B

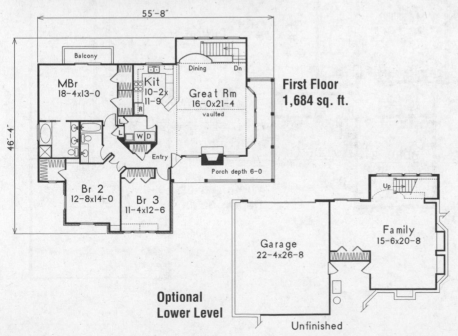

Rear View

Special features

- Delightful wrap-around porch anchored by full masonry fireplace

- The vaulted great room includes a large bay window, fireplace, dining balcony and atrium window wall

- His and hers walk-in closets, large luxury bath and sliding doors to exterior balcony are a few fantastic features of the master bedroom

- Atrium open to 611 square feet of optional living area on the lower level

- 3 bedrooms, 2 baths, 2-car drive under garage

- Walk-out basement foundation

55'-8"

Balcony

MBr
18-4x13-0

Kit
10-2x
11-9

Dining   Dn

Great Rm
16-0x21-4
vaulted

**First Floor
1,684 sq. ft.**

46-4"

W D

Entry

Br 2
12-8x14-0

Br 3
11-4x12-6

Porch depth 6-0

Up

Garage
22-4x26-8

Family
15-6x20-8

**Optional
Lower Level**

Unfinished

Fabulous Curb Appeal

1,588 total square feet of living area

Price Code B

Special features

- Workshop in garage ideal for storage and projects
- 12' vaulted master suite has his and hers closets as well as a lovely bath with bayed soaking tub and compartmentalized shower and toilet area
- Lovely arched entry to 14' vaulted great room that flows open to the dining room and sky-lit kitchen
- 3 bedrooms, 2 baths, 2-car garage
- Basement foundation

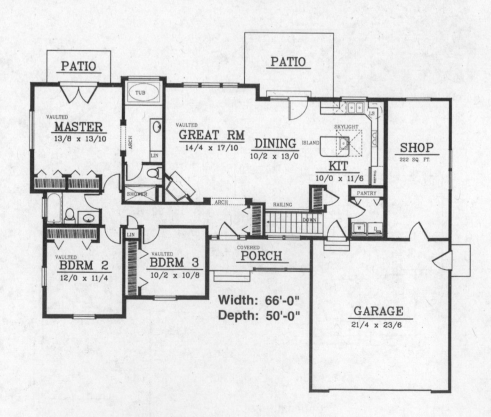

PATIO

PATIO

VAULTED
MASTER
13/8 x 13/10

TUB

VAULTED
GREAT RM
14/4 x 17/10

DINING
10/2 x 13/0

ISLAND

SKYLIGHT

KIT
10/0 x 11/6

SHOP
222 SQ. FT.

ARCH

LIN

SHOWER

PANTRY

ARCH

RAILING

DOWN

W D

VAULTED
BDRM 2
12/0 x 11/4

LIN

VAULTED
BDRM 3
10/2 x 10/8

COVERED
PORCH

GARAGE
21/4 x 23/6

Width: 66'-0"
Depth: 50'-0"

Outdoor Living With Wrap-Around Covered Porch

1,784 total square feet of living area

Price Code B

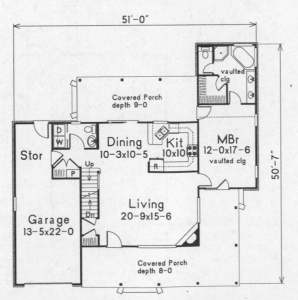

Second Floor
672 sq. ft.

Br 2
10-0x11-0
vaulted clg

Br 3
10-0x11-0
vaulted clg

L

Dn

Ga thering Rm
15-5x15-5
vaulted clg

First Floor
1,112 sq. ft.

51'-0"

50'-7"

Covered Porch
depth 9-0

vaulted clg

Stor

D
W

Dining
10-3x10-5

Kit
10x10

MBr
12-0x17-6
vaulted clg

Up

Garage
13-5x22-0

Dn

P

R

Living
20-9x15-6

Covered Porch
depth 8-0

Special features

- Spacious living area with corner fireplace offers a cheerful atmosphere with large windows
- Large second floor gathering room is great for kid's play area
- Secluded master suite has separate porch entrances and large master bath with walk-in closet
- 3 bedrooms, 2 1/2 baths, 1-car garage
- Basement foundation, drawings also include crawl space foundation

TO ORDER BLUEPRINTS USE THE FORM ON PAGE 15 OR CALL TOLL-FREE 1-877-671-6036
View thousands more home plans online at www.familyhandyman.com/homeplans

139

Quaint Country Home Is Ideal

1,028 total square feet of living area

Price Code AA

Special features

- Master bedroom conveniently located on first floor
- Well-designed bath contains laundry facilities
- L-shaped kitchen has a handy pantry
- Tall windows flank family room fireplace
- Cozy covered porch provides unique angled entry into home
- 3 bedrooms, 1 bath
- Crawl space foundation

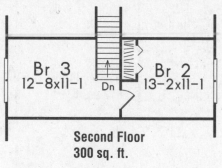

Second Floor
300 sq. ft.

Br 3
12-8x11-1

Br 2
13-2x11-1

Dn

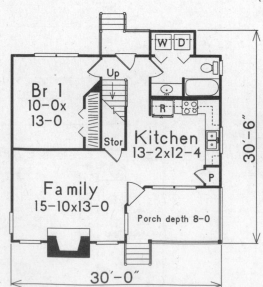

First Floor
728 sq. ft.

W/D

Up

Br 1
10-0x 13-0

Stor

Kitchen
13-2x12-4

R

P

Family
15-10x13-0

Porch depth 8-0

30'-6"

30'-0"

140

TO ORDER BLUEPRINTS USE THE FORM ON PAGE 15 OR CALL TOLL-FREE 1-877-671-6036
View thousands more home plans online at www.familyhandyman.com/homeplans

Large Windows Grace This Split-Level Home

1,427 total square feet of living area

Price Code A

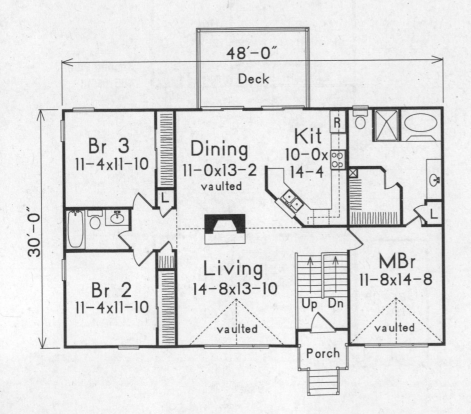

48'-0"

Deck

30'-0"

Br 3
11-4x11-10

Dining
11-0x13-2
vaulted

Kit
10-0x
14-4

R

L

L

Living
14-8x13-10

vaulted

Up Dn

MBr
11-8x14-8

vaulted

Br 2
11-4x11-10

Porch

Special features

- Practical storage space situated in the garage
- Convenient laundry closet located on lower level
- Kitchen and dining area both have sliding doors that access the deck
- Large expansive space created by vaulted living and dining rooms
- 3 bedrooms, 2 baths, 2-car drive under garage
- Basement foundation

TO ORDER BLUEPRINTS USE THE FORM ON PAGE 15 OR CALL TOLL-FREE 1-877-671-6036
View thousands more home plans online at www.familyhandyman.com/homeplans

141

Dramatic Sloping Ceiling In Living Room

1,432 total square feet of living area

Price Code B

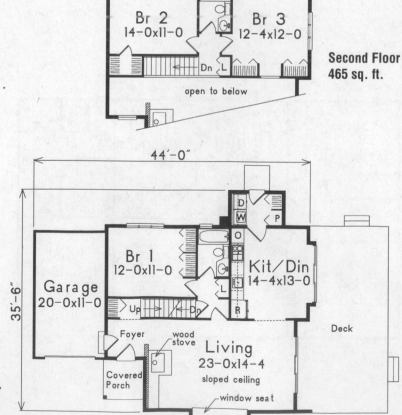

**Second Floor
465 sq. ft.**

Br 2
14-0x11-0

Br 3
12-4x12-0

Dn

open to below

44'-0"

35'-6"

Garage
20-0x11-0

Br 1
12-0x11-0

Kit/Din
14-4x13-0

Up

Foyer

wood
stove

Living
23-0x14-4
sloped ceiling

Deck

window seat

Covered
Porch

**First Floor
967 sq. ft.**

Special features

- Enter the two-story foyer from covered porch or garage

- Living room has square bay and window seat, glazed end wall with floor-to-ceiling windows and access to the deck

- Kitchen/dining room also opens to the deck for added convenience

- 3 bedrooms, 2 baths, 1-car garage

- Basement foundation, drawings also include slab foundation

A Great Country Farmhouse

1,669 total square feet of living area

Price Code B

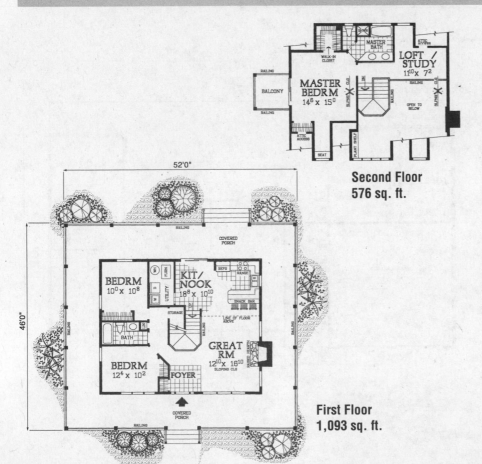

Second Floor 576 sq. ft.

First Floor 1,093 sq. ft.

Special features

- Generous use of windows add exciting visual elements to the exterior as well as plenty of natural light to the interior
- Two-story great room has a raised hearth
- Second floor loft/study would easily make a terrific home office
- 3 bedrooms, 2 baths
- Crawl space foundation

Private Master Suite

1,458 total square feet of living area

Price Code A

Special features

- Divider wall allows for some privacy in the formal dining area

- Two secondary bedrooms share a full bath

- Covered front and rear porches create enjoyable outdoor living spaces

- 3 bedrooms, 2 baths, 2-car garage

- Slab or crawl space foundation, please specify when ordering

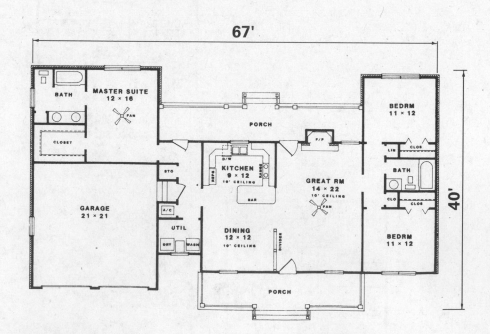

Distinctive Home For Sloping Terrain

1,340 total square feet of living area

Price Code A

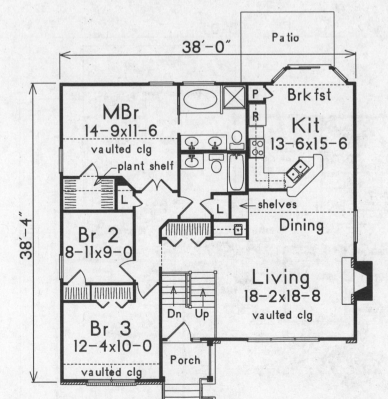

Special features

- Grand-sized vaulted living and dining rooms offer fireplace, wet bar and breakfast counter open to spacious kitchen

- Vaulted master suite features double entry doors, walk-in closet and elegant bath

- Basement includes a huge two-car garage and space for a bedroom/bath expansion

- 3 bedrooms, 2 baths, 2-car drive under garage with storage area

- Basement foundation

Bedrooms Separated From Living Areas

1,734 total square feet of living area

Price Code B

Special features

- Large entry with coffered ceiling and display niches
- Sunken great room has 10' ceiling
- Kitchen island includes eating counter
- 9' ceiling in master bedroom
- Master bath features corner tub and double sinks
- 3 bedrooms, 2 baths, 2-car garage
- Crawl space foundation

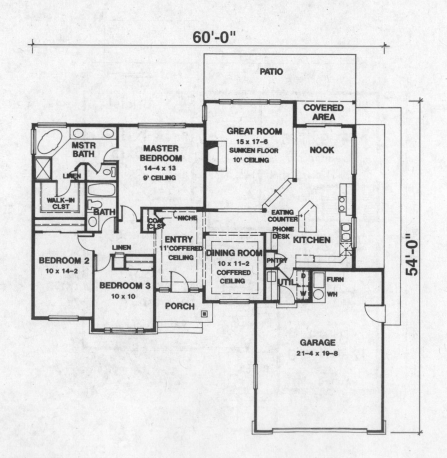

Cozy And Functional Design

1,285 total square feet of living area

Price Code A

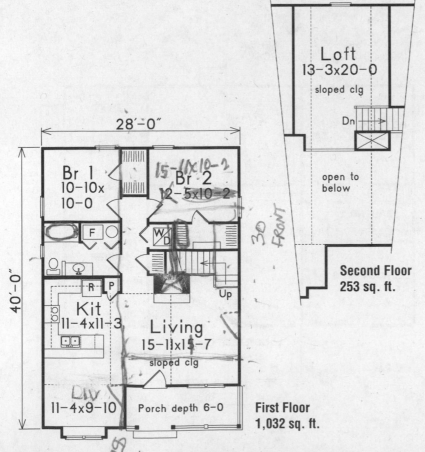

28'-0"

40'-0"

Br 1
10-10x
10-0

Br 2
15-11x10-2
12-5x10-2

F

W/D

Kit
11-4x11-3

R P

3D FRONT

Living
15-11x15-7
sloped clg

Up

DIN
11-4x9-10

Porch depth 6-0

First Floor
1,032 sq. ft.

Loft
13-3x20-0
sloped clg

Dn

open to below

Second Floor
253 sq. ft.

Special features

- Dining nook creates warm feeling with sunny box bay window
- Second floor loft perfect for recreation space or office hideaway
- Bedrooms include walk-in closets allowing extra storage space
- Kitchen, dining and living areas combine making perfect gathering place
- 2 bedrooms, 1 bath
- Crawl space foundation

TO ORDER BLUEPRINTS USE THE FORM ON PAGE 15 OR CALL TOLL-FREE 1-877-671-6036
View thousands more home plans online at www.familyhandyman.com/homeplans

147

Perfect Home For Family Living

1,700 total square feet of living area

Price Code B

Special features

- Oversized laundry room has large pantry and storage area as well as access to the outdoors
- Master bedroom is separated from other bedrooms for privacy
- Raised snack bar in kitchen allows extra seating for dining
- 3 bedrooms, 2 baths
- Crawl space foundation

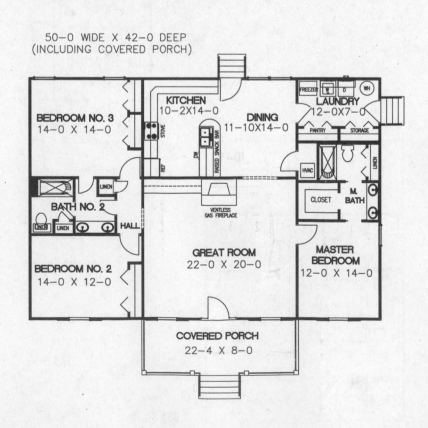

50–0 WIDE X 42–0 DEEP
(INCLUDING COVERED PORCH)

BEDROOM NO. 3
14–0 X 14–0

KITCHEN
10–2X14–0

DINING
11–10X14–0

FREEZER

LAUNDRY
12–0X7–0

PANTRY STORAGE

HVAC

BATH NO. 2

HALL

CLOSET

M.
BATH

VENTLESS
GAS FIREPLACE

BEDROOM NO. 2
14–0 X 12–0

GREAT ROOM
22–0 X 20–0

MASTER
BEDROOM
12–0 X 14–0

COVERED PORCH
22–4 X 8–0

Bright Spacious Living Area

1,844 total square feet of living area

Price Code C

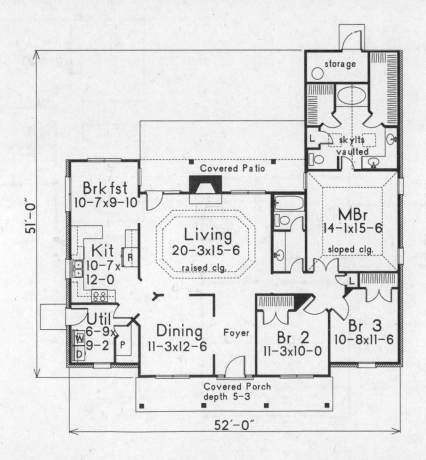

storage

Covered Patio

Brkfst
10-7x9-10

Kit
10-7x
12-0

Living
20-3x15-6
raised clg.

MBr
14-1x15-6
sloped clg.

Util
6-9x
9-2

W
D

P

Dining
11-3x12-6

Foyer

Br 2
11-3x10-0

Br 3
10-8x11-6

Covered Porch
depth 5-3

51'-0"

52'-0"

skylts
vaulted

Special features

- Luxurious master bath is impressive with vaulted ceiling, large walk-in closets and an oversized tub
- Living room has high ceiling and large windows that flank the fireplace
- Front and rear covered porches add a charming feel
- Cozy breakfast room is adjacent to kitchen for easy access
- Spacious utility room includes pantry and is accessible to both the kitchen and the outdoors
- 3 bedrooms, 2 baths
- Slab foundation

TO ORDER BLUEPRINTS USE THE FORM ON PAGE 15 OR CALL TOLL-FREE 1-877-671-6036
View thousands more home plans online at www.familyhandyman.com/homeplans

149

Spacious Vaulted Great Room

1,189 total square feet of living area

Price Code AA

Special features

- All bedrooms are located on the second floor
- Dining room and kitchen both have views of the patio
- Convenient half bath located near the kitchen
- Master bedroom has private bath
- 3 bedrooms, 2 1/2 baths, 2-car garage
- Basement foundation

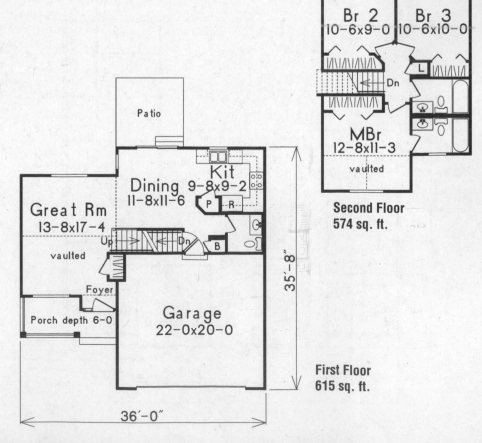

Second Floor
574 sq. ft.

First Floor
615 sq. ft.

TO ORDER BLUEPRINTS USE THE FORM ON PAGE 15 OR CALL TOLL-FREE 1-877-671-6036
View thousands more home plans online at www.familyhandyman.com/homeplans

Balcony Provides Dramatic View Below To Great Room

2,157 total square feet of living area

Price Code C

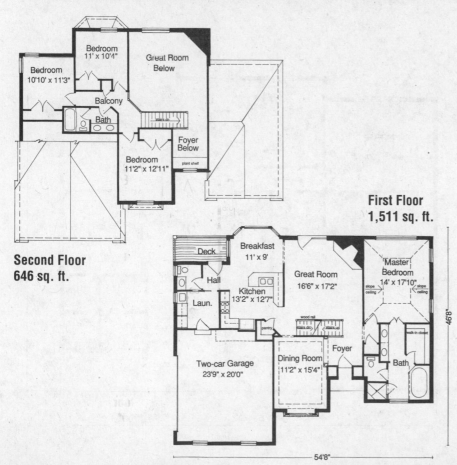

Second Floor 646 sq. ft.

First Floor 1,511 sq. ft.

Special features

- Varied ceiling treatments, spacious rooms and lots of windows combine to set this home apart from the ordinary
- A spacious kitchen has a peninsula and walk-in pantry
- The master bedroom has every luxury imagined
- 4 bedrooms, 2 1/2 baths, 2-car side entry garage
- Basement or walk-out basement foundation, please specify when ordering

Plan #706-JA-59195

Superb Ranch Style

1,739 total square feet of living area

Price Code B

Special features

- Cheerful and bright living room has an open, airy feel with lots of windows and a cathedral ceiling

- Two secondary bedrooms have direct access to a jack and jill bath

- U-shaped kitchen has an adjacent dining room

- 3 bedrooms, 2 1/2 baths, 2-car garage

- Basement foundation

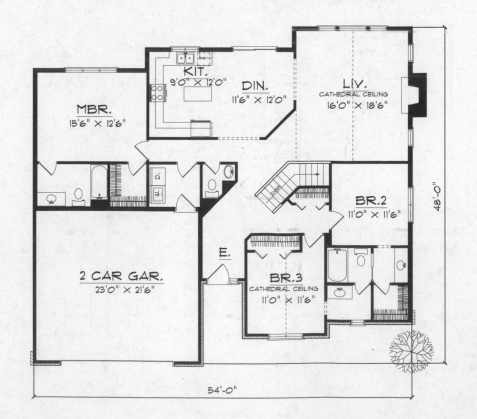

Open Living Spaces

1,000 total square feet of living area

Price Code AA

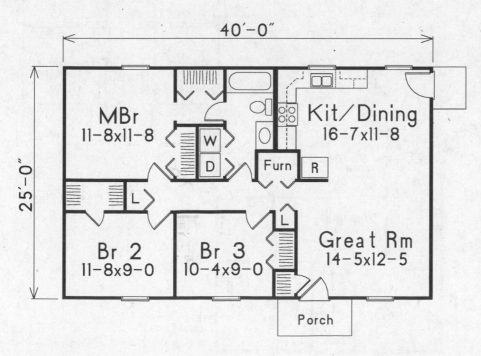

40'-0"

25'-0"

MBr
11-8x11-8

W
D

Kit/Dining
16-7x11-8

Furn

R

L

Br 2
11-8x9-0

Br 3
10-4x9-0

L

Great Rm
14-5x12-5

Porch

Special features

- Bath includes convenient closeted laundry area
- Master bedroom includes double closets and private access to bath
- Foyer features handy coat closet
- L-shaped kitchen provides easy access outdoors
- 3 bedrooms, 1 bath
- Crawl space foundation, drawings also include basement and slab foundations

Quaint Porch Adds Charm

1,735 total square feet of living area

Price Code B

Special features

- Angled kitchen wall expands space into the dining room
- Second floor has cozy sitting area with cheerful window
- Two spacious bedrooms on second floor share a bath
- 3 bedrooms, 2 1/2 baths, 2-car drive under garage
- Basement foundation

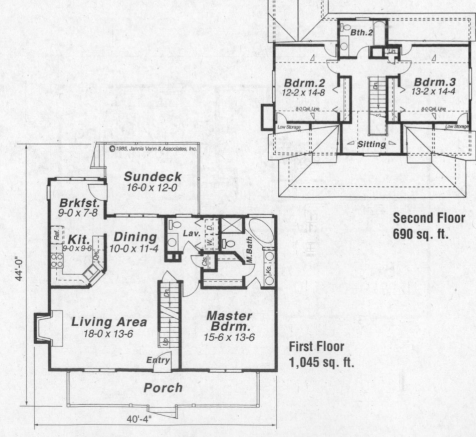

Second Floor
690 sq. ft.

First Floor
1,045 sq. ft.

TO ORDER BLUEPRINTS USE THE FORM ON PAGE 15 OR CALL TOLL-FREE 1-877-671-6036
View thousands more home plans online at www.familyhandyman.com/homeplans

Covered Deck Off Breakfast Room

1,231 total square feet of living area

Price Code A

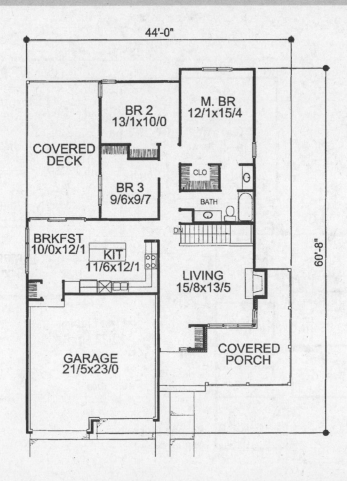

44'-0"

60'-8"

BR 2
13/1x10/0

M. BR
12/1x15/4

COVERED DECK

CLO

BR 3
9/6x9/7

BATH

DN

BRKFST
10/0x12/1

KIT
11/6x12/1

LIVING
15/8x13/5

GARAGE
21/5x23/0

COVERED PORCH

Special features
- Covered front porch
- Master bedroom has separate sink area
- Large island in kitchen for eat-in dining or preparation area
- 3 bedrooms, 1 bath, 2-car garage
- Basement foundation

Affordable Home Features Five Bedrooms

2,012 total square feet of living area

Price Code C

Special features

- Gables, cantilevers, angled and box bay windows all contribute to an elegant exterior

- Two-story entry leads to an efficient kitchen and bayed breakfast area with morning room

- Garage contains bonus area for a shop, bicycles and miscellaneous storage

- 5 bedrooms, 2 1/2 baths, 2-car garage

- Basement foundation

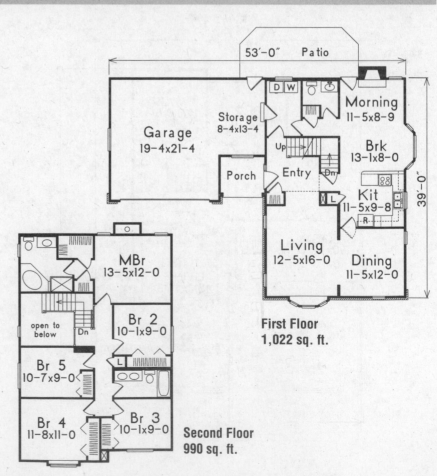

53'-0" Patio

Garage
19-4x21-4

Storage
8-4x13-4

D W

Morning
11-5x8-9

Brk
13-1x8-0

Porch

Up

Entry

Dn

Kit
11-5x9-8

39'-0"

Living
12-5x16-0

Dining
11-5x12-0

First Floor
1,022 sq. ft.

MBr
13-5x12-0

open to below

Dn

Br 2
10-1x9-0

Br 5
10-7x9-0

Br 4
11-8x11-0

Br 3
10-1x9-0

Second Floor
990 sq. ft.

Innovative Ranch Has Cozy Corner Patio

1,092 total square feet of living area

Price Code AA

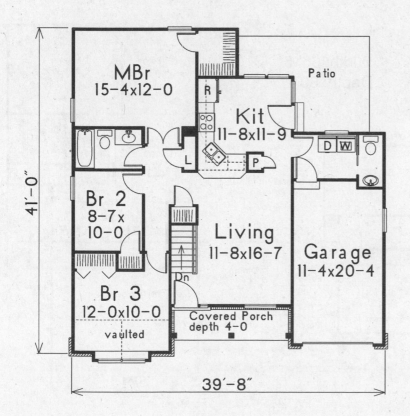

MBr
15-4x12-0

R

Patio

Kit
11-8x11-9

L

P

D W

Br 2
8-7 x
10-0

Living
11-8x16-7

Garage
11-4x20-4

Dn

Br 3
12-0x10-0

vaulted

Covered Porch
depth 4-0

41'-0"

39'-8"

Special features

- Box window and inviting porch with dormers create a charming facade

- Eat-in kitchen offers a pass-through breakfast bar, corner window wall to patio, pantry and convenient laundry with half bath

- Master bedroom features double entry doors and walk-in closet

- 3 bedrooms, 1 1/2 baths, 1-car garage

- Basement foundation

Vaulted Rear Porch

1,849 total square feet of living area   **Price Code C**

Special features

- Open floor plan creates an airy feeling

- Kitchen and breakfast area include center island, pantry and built-in desk

- Master bedroom has private entrance off breakfast area and a view of vaulted porch

- 3 bedrooms, 2 baths, 2-car garage

- Crawl space or slab foundation, please specify when ordering

Width: 66'-5"
Depth: 60'-0"

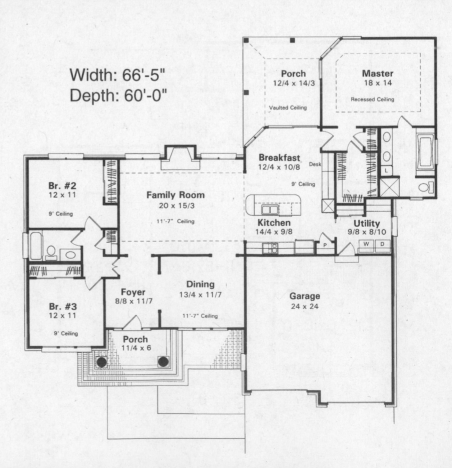

Circle-Top Details

1,932 total square feet of living area

Price Code C

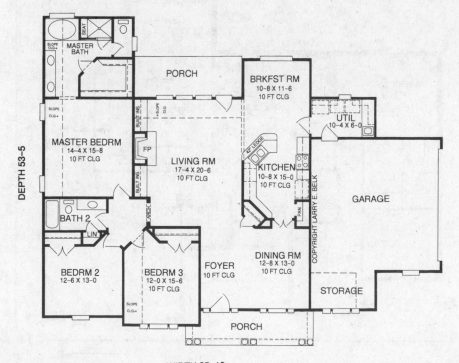

DEPTH 53–5

MASTER BATH
SEAT
SLOPE CLG

PORCH

BRKFST RM
10–8 X 11–6
10 FT CLG

UTIL
10–4 X 6–0

SLOPE CLG→

MASTER BEDRM
14–4 X 15–8
10 FT CLG

FP
BUILT INS

LIVING RM
17–4 X 20–6
10 FT CLG

42" LEDGE

KITCHEN
10–8 X 15–0
10 FT CLG

GARAGE

COPYRIGHT LARRY E. BELK

BATH 2
LIN

BEDRM 2
12–6 X 13–0

BEDRM 3
12–0 X 15–6
10 FT CLG

FOYER
10 FT CLG

DINING RM
12–8 X 13–0
10 FT CLG

STORAGE

SLOPE CLG→

PORCH

WIDTH 65–10

Special features

- Double arches form entrance to this elegantly styled home
- Two palladian windows add distinction to facade
- Kitchen has angled eating bar opening to the breakfast and living rooms
- 3 bedrooms, 2 baths, 2-car side entry garage
- Crawl space or slab foundation, please specify when ordering

Spacious Foyer Welcomes Guests

1,593 total square feet of living area

Price Code B

Special features

- The rear porch is a pleasant surprise and perfect for enjoying the outdoors
- Great room is filled with extras like a corner fireplace, sloping ceiling and view to the outdoors
- Separating the kitchen from the dining area is a large island with seating
- 3 bedrooms, 2 baths, 2-car garage
- Basement foundation

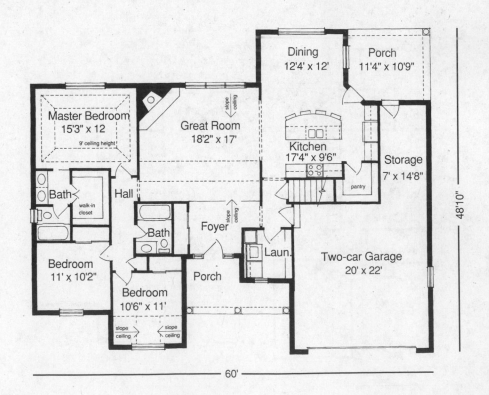

Dining 12'4" x 12'
Porch 11'4" x 10'9"
Master Bedroom 15'3" x 12
9' ceiling height
Great Room 18'2" x 17'
Kitchen 17'4" x 9'6"
Storage 7' x 14'8"
Bath
walk-in closet
Hall
pantry
Bath
Foyer
slope ceiling
Laun.
Two-car Garage 20' x 22'
Bedroom 11' x 10'2"
Porch
Bedroom 10'6" x 11'
slope ceiling
slope ceiling
48'10"
60'

Appealing Ranch Has Attractive Front Dormers

1,642 total square feet of living area   **Price Code B**

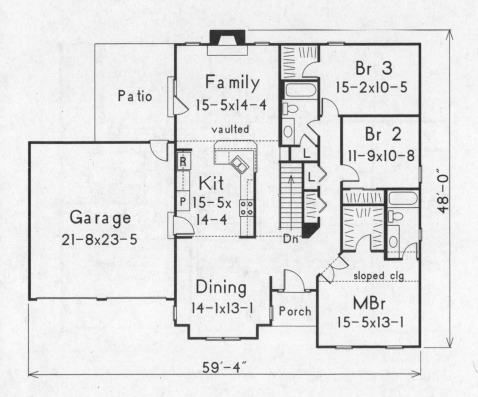

Patio

Family
15-5x14-4

vaulted

Kit
15-5x
14-4

Garage
21-8x23-5

Dining
14-1x13-1

Br 3
15-2x10-5

Br 2
11-9x10-8

48'-0"

sloped clg

Porch

MBr
15-5x13-1

Dn

59'-4"

Special features

- Walk-through kitchen boasts vaulted ceiling and corner sink overlooking family room

- Vaulted family room features cozy fireplace and access to rear patio

- Master bedroom includes sloped ceiling, walk-in closet and private bath

- 3 bedrooms, 2 baths, 2-car garage

- Basement foundation, drawings also include slab and crawl space foundations

TO ORDER BLUEPRINTS USE THE FORM ON PAGE 15 OR CALL TOLL-FREE 1-877-671-6036
View thousands more home plans online at www.familyhandyman.com/homeplans

161

Private Master Suite

1,783 total square feet of living area

Price Code B

Special features

- Grand foyer leads to family room
- Walk-in pantry in kitchen
- Master bath has step down doorless shower, huge vanity and large walk-in closet
- 3 bedrooms, 2 baths, 2-car garage
- Slab foundation

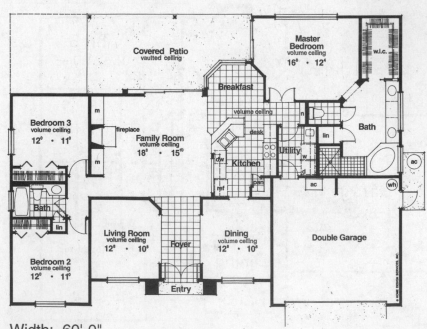

Width: 60'-0"
Depth: 45'-0"

162

TO ORDER BLUEPRINTS USE THE FORM ON PAGE 15 OR CALL TOLL-FREE 1-877-671-6036
View thousands more home plans online at www.familyhandyman.com/homeplans

Vaulted Ceilings Highlight This Home

1,560 total square feet of living area

Price Code B

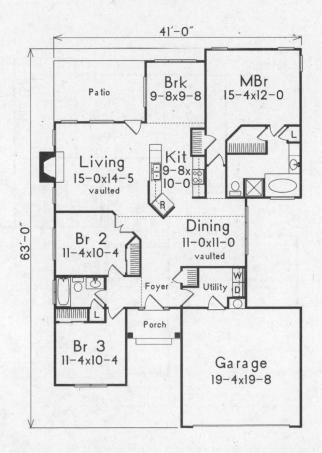

Special features

■ Cozy breakfast room is tucked at the rear of this home and features plenty of windows for natural light

■ Large entry has easy access to secondary bedrooms, laundry/utility, dining and living rooms

■ Private master suite

■ Kitchen overlooks living room with fireplace and patio access

■ 3 bedrooms, 2 baths, 2-car garage

■ Slab foundation

TO ORDER BLUEPRINTS USE THE FORM ON PAGE 15 OR CALL TOLL-FREE 1-877-671-6036
View thousands more home plans online at www.familyhandyman.com/homeplans

163

Upscale Ranch Boasts Both Formal And Casual Areas

1,950 total square feet of living area

Price Code C

Special features

- Large corner kitchen with island cooktop opens to family room
- Master suite features double-door entry, raised ceiling, double-bowl vanity and walk-in closet
- Plant shelf accents hall
- 4 bedrooms, 2 baths, 3-car garage
- Crawl space foundation

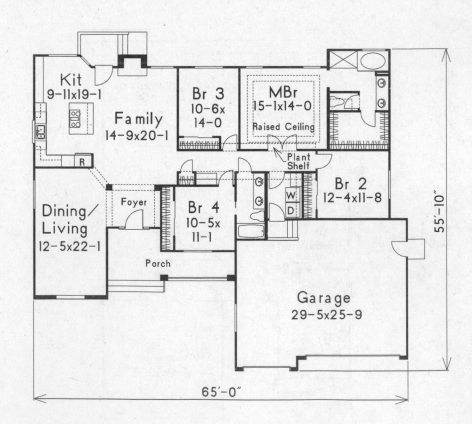

Kit
9-11x19-1

Family
14-9x20-1

Br 3
10-6x14-0

MBr
15-1x14-0
Raised Ceiling

Plant Shelf

Br 2
12-4x11-8

Dining/
Living
12-5x22-1

Foyer

Br 4
10-5x11-1

W
D

Porch

Garage
29-5x25-9

55'-10"

65'-0"

164

TO ORDER BLUEPRINTS USE THE FORM ON PAGE 15 OR CALL TOLL-FREE 1-877-671-6036
View thousands more home plans online at www.familyhandyman.com/homeplans

Secluded Master Suite

1,937 total square feet of living area

Price Code C

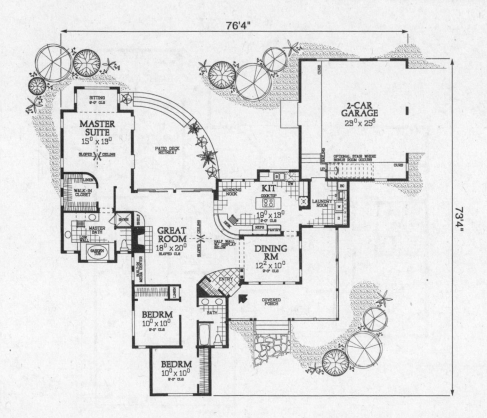

Special features

- Upscale great room offers a sloped ceiling, fireplace with extended hearth and built-in shelves for an entertainment center

- Gourmet kitchen includes a cooktop island counter and a quaint morning room

- Master suite features a sloped ceiling, cozy sitting room, walk-in closet and a private bath with whirlpool tub

- 3 bedrooms, 2 baths, 2-car side entry garage

- Crawl space foundation

Central Living Room

1,420 total square feet of living area

Price Code A

Special features

- Energy efficient home with 2" x 6" exterior walls

- Living room has 12' ceiling, corner fireplace and atrium doors leading to covered porch

- Separate master suite has garden bath and walk-in closet

- 3 bedrooms, 2 baths, 2-car garage

- Slab or crawl space foundation, please specify when ordering

Wrap-Around Porch Adds Outdoor Living

1,814 total square feet of living area

Price Code C

Second Floor
890 sq. ft.

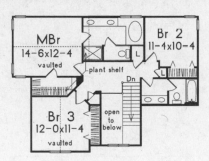

MBr
14-6x12-4
vaulted

Br 2
11-4x10-4

plant shelf

Dn

Br 3
12-0x11-4
vaulted

open to below

Special features

■ Vaulted master bedroom features a walk-in closet and a private bath

■ Exciting two-story entry with views into the dining room

■ Kitchen, family and dining rooms combine to make a great entertaining space with lots of windows

■ 3 bedrooms, 2 1/2 baths, 2-car garage

■ Basement foundation

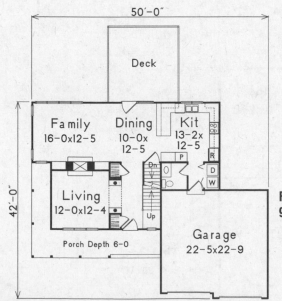

50'-0"

Deck

Family
16-0x12-5

Dining
10-0x
12-5

Kit
13-2x
12-5

R

P

D
W

42'-0"

Living
12-0x12-4

Dn

Up

First Floor
924 sq. ft.

Porch Depth 6-0

Garage
22-5x22-9

TO ORDER BLUEPRINTS USE THE FORM ON PAGE 15 OR CALL TOLL-FREE 1-877-671-6036
View thousands more home plans online at www.familyhandyman.com/homeplans

167

Floor-To-Ceiling Window

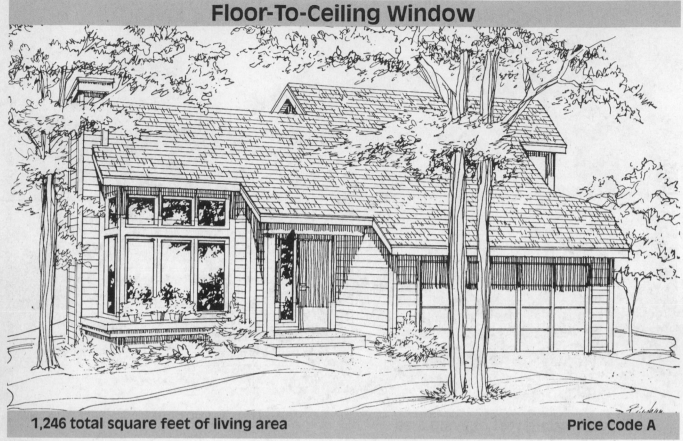

1,246 total square feet of living area

Price Code A

Special features

- Corner living room window adds openness and light
- Out-of-the-way kitchen with dining area accesses the outdoors
- Private first floor master bedroom with corner window
- Large walk-in closet is located in bedroom #3
- Easily built perimeter allows economical construction
- 3 bedrooms, 2 baths, 2-car garage
- Basement foundation

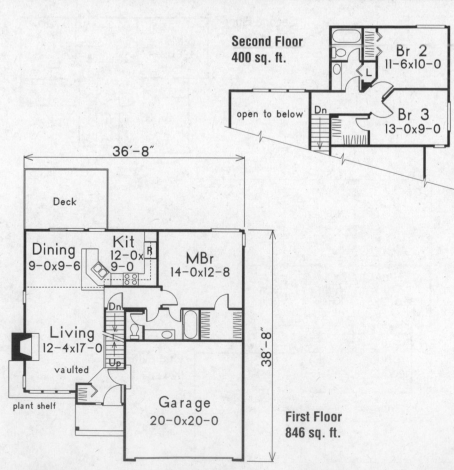

Second Floor
400 sq. ft.

Br 2
11-6x10-0

open to below   Dn

Br 3
13-0x9-0

36'-8"

Deck

Dining
9-0x9-6

Kit
12-0x
9-0

MBr
14-0x12-8

Dn

Living
12-4x17-0

vaulted

Up

plant shelf

Garage
20-0x20-0

38'-8"

First Floor
846 sq. ft.

168

TO ORDER BLUEPRINTS USE THE FORM ON PAGE 15 OR CALL TOLL-FREE 1-877-671-6036
View thousands more home plans online at www.familyhandyman.com/homeplans

One-Level Living At Its Best

1,653 total square feet of living area

Price Code B

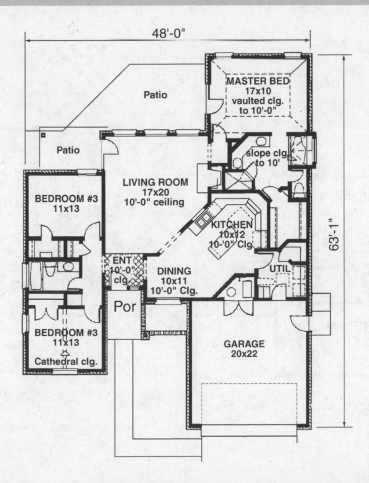

48'-0"

Patio

MASTER BED
17x10
vaulted clg.
to 10'-0"

Patio

slope clg.
to 10'

LIVING ROOM
17x20
10'-0" ceiling

BEDROOM #3
11x13

KITCHEN
10x12
10'-0" Clg.

63'-1"

ENT
10'-0"
clg.

DINING
10x11
10'-0" Clg.

UTIL

Por

BEDROOM #3
11x13
Cathedral clg.

GARAGE
20x22

Special features

- Open kitchen accesses living room and backyard through sliding glass doors

- Master suite is separated from rest of the bedrooms for privacy

- Handy work island in kitchen

- 3 bedrooms, 2 baths, 2-car garage

- Slab foundation

Easy Living

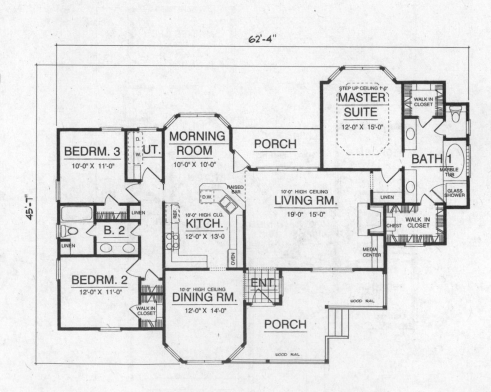

1,753 total square feet of living area

Price Code B

Special features

- Large front porch has charming appeal
- Kitchen with breakfast bar overlooks morning room and accesses covered porch
- Master suite with amenities like private bath, spacious closets and sunny bay window
- 3 bedrooms, 2 baths
- Slab or crawl space foundation, please specify when ordering

62'-4"

45'-7"

STEP UP CEILING 1'-0"
MASTER SUITE 12'-0" X 15'-0"
WALK IN CLOSET

BEDRM. 3 10'-0" X 11'-0"

UT. D.W.

MORNING ROOM 10'-0" X 10'-0"

PORCH

BATH 1
MARBLE TUB
GLASS SHOWER

LINEN

RAISED BAR
D.W.

10'-0" HIGH CEILING **LIVING RM.** 19'-0" 15'-0"

LINEN

LINEN

B. 2

10'-0" HIGH CLG. **KITCH.** 12'-0" X 13'-0

OVEN

WALK IN CLOSET
CHEST

MEDIA CENTER

BEDRM. 2 12'-0" X 11'-0"

10'-0" HIGH CEILING **DINING RM.** 12'-0" X 14'-0"

ENT.

WOOD RAIL

WALK IN CLOSET

PORCH

WOOD RAIL

Dramatic Expanse Of Windows

1,660 total square feet of living area   **Price Code C**

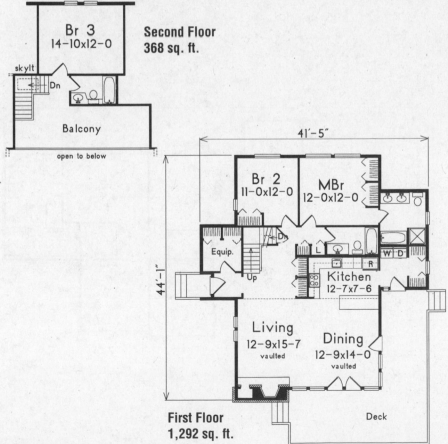

Br 3
14-10x12-0

Second Floor
368 sq. ft.

skylt

Dn

Balcony

open to below

41'-5"

Br 2
11-0x12-0

MBr
12-0x12-0

Equip.

Up

Kitchen
12-7x7-6

44'-1"

W/D

L

R

Living
12-9x15-7
vaulted

Dining
12-9x14-0
vaulted

First Floor
1,292 sq. ft.

Deck

Special features

- Convenient gear and equipment room
- Spacious living and dining rooms look even larger with the openness of the foyer and kitchen
- Large wrap-around deck, a great plus for outdoor living
- Broad balcony overlooks living and dining rooms
- 3 bedrooms, 3 baths
- Partial basement/crawl space foundation, drawings also include slab foundation

Distinctive Turret Surrounds The Dining Bay

1,742 total square feet of living area

Price Code B

Special features

- Efficient kitchen combines with breakfast area and great room creating a spacious living area

- Master bedroom includes private bath with huge walk-in closet, shower and corner tub

- Great room boasts a fireplace and access outdoors

- Laundry room conveniently located near kitchen and garage

- 3 bedrooms, 2 baths, 2-car garage

- Slab foundation, drawings also include crawl space foundation

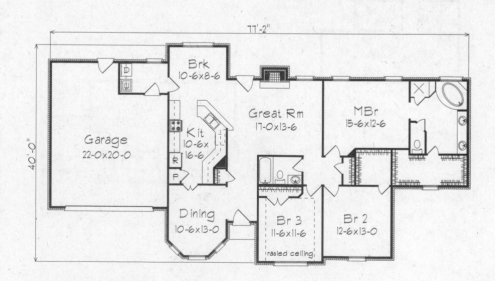

Sleeping Quarters On Second Floor

1,805 total square feet of living area

Price Code D

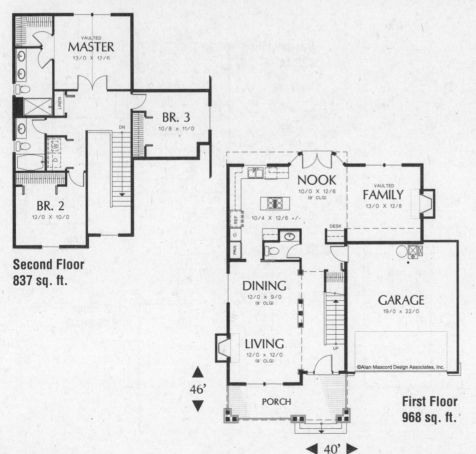

Second Floor
837 sq. ft.

First Floor
968 sq. ft.

©Alan Mascord Design Associates, Inc.

Special features

- Cooktop island, a handy desk and dining area make the kitchen highly functional
- Open floor plan with tall ceilings creates an airy atmosphere
- Family and living rooms enhanced with fireplaces
- 3 bedrooms, 2 1/2 baths, 2-car garage
- Crawl space foundation

TO ORDER BLUEPRINTS USE THE FORM ON PAGE 15 OR CALL TOLL-FREE 1-877-671-6036
View thousands more home plans online at www.familyhandyman.com/homeplans

173

Balcony Overlooks Skylighted Family Room

2,128 total square feet of living area

Price Code C

Special features

- Large bonus room offers many possibilities
- Convenient laundry room located near kitchen
- Private master bath features raised ceiling, large walk-in closet and deluxe bath
- 829 square feet on the second floor includes the bonus room above the garage
- 3 bedrooms, 2 1/2 baths, 2-car garage
- Basement foundation

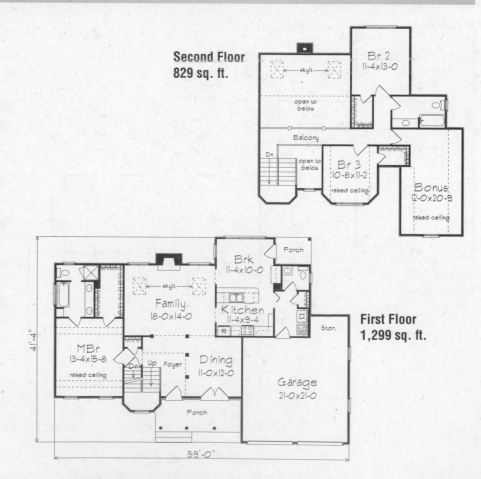

Second Floor 829 sq. ft.

skylt

Br 2
11-4x13-0

open to below

Balcony

open to below

Dn

Br 3
10-8x11-2
raised ceiling

Bonus
12-0x20-9
raised ceiling

First Floor 1,299 sq. ft.

Brk
11-4x10-0

Porch

skylt

Family
18-0x14-0

Kitchen
11-4x9-4

Stor.

41'-4"

MBr
13-4x15-8
raised ceiling

Dn Up Foyer

Dining
11-0x12-0

Garage
21-0x21-0

Porch

59'-0"

Stone Entry Accents This Stately Two-Story

1,776 total square feet of living area

Price Code B

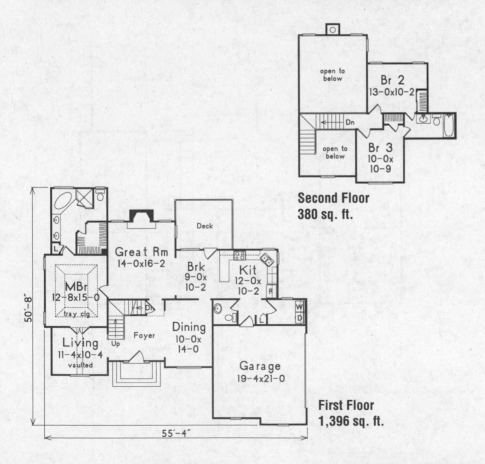

Second Floor
380 sq. ft.

First Floor
1,396 sq. ft.

Special features

- Master bedroom has double-door entry into formal living room
- Large foyer has plenty of room for greeting guests
- Great room is open to second floor and features fireplace flanked by windows
- 3 bedrooms, 2 1/2 baths, 2-car side entry garage
- Basement foundation

TO ORDER BLUEPRINTS USE THE FORM ON PAGE 15 OR CALL TOLL-FREE 1-877-671-6036
View thousands more home plans online at www.familyhandyman.com/homeplans

175

Cedar Shakes Create A Charming Feel

1,842 total square feet of living area

Price Code C

Special features

- Vaulted family room features fireplace and elegant bookcase

- Island countertop in kitchen makes cooking convenient

- Rear facade has intimate porch area ideal for relaxing

- 3 bedrooms, 2 baths, 2-car garage

- Slab or crawl space foundation, please specify when ordering

Width: 56'-4"
Depth: 68'-6"

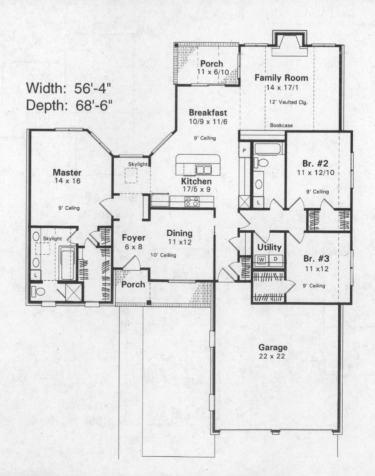

Covered Porch Highlights This Home

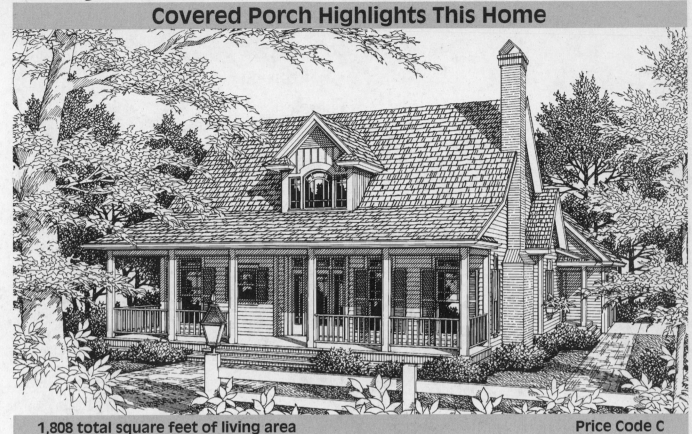

1,808 total square feet of living area

Price Code C

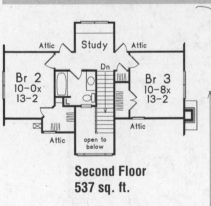

Attic Study Attic

Br 2
10-0x
13-2

Dn

Br 3
10-8x
13-2

Attic

Attic

open to
below

**Second Floor
537 sq. ft.**

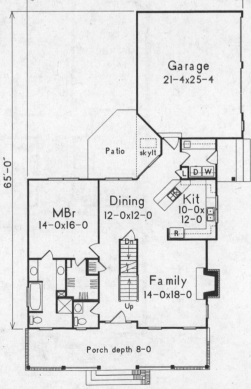

44'-4"

Garage
21-4x25-4

65'-0"

Patio skylt

L D W

MBr
14-0x16-0

Dining
12-0x12-0

Kit
10-0x
12-0

R

Dn

Family
14-0x18-0

Up

**First Floor
1,271 sq. ft.**

Porch depth 8-0

Special features

- Master bedroom has a walk-in closet, double vanities and separate tub and shower

- Two second floor bedrooms share a study area and full bath

- Partially covered patio is complete with a skylight

- Side entrance opens to utility room with convenient counterspace and laundry sink

- 3 bedrooms, 2 1/2 baths, 2-car side entry garage

- Basement foundation

Study Off Main Entrance

1,760 total square feet of living area

Price Code B

Special features

- Stone and brick exterior has old world charm

- Master suite includes a sitting area and is situated away from other bedrooms for privacy

- Kitchen and dinette access the outdoors

- Great room includes fireplace, built-in bookshelves and entertainment center

- 3 bedrooms, 2 baths, 2-car side entry garage

- Slab foundation

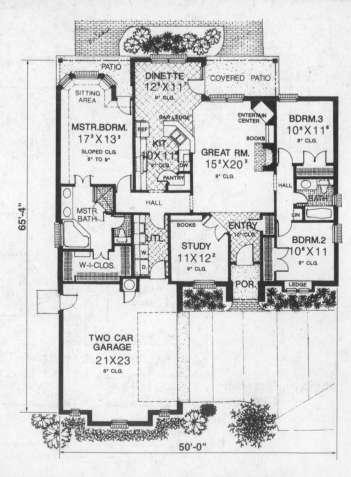

Unique Angled Entry

1,150 total square feet of living area

Price Code AA

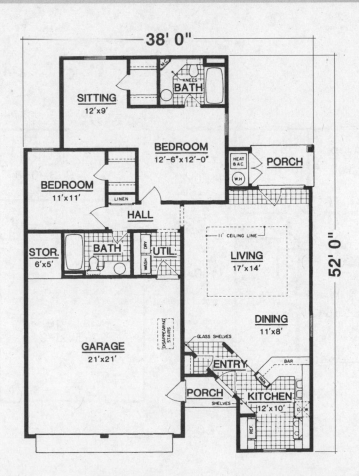

38' 0"

SITTING
12'x9'

BATH
KNEES

BEDROOM
12'-6"x12'-0"

HEAT
B A.C.
WH

PORCH

BEDROOM
11'x11'

LINEN

HALL

STOR.
6'x5'

BATH

WASH DRY

UTIL.

11' CEILING LINE

LIVING
17'x14'

52' 0"

GARAGE
21'x21'

DISAPPEARING STAIRS

GLASS SHELVES

DINING
11'x8'

BAR

ENTRY

FAN

PORCH

SHELVES

KITCHEN
12'x10'

REF

Special features

- Master suite has its own private sitting area
- Living and dining rooms have 11' high box ceilings
- Ornate trim work accents the wood sided exterior
- 2 bedrooms, 2 baths, 2-car garage
- Slab or crawl space foundation, please specify when ordering

See-Through Fireplace Joins Gathering Rooms

1,684 total square feet of living area

Price Code B

Special features

- Convenient double-doors in dining area provide access to large deck

- Family room features several large windows for brightness

- Bedrooms separate from living areas for privacy

- Master bedroom suite offers bath with walk-in closet, double-bowl vanity and both a shower and whirlpool tub

- 3 bedrooms, 2 1/2 baths, 2-car garage

- Basement foundation

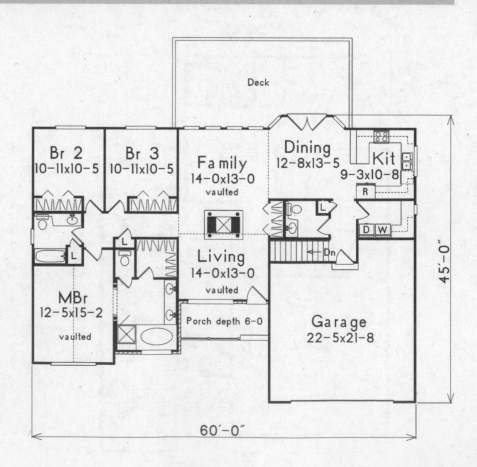

Spacious And Open Family Living Area

1,416 total square feet of living area

Price Code A

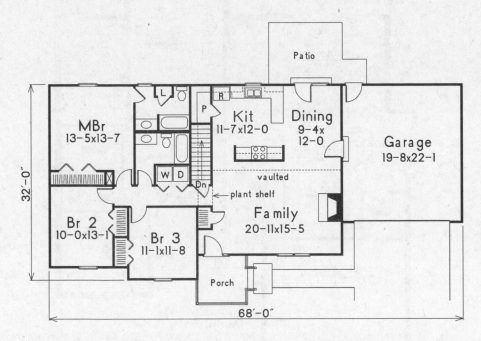

Special features

- Family room includes fireplace, elevated plant shelf and vaulted ceiling
- Patio is accessible from dining area and garage
- Centrally located laundry area
- Oversized walk-in pantry
- 3 bedrooms, 2 baths, 2-car garage
- Basement foundation, drawings also include crawl space and slab foundations

TO ORDER BLUEPRINTS USE THE FORM ON PAGE 15 OR CALL TOLL-FREE 1-877-671-6036
View thousands more home plans online at www.familyhandyman.com/homeplans

181

Quaint Box Window Seat

1,665 total square feet of living area

Price Code B

Special features

- Oversized family room has a corner fireplace and double-doors leading to the patio
- Bedroom locations give privacy from gathering areas
- 3 bedrooms, 2 baths, 2-car garage
- Slab foundation

Width: 50'-0"
Depth: 55'-0"

Efficient Layout In This Multi-Level Home

1,617 total square feet of living area

Price Code B

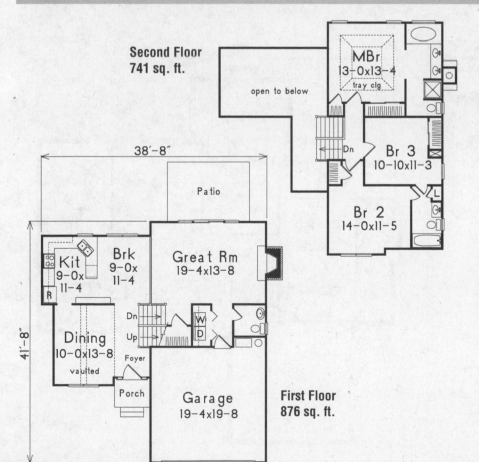

Second Floor
741 sq. ft.

open to below

MBr
13-0x13-4
tray clg

Br 3
10-10x11-3

Br 2
14-0x11-5

38'-8"

Patio

Kit
9-0x 11-4

Brk
9-0x 11-4

Great Rm
19-4x13-8

41'-8"

Dining
10-0x13-8
vaulted

Dn
Up
W
D

Foyer

Porch

Garage
19-4x19-8

First Floor
876 sq. ft.

Special features

- Kitchen and breakfast area overlook great room with fireplace

- Formal dining room features vaulted ceiling and elegant circle-top window

- All bedrooms are located on the second floor for privacy

- 3 bedrooms, 2 1/2 baths, 2-car garage

- Partial crawl space/slab foundation

TO ORDER BLUEPRINTS USE THE FORM ON PAGE 15 OR CALL TOLL-FREE 1-877-671-6036
View thousands more home plans online at www.familyhandyman.com/homeplans

183

Traditional Styling

2,050 total square feet of living area

Price Code C

Special features

- Living room immersed in sunlight from wall of windows

- Master suite with amenities like double walk-in closets, private bath and view onto covered porch

- Cozy family room with built-in shelves and fireplace

- 3 bedrooms, 2 baths, 2-car side entry garage

- Slab or crawl space foundation, please specify when ordering

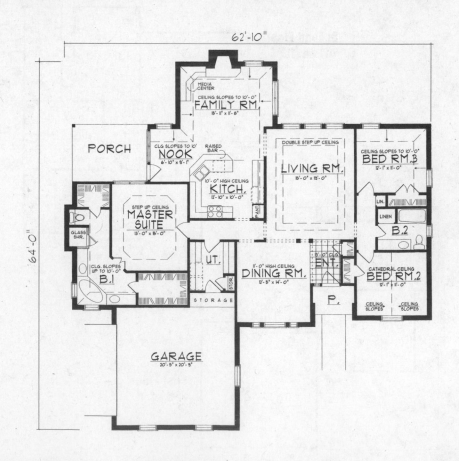

Columns Grace The Interior And Exterior

1,476 total square feet of living area   **Price Code B**

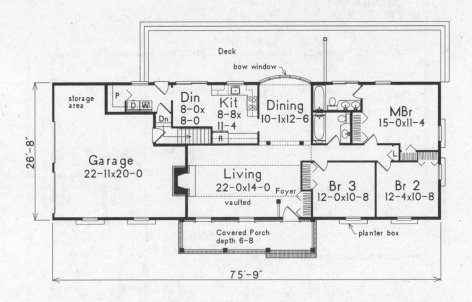

Special features

- Energy efficient home with 2" x 6" exterior walls
- Living room made more spacious by vaulted ceiling
- Laundry/mud room has a large pantry and accesses dining area, garage, stairs and the outdoors
- Master bedroom features bath and private deck
- Dining room is defined by columns and a large bow window
- 3 bedrooms, 2 baths, 2-car side entry garage
- Basement foundation, drawings also include slab foundation

Gabled Front Porch Gives A Country Flair

1,379 total square feet of living area

Price Code A

Special features

- Living area has spacious feel with 11'-6" ceiling
- Kitchen has eat-in breakfast bar open to dining area
- Laundry located near bedrooms
- Large cased opening with columns opens the living and dining areas
- 3 bedroom, 2 baths, 2-car drive under garage
- Basement foundation

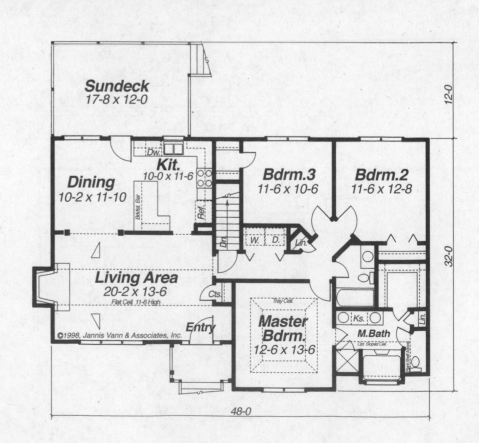

Sundeck 17-8 x 12-0

Kit. 10-0 x 11-6

Dining 10-2 x 11-10

Bdrm.3 11-6 x 10-6

Bdrm.2 11-6 x 12-8

Living Area 20-2 x 13-6
Flat Ceil. 11-6 High

Entry

©1998, Jannis Vann & Associates, Inc.

Master Bdrm. 12-6 x 13-6

M.Bath

W. D. Ldn.

Dw.

Ref.

Brkfst. Bar

Dn

Cts.

Ks.

Tray Ceil.

Clg. Sloped Ceil.

12-0

32-0

48-0

Innovative Design For That Narrow Lot

1,558 total square feet of living area

Price Code B

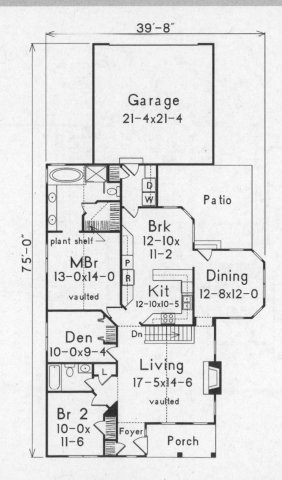

39'-8"

Garage
21-4x21-4

75'-0"

Patio

plant shelf

D
W

MBr
13-0x14-0

Brk
12-10x
11-2

vaulted

P
R

Dining
12-8x12-0

Kit
12-10x10-5

Den
10-0x9-4

Dn

Living
17-5x14-6

vaulted

Br 2
10-0x
11-6

Foyer

Porch

Special features

- Illuminated spaces created by visual access to outdoor living areas

- Vaulted master bedroom features private bath with whirlpool tub, separate shower and large walk-in closet

- Convenient first floor laundry has garage access

- Practical den or third bedroom

- U-shaped kitchen adjacent to sunny breakfast area

- 2 bedrooms, 2 baths, 2-car rear entry garage

- Basement foundation

Distinctive Ranch

FREILING

1,962 total square feet of living area

Price Code C

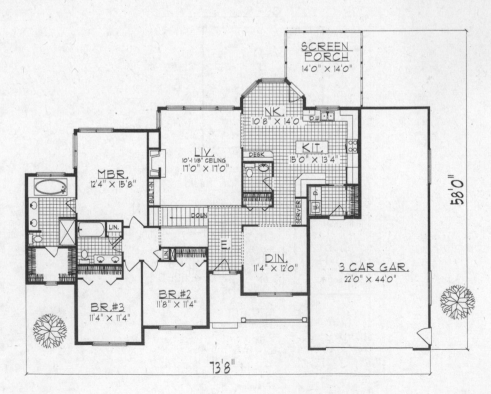

Special features

- Formal dining room has a butler's pantry for entertaining

- Open living room offers a fireplace, built-in cabinetry and exceptional views to the outdoors

- Kitchen has work island and planning desk

- 3 bedrooms, 2 1/2 baths, 3-car garage

- Basement foundation

TO ORDER BLUEPRINTS USE THE FORM ON PAGE 15 OR CALL TOLL-FREE 1-877-671-6036
View thousands more home plans online at www.familyhandyman.com/homeplans

Circle-Top Windows Adorn The Foyer

1,516 total square feet of living area

Price Code B

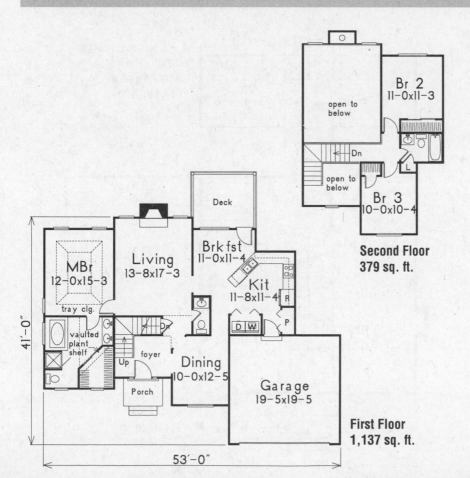

Br 2
11-0x11-3

open to below

Dn

open to below

Br 3
10-0x10-4

Second Floor
379 sq. ft.

Deck

MBr
12-0x15-3

tray clg.

vaulted
plant
shelf

Living
13-8x17-3

Brkfst
11-0x11-4

Kit
11-8x11-4

R

P

D W

Up

foyer

Dining
10-0x12-5

Garage
19-5x19-5

Porch

41'-0"

53'-0"

First Floor
1,137 sq. ft.

Special features

- On the second floor the stair-way looks out over the living room
- Master bedroom enjoys first floor privacy and luxurious bath
- Kitchen has easy access to the deck, laundry closet and garage
- 3 bedrooms, 2 1/2 baths, 2-car garage
- Basement foundation

TO ORDER BLUEPRINTS USE THE FORM ON PAGE 15 OR CALL TOLL-FREE 1-877-671-6036
View thousands more home plans online at www.familyhandyman.com/homeplans

189

Roomy Two-Story Has Screened-In Rear Porch

1,600 total square feet of living area

Price Code B

Special features

- Energy efficient home with 2" x 6" exterior walls

- First floor master suite accessible from two points of entry

- Master suite dressing area includes separate vanities and a mirrored make-up counter

- Second floor bedrooms with generous storage, share a full bath

- 3 bedrooms, 2 baths, 2-car side entry garage

- Crawl space foundation, drawings also include slab foundation

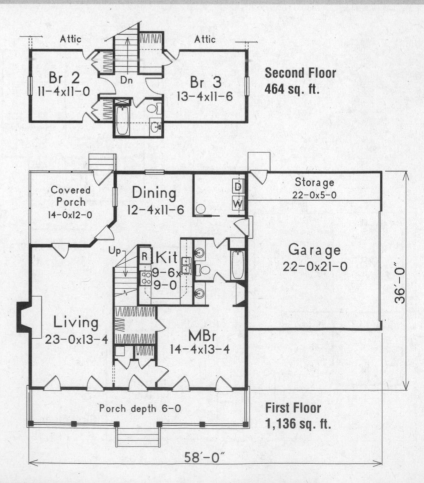

Attic

Attic

Br 2
11-4x11-0

Dn

Br 3
13-4x11-6

**Second Floor
464 sq. ft.**

Covered Porch
14-0x12-0

Dining
12-4x11-6

D
W

Storage
22-0x5-0

Up

R Kit
9-6x
9-0

Garage
22-0x21-0

Living
23-0x13-4

MBr
14-4x13-4

36'-0"

Porch depth 6-0

**First Floor
1,136 sq. ft.**

58'-0"

Lovely Front Dormers

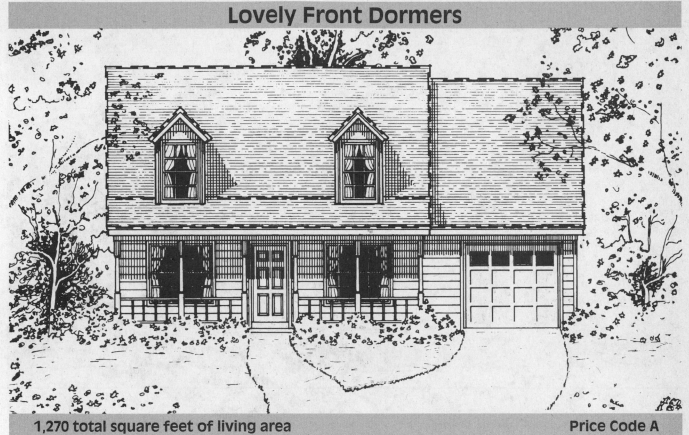

1,270 total square feet of living area   **Price Code A**

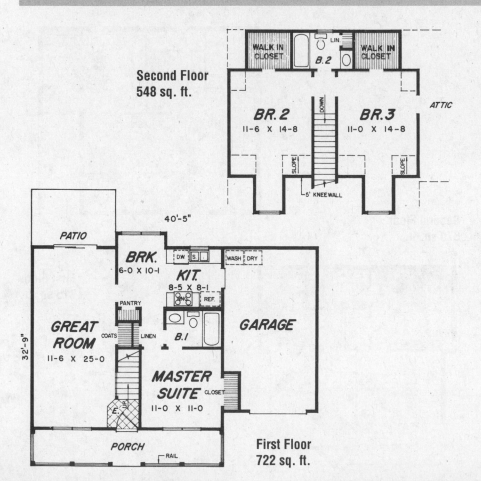

**Second Floor
548 sq. ft.**

WALK IN CLOSET   B.2   LIN.   WALK IN CLOSET

BR. 2
11-6 X 14-8

DOWN

BR. 3
11-0 X 14-8

ATTIC

SLOPE   SLOPE

5' KNEE WALL

PATIO

40'-5"

BRK.
6-0 X 10-1

DW S.   WASH DRY

KIT.
8-5 X 8-1

RNG. REF.

PANTRY

32'-9"

GREAT
ROOM
11-6 X 25-0

COATS LINEN

B.1

GARAGE

E. UP

MASTER
SUITE
11-0 X 11-0

CLOSET

PORCH   RAIL

**First Floor
722 sq. ft.**

Special features

- Convenient master suite on first floor
- Two secondary bedrooms on second floor each have a large walk-in closet and share a full bath
- Sunny breakfast room has lots of sunlight and easy access to great room and kitchen
- 3 bedrooms, 2 baths, 1-car garage
- Slab or crawl space foundation, please specify when ordering

TO ORDER BLUEPRINTS USE THE FORM ON PAGE 15 OR CALL TOLL-FREE 1-877-671-6036
View thousands more home plans online at www.familyhandyman.com/homeplans

191

Lots Of Windows Creates A Cheerful Home

1,285 total square feet of living area

Price Code A

Special features

- Energy efficient home with 2" x 6" exterior walls
- Dining and living areas both access a large wrap-around porch
- First floor bath has convenient laundry closet as well as a shower
- 2 bedrooms, 2 baths
- Basement foundation

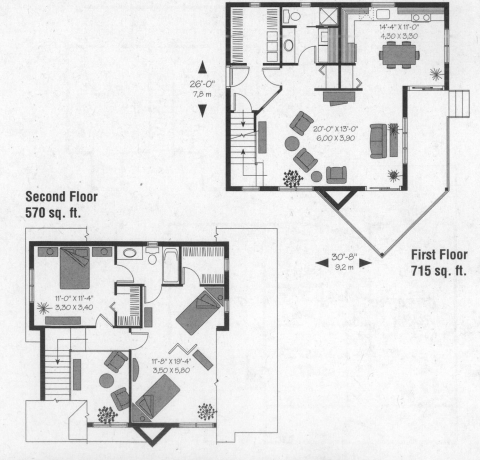

26'-0"
7,8 m

14'-4" X 11'-0"
4,30 X 3,30

20'-0" X 13'-0"
6,00 X 3,90

**Second Floor
570 sq. ft.**

30'-8"
9,2 m

**First Floor
715 sq. ft.**

11'-0" X 11'-4"
3,30 X 3,40

11'-8" X 19'-4"
3,50 X 5,80

192

TO ORDER BLUEPRINTS USE THE FORM ON PAGE 15 OR CALL TOLL-FREE 1-877-671-6036
View thousands more home plans online at www.familyhandyman.com/homeplans

Terrific Design For Family Living

1,345 total square feet of living area

Price Code A

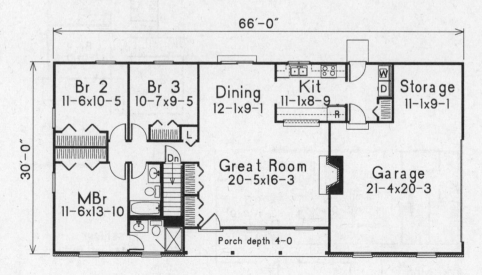

66'-0"

Br 2
11-6x10-5

Br 3
10-7x9-5

Dining
12-1x9-1

Kit
11-1x8-9

Storage
11-1x9-1

MBr
11-6x13-10

Great Room
20-5x16-3

Garage
21-4x20-3

30'-0"

Porch depth 4-0

Special features

- Brick front details add a touch of elegance
- Master suite has private full bath
- Great room combined with dining area adds spaciousness
- Garage includes handy storage area which could easily convert to a workshop space
- 3 bedrooms, 2 baths, 2-car side entry garage
- Basement foundation, drawings also include crawl space and slab foundations

TO ORDER BLUEPRINTS USE THE FORM ON PAGE 15 OR CALL TOLL-FREE 1-877-671-6036
View thousands more home plans online at www.familyhandyman.com/homeplans

193

Vaulted Ceilings Enhance Spacious Home

2,073 total square feet of living area

Price Code D

Special features

- Family room provides ideal gathering area with a fireplace, large windows and vaulted ceiling

- Private first floor master bedroom suite with a vaulted ceiling and luxury bath

- Kitchen features angled bar connecting kitchen and breakfast area

- 4 bedrooms, 2 1/2 baths, 2-car side entry garage

- Basement foundation

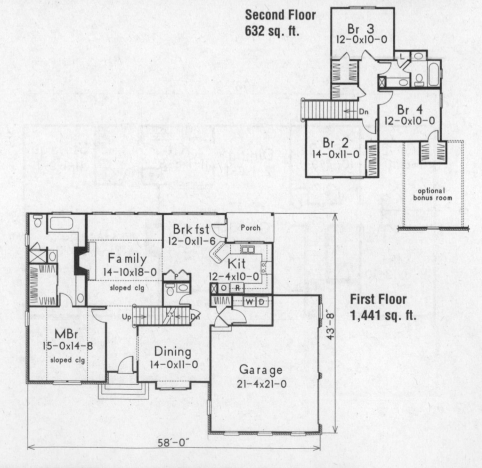

Second Floor 632 sq. ft.

Br 3
12-0x10-0

Br 4
12-0x10-0

Br 2
14-0x11-0

Dn

optional bonus room

First Floor 1,441 sq. ft.

Brk fst
12-0x11-6

Porch

Family
14-10x18-0
sloped clg

Kit
12-4x10-0

MBr
15-0x14-8
sloped clg

Up

Dn

Dining
14-0x11-0

Garage
21-4x21-0

43'-8"

58'-0"

Lovely Ranch Home

1,123 total square feet of living area

Price Code AA

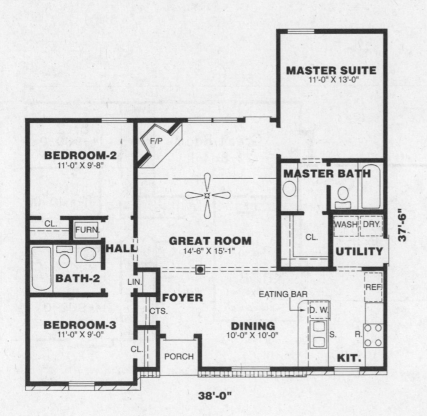

Special features

- Eating bar in kitchen extends dining area
- Dining area and great room flow together creating a sense of spaciousness
- Master suite has privacy from other bedrooms as well as a private bath
- Utility room is conveniently located near kitchen
- 3 bedrooms, 2 baths
- Crawl space or slab foundation, please specify when ordering

Cheerful And Sunny Kitchen

1,540 total square feet of living area

Price Code B

Special features

- Porch entrance into foyer leads to an impressive dining area with full window and a half-circle window above

- Kitchen/breakfast room features a center island and cathedral ceiling

- Great room with cathedral ceiling and exposed beams is accessible from foyer

- Master bedroom includes full bath and walk-in closet

- Two additional bedrooms share a full bath

- 3 bedrooms, 2 baths, 2-car garage

- Basement foundation, drawings also include crawl space and slab foundations

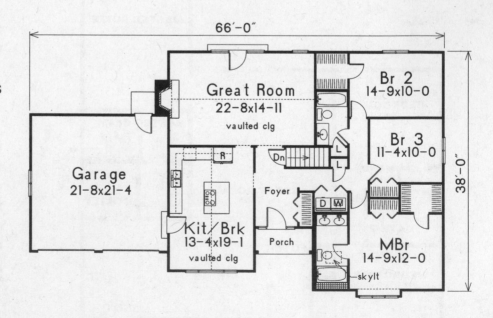

Country-Style Home With Large Front Porch

1,501 total square feet of living area

Price Code B

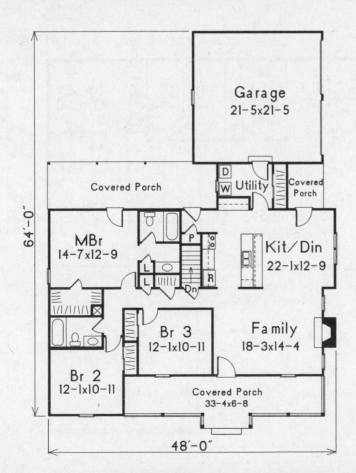

Special features

- Spacious kitchen with dining area is open to the outdoors
- Convenient utility room is adjacent to garage
- Master suite with private bath, dressing area and access to large covered porch
- Large family room creates openness
- 3 bedrooms, 2 baths, 2-car side entry garage
- Basement foundation, drawings also include crawl space and slab foundations

TO ORDER BLUEPRINTS USE THE FORM ON PAGE 15 OR CALL TOLL-FREE 1-877-671-6036
View thousands more home plans online at www.familyhandyman.com/homeplans

197

Plan #706-1117

An Enhancement To Any Neighborhood

1,440 total square feet of living area

Price Code A

Special features

- Foyer adjoins massive-sized great room with sloping ceiling and tall masonry fireplace

- Kitchen adjoins spacious dining room and features pass-through breakfast bar

- Master suite enjoys private bath and two closets

- An oversized two-car side entry garage offers plenty of storage for bicycles, lawn equipment, etc.

- 3 bedrooms, 2 baths, 2-car side entry garage

- Basement foundation, drawings also include crawl space and slab foundations

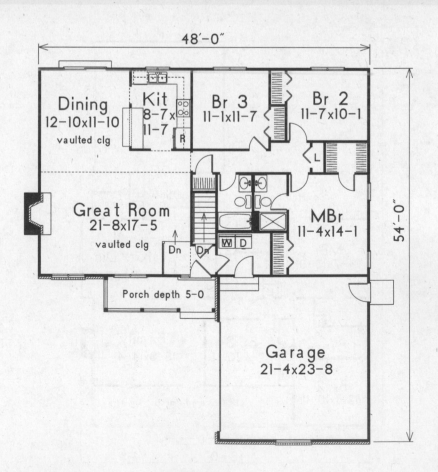

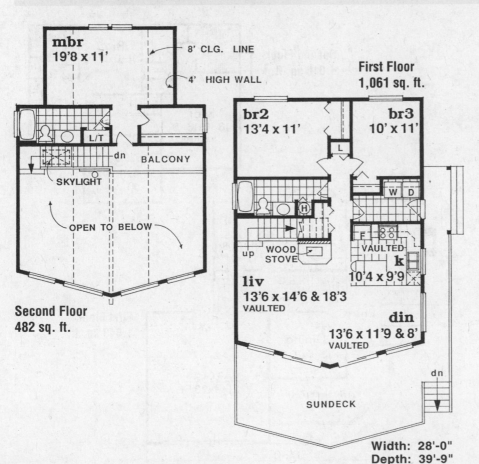

The Family Handyman

Expansive Glass Wall In Living Areas

1,543 total square feet of living area

Price Code B

---

mbr
19'8 x 11'

8' CLG. LINE

4' HIGH WALL

First Floor
1,061 sq. ft.

dn   BALCONY

L/T

SKYLIGHT

OPEN TO BELOW

Second Floor
482 sq. ft.

br2
13'4 x 11'

br3
10' x 11'

L

W   D

H

up   WOOD
STOVE

VAULTED

F

k
10'4 x 9'9

liv
13'6 x 14'6 & 18'3
VAULTED

din
13'6 x 11'9 & 8'
VAULTED

dn

SUNDECK

Width: 28'-0"
Depth: 39'-9"

Special features

- Enormous sundeck makes this a popular vacation style
- A woodstove warms the vaulted living and dining rooms
- A vaulted kitchen has a prep island and breakfast bar
- Second floor vaulted master bedroom has private bath and walk-in closet
- 3 bedrooms, 2 baths
- Crawl space foundation

TO ORDER BLUEPRINTS USE THE FORM ON PAGE 15 OR CALL TOLL-FREE 1-877-671-6036

View thousands more home plans online at www.familyhandyman.com/homeplans

Angled Porch Greets Guests

2,059 total square feet of living area

Price Code C

Special features

- Large desk and pantry add to the breakfast room
- Laundry is located on second floor near bedrooms
- Vaulted ceiling in master suite
- Mud room is conveniently located near garage
- 3 bedrooms, 2 1/2 baths, 2-car garage
- Basement foundation

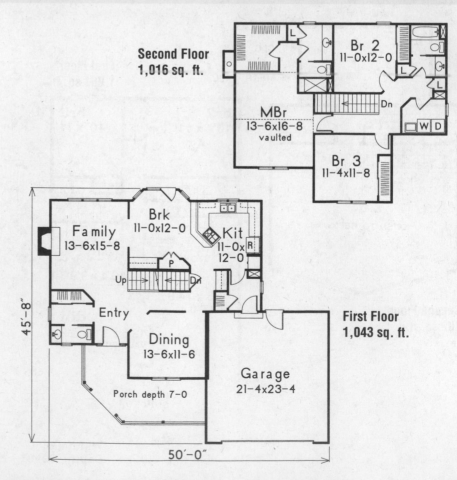

Second Floor 1,016 sq. ft.

Br 2 11-0x12-0

MBr 13-6x16-8 vaulted

Br 3 11-4x11-8

First Floor 1,043 sq. ft.

Family 13-6x15-8

Brk 11-0x12-0

Kit 11-0x 12-0

Up

Entry

Dining 13-6x11-6

Garage 21-4x23-4

Porch depth 7-0

45'-8"

50'-0"

Home Designed For Outdoor Lifestyle

1,230 total square feet of living area

Price Code A

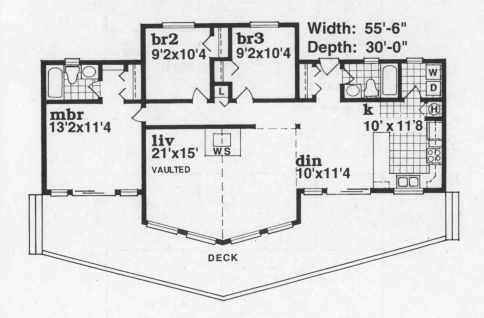

Width: 55'-6"
Depth: 30'-0"

br2 9'2x10'4
br3 9'2x10'4
mbr 13'2x11'4
liv 21'x15' VAULTED
W S
din 10'x11'4
k 10' x 11'8
W D H
DECK

Special features

- Full-width deck creates plenty of outdoor living area
- The master bedroom accesses the deck through sliding glass doors and features a private bath
- Vaulted living room has a woodstove
- 3 bedrooms, 2 baths
- Crawl space or basement foundation, please specify when ordering

TO ORDER BLUEPRINTS USE THE FORM ON PAGE 15 OR CALL TOLL-FREE 1-877-671-6036
View thousands more home plans online at www.familyhandyman.com/homeplans

201

Practical Two-Story, Full Of Features

2,058 total square feet of living area

Price Code C

Special features

- Handsome two-story foyer with balcony creates a spacious entrance area

- Vaulted ceiling in the master bedroom with private dressing area and large walk-in closet

- Skylights furnish natural lighting in the hall and master bath

- Conveniently located second floor laundry near bedrooms

- 3 bedrooms, 2 1/2 baths, 2-car garage

- Basement foundation, drawings also include slab and crawl space foundations

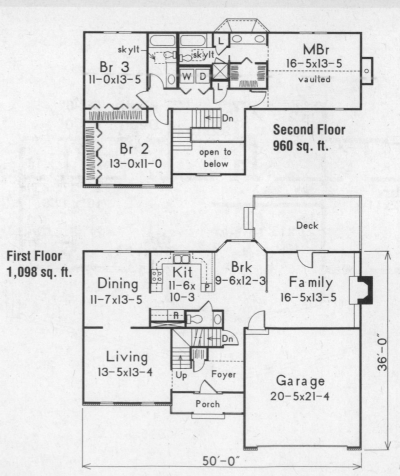

**Second Floor
960 sq. ft.**

Br 3
11-0x13-5

MBr
16-5x13-5
vaulted

W D

Br 2
13-0x11-0

open to below

Dn

**First Floor
1,098 sq. ft.**

Deck

Dining
11-7x13-5

Kit
11-6x
10-3

Brk
9-6x12-3

Family
16-5x13-5

Living
13-5x13-4

Up

Dn

Foyer

Garage
20-5x21-4

Porch

36'-0"

50'-0"

Classic Atrium Ranch With Rooms To Spare

1,977 total square feet of living area

Price Code C

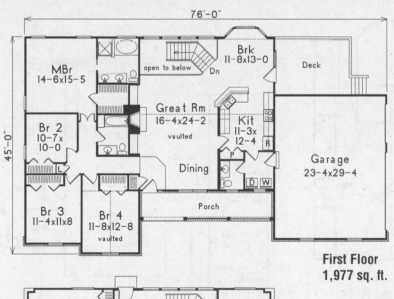

76'-0"

45'-0"

MBr
14-6x15-5

Br 2
10-7x
10-0

Br 3
11-4x11x8

Br 4
11-8x12-8
vaulted

open to below

Great Rm
16-4x24-2
vaulted

Dining

Porch

Brk
11-8x13-0

Dn

Kit
11-3x
12-4

Deck

Garage
23-4x29-4

D W

P

First Floor
1,977 sq. ft.

Br 5
15-3x15-6

Br 6
11-5x12-7

Up
Atrium

Study
10-9x
13-2

Family
18-4x23-6

storage

storage

G

F

L

Optional
Lower Level

Special features

- Classic traditional exterior always in style
- Spacious great room boasts a vaulted ceiling, dining area, atrium with elegant staircase and feature windows
- Atrium open to 1,416 square feet of optional living area below which consists of an optional family room, two bedrooms, two baths and a study
- 4 bedrooms, 2 1/2 baths, 3-car side entry garage
- Walk-out basement foundation

TO ORDER BLUEPRINTS USE THE FORM ON PAGE 15 OR CALL TOLL-FREE 1-877-671-6036
View thousands more home plans online at www.familyhandyman.com/homeplans

203

Open And Airy Grand Room

© 2003, Garrell Associates, Inc.

Christine Canova 2/02

2,111 total square feet of living area   **Price Code H**

Special features

- 9' ceilings throughout first floor
- Formal dining room has columns separating it from other areas while allowing it to maintain an open feel
- Master bedroom has privacy from other bedrooms
- Bonus room on the second floor has an additional 345 square feet of living area
- 3 bedrooms, 2 baths, 2-car side entry garage
- Basement foundation

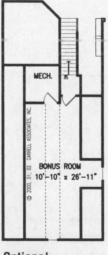

Optional Second Floor

MECH.

© 2000, 01, 02 GARRELL ASSOCIATES, INC.

BONUS ROOM
10'-10" x 26'-11"

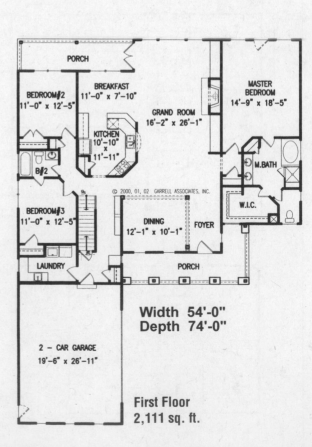

PORCH

BEDROOM#2
11'-0" x 12'-5"

BREAKFAST
11'-0" x 7'-10"

GRAND ROOM
16'-2" x 26'-1"

MASTER BEDROOM
14'-9" x 18'-5"

KITCHEN
10'-10" x 11'-11"

B/2

M.BATH

© 2000, 01, 02 GARRELL ASSOCIATES, INC.

BEDROOM#3
11'-0" x 12'-5"

DINING
12'-1" x 10'-1"

FOYER

W.I.C.

LAUNDRY

PORCH

Width 54'-0"
Depth 74'-0"

2 - CAR GARAGE
19'-6" x 26'-11"

First Floor
2,111 sq. ft.

Plan #706-NDG-788

Beautiful Arched Windows Enhance Facade

2,050 total square feet of living area

Price Code C

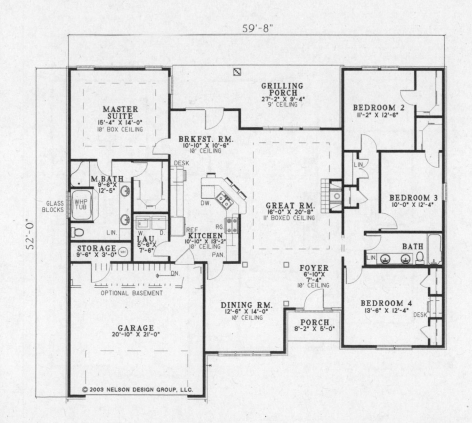

Special features

- Open living spaces allow for dining area, great room and breakfast room to flow together

- Bedroom #4 has unique design with double closets and a built-in desk

- Plenty of closet space throughout

- 4 bedrooms, 2 baths, 2-car garage

- Crawl space or slab foundation, please specify when ordering

TO ORDER BLUEPRINTS USE THE FORM ON PAGE 15 OR CALL TOLL-FREE 1-877-671-6036
View thousands more home plans online at www.familyhandyman.com/homeplans

205

Organized Kitchen, Center Of Activity

1,882 total square feet of living area

Price Code C

Special features

- Handsome brick facade
- Spacious great room and dining room combination brightened by unique corner windows and patio access
- Well-designed kitchen incorporates breakfast bar peninsula, sweeping casement window above sink and walk-in pantry island
- Master suite features large walk-in closet and private bath with bay window
- 4 bedrooms, 2 baths, 2-car side entry garage
- Basement foundation

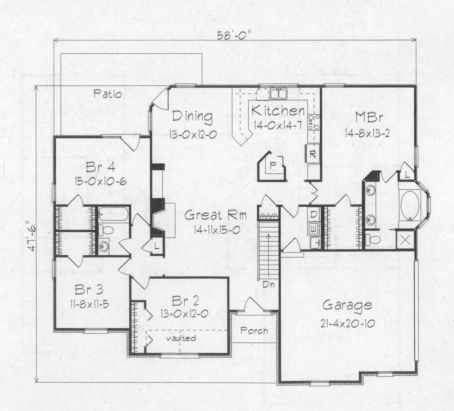

Spacious A-Frame

1,769 total square feet of living area

Price Code B

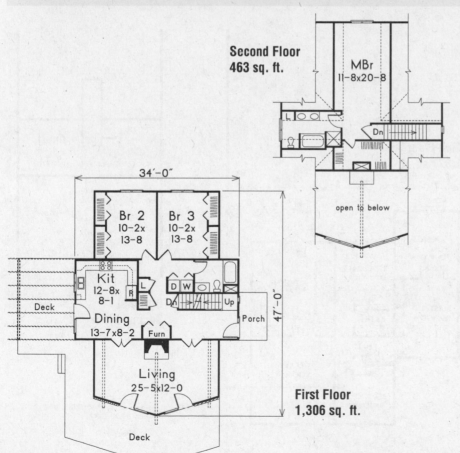

Second Floor 463 sq. ft.

MBr
11-8x20-8

open to below

Dn

First Floor 1,306 sq. ft.

34'-0"

47'-0"

Br 2
10-2x
13-8

Br 3
10-2x
13-8

Kit
12-8x
8-1

Deck

Dining
13-7x8-2

Furn

Dn   Up

Porch

Living
25-5x12-0

Deck

Special features

- Living room boasts elegant cathedral ceiling and fireplace
- U-shaped kitchen and dining area combine for easy living
- Secondary bedrooms include double closets
- Secluded master bedroom with sloped ceiling, large walk-in closet and private bath
- 3 bedrooms, 2 baths
- Basement foundation, drawings also include crawl space and slab foundations

TO ORDER BLUEPRINTS USE THE FORM ON PAGE 15 OR CALL TOLL-FREE 1-877-671-6036
View thousands more home plans online at www.familyhandyman.com/homeplans

207

Country Colonial Feel To This Home

1,377 total square feet of living area   **Price Code A**

Special features

- Master bedroom has double-door access into screened porch

- Cozy dining area is adjacent to kitchen for convenience

- Great room includes fireplace

- Optional second floor has an additional 349 square feet of living area

- 3 bedrooms, 1 bath

- Crawl space or slab foundation, please specify when ordering

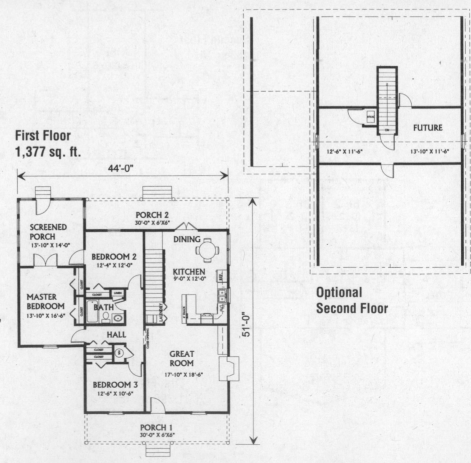

First Floor
1,377 sq. ft.

44'-0"

SCREENED PORCH
13'-10" X 14'-0"

PORCH 2
30'-0" X 6'X6"

DINING

BEDROOM 2
12'-4" X 12'-0"

KITCHEN
9'-0" X 12'-0"

MASTER BEDROOM
13'-10" X 16'-6"

BATH

HALL

LAUNDRY

51'-0"

GREAT ROOM
17'-10" X 18'-6"

BEDROOM 3
12'-6" X 10'-6"

PORCH 1
30'-0" X 6'X6"

FUTURE

12'-6" X 11'-6"   13'-10" X 11'-6"

Optional Second Floor

Plan #706-FB-1148

Southern Styling With Covered Porch

1,491 total square feet of living area

Price Code A

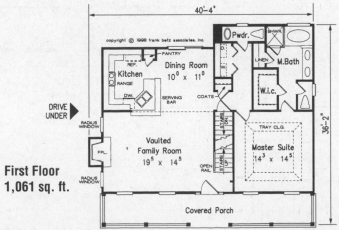

Second Floor 430 sq. ft.

Bedroom 2 12⁰ x 10⁹

Bath

Bedroom 3 12⁰ x 10⁹

OVERLOOK · OPEN RAIL · LINEN

Family Room Below

Attic

VAULT · VAULT · STAIRS DN

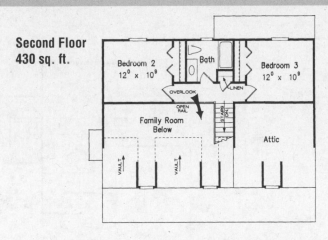

First Floor 1,061 sq. ft.

40'-4"

copyright © 1998 frank betz associates, inc.

PANTRY · REF. · Kitchen · RANGE · DW.

Dining Room 10⁰ x 11⁰

Pwdr. · SHWR · D. · W · LINEN · M.Bath

SERVING BAR · COATS · W.i.c.

DRIVE UNDER · RADIUS WINDOW

FPL.

Vaulted Family Room 19⁵ x 14⁵

STAIRS DN · STAIRS UP · OPEN RAIL

TRAY CLG.

Master Suite 14³ x 14⁵

36'-2"

Covered Porch

Special features

- Two-story family room has vaulted ceiling
- Well-organized kitchen has serving bar which overlooks family and dining rooms
- First floor master suite has tray ceiling, walk-in closet and master bath
- 3 bedrooms, 2 1/2 baths, 2-car drive under garage
- Walk-out basement foundation

TO ORDER BLUEPRINTS USE THE FORM ON PAGE 15 OR CALL TOLL-FREE 1-877-671-6036

View thousands more home plans online at www.familyhandyman.com/homeplans

209

Breezeway Joins Living Space With Garage

1,874 total square feet of living area

Price Code C

Special features

- 9' ceilings throughout first floor
- Two-story foyer opens into large family room with fireplace
- First floor master suite includes private bath with tub and shower
- 4 bedrooms, 2 1/2 baths, 2-car garage
- Basement foundation, drawings also include slab foundation

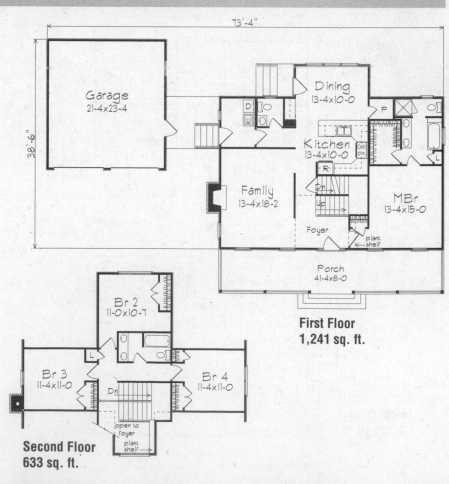

First Floor
1,241 sq. ft.

Second Floor
633 sq. ft.

TO ORDER BLUEPRINTS USE THE FORM ON PAGE 15 OR CALL TOLL-FREE 1-877-671-6036
View thousands more home plans online at www.familyhandyman.com/homeplans

Dormer And Covered Porch Add To Country Charm

954 total square feet of living area

Price Code AA

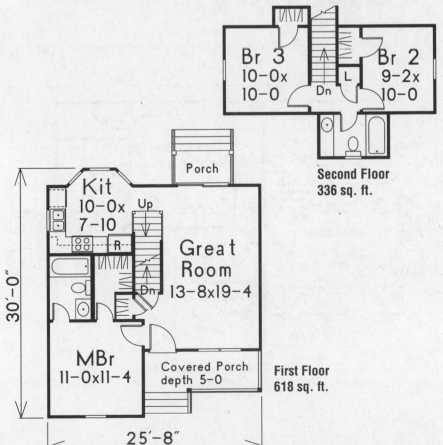

**Second Floor
336 sq. ft.**

Kit
10-0x
7-10

Up

R

Great
Room
13-8x19-4

Dn

MBr
11-0x11-4

Porch

Covered Porch
depth 5-0

**First Floor
618 sq. ft.**

30'-0"

25'-8"

Br 3
10-0x
10-0

Dn

L

Br 2
9-2x
10-0

Special features

- Kitchen has cozy bayed eating area
- Master bedroom has a walk-in closet and private bath
- Large great room has access to the back porch
- Convenient coat closet near front entry
- 3 bedrooms, 2 baths
- Basement foundation

TO ORDER BLUEPRINTS USE THE FORM ON PAGE 15 OR CALL TOLL-FREE 1-877-671-6036
View thousands more home plans online at www.familyhandyman.com/homeplans

211

Handsome Stonework

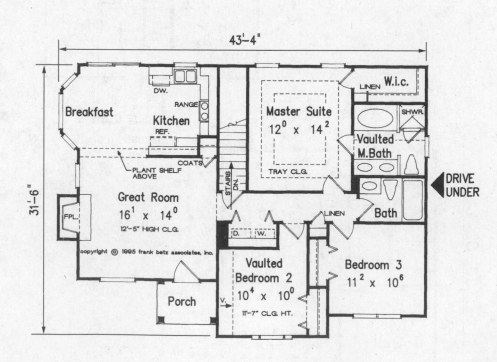

1,124 total square feet of living area　　　**Price Code AA**

Special features

- Varied ceiling heights through-out this home
- Enormous bayed breakfast room overlooks great room with fireplace
- Conveniently located washer and dryer closet
- 3 bedrooms, 2 baths, 2-car drive under garage
- Walk-out basement foundation

Great Room And Kitchen Symmetry Dominates Design

KURT KAUSS
ORLANDO

1,712 total square feet of living area

Price Code B

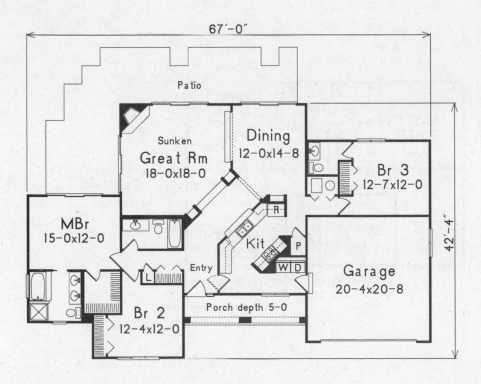

67'-0"

Patio

Sunken
Great Rm
18-0x18-0

Dining
12-0x14-8

Br 3
12-7x12-0

MBr
15-0x12-0

Kit

R

P

W D

42'-4"

L

Entry

Garage
20-4x20-8

Br 2
12-4x12-0

Porch depth 5-0

Special features

- Stylish stucco exterior enhances curb appeal
- Sunken great room offers corner fireplace flanked by 9' wide patio doors
- Well-designed kitchen features ideal view of great room and fireplace through breakfast bar opening
- 3 bedrooms, 2 1/2 baths, 2-car garage
- Crawl space foundation

TO ORDER BLUEPRINTS USE THE FORM ON PAGE 15 OR CALL TOLL-FREE 1-877-671-6036
View thousands more home plans online at www.familyhandyman.com/homeplans

213

Arched Window Is A Focal Point

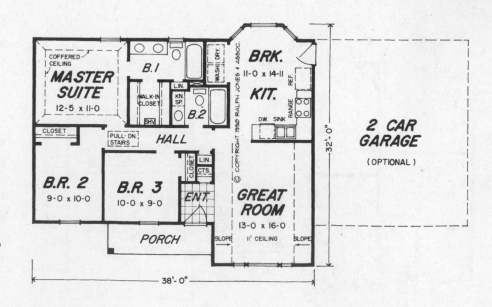

© COPYRIGHT 1990 RALPH JONES & ASSOC.

1,021 total square feet of living area

Price Code AA

Special features

- 11' ceiling in great room expands living area
- Kitchen and breakfast room combine allowing for easier preparation and cleanup
- Master suite features private bath and oversized walk-in closet
- 3 bedrooms, 2 baths, optional 2-car garage
- Slab or crawl space foundation, please specify when ordering

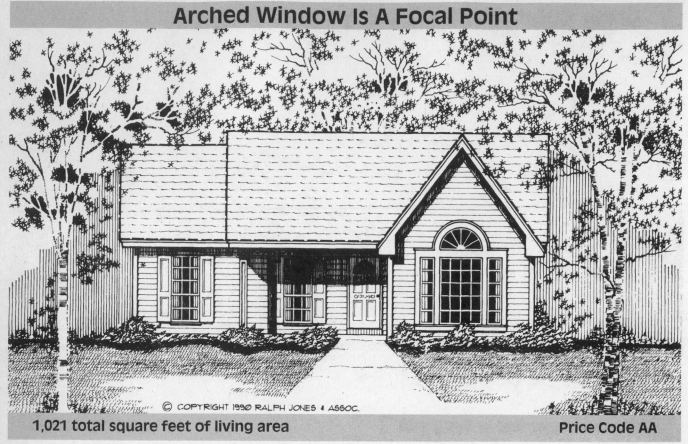

Contemporary Elegance With Efficiency

1,321 total square feet of living area

Price Code A

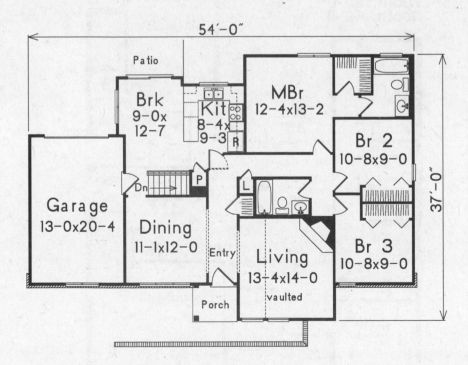

54'-0"

Patio

Brk
9-0x
12-7

Kit
8-4x
9-3

MBr
12-4x13-2

Garage
13-0x20-4

Dn

P

Dining
11-1x12-0

Entry

L

Living
13-4x14-0
vaulted

Porch

Br 2
10-8x9-0

Br 3
10-8x9-0

37'-0"

Special features

- Rear garage and elongated brick wall adds to appealing facade
- Dramatic vaulted living room includes corner fireplace and towering feature windows
- Kitchen and breakfast room are immersed in light from two large windows and glass sliding doors
- 3 bedrooms, 2 baths, 1-car rear entry garage
- Basement foundation

TO ORDER BLUEPRINTS USE THE FORM ON PAGE 15 OR CALL TOLL-FREE 1-877-671-6036
View thousands more home plans online at www.familyhandyman.com/homeplans

215

Beautiful Brickwork Adds Elegance

1,960 total square feet of living area

Price Code C

Special features

- Open floor plan suitable for an active family
- Desk space in bedroom #3 is ideal for a young student
- Effective design creates enclosed courtyard in rear of home
- 3 bedrooms, 2 baths, 2-car garage
- Slab foundation

Width: 50'-0"
Depth: 60'-8"

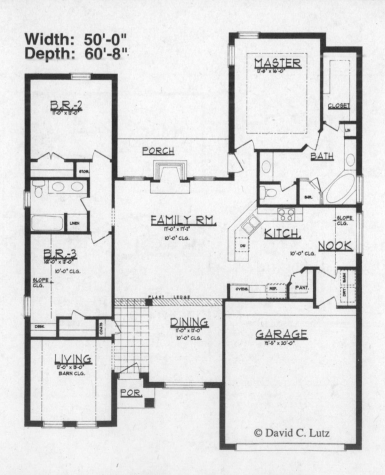

© David C. Lutz

Master Bedroom Provides Retreat

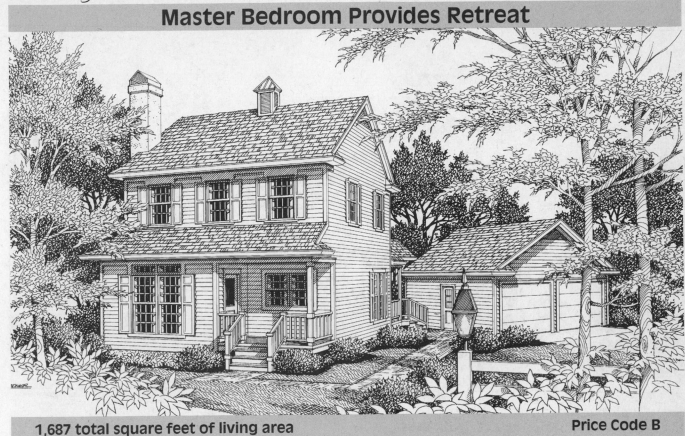

1,687 total square feet of living area

Price Code B

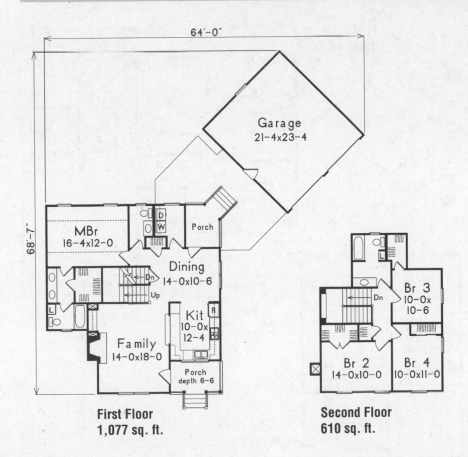

First Floor
1,077 sq. ft.

Second Floor
610 sq. ft.

Special features

- Family room with built-in cabinet and fireplace is focal point of this home
- U-shaped kitchen has bar that opens to the family room
- Back porch opens to dining room and leads to the garage via a walkway
- Convenient laundry room
- 4 bedrooms, 2 1/2 baths, 2-car detached garage
- Basement foundation

TO ORDER BLUEPRINTS USE THE FORM ON PAGE 15 OR CALL TOLL-FREE 1-877-671-6036
View thousands more home plans online at www.familyhandyman.com/homeplans

217

Private Master Bedroom

2,018 total square feet of living area

Price Code C

Special features

- Family room situated near dining area and kitchen create a convenient layout
- First floor master suite features private bath with step-up tub and bay window
- Laundry area located on the first floor
- 4 bedrooms, 2 1/2 baths, 2-car garage
- Basement foundation

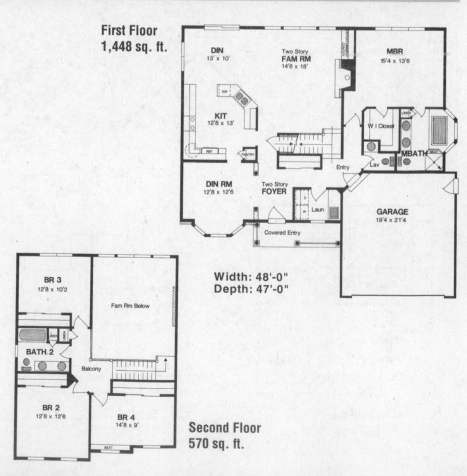

First Floor
1,448 sq. ft.

DIN 13' x 10'	Two Story FAM RM 14'6 x 18'	MBR 15'4 x 13'6
KIT 12'8 x 13'		W I Closet
		MBATH
DIN RM 12'8 x 12'6	Two Story FOYER	
	Laun	GARAGE 19'4 x 21'4
	Covered Entry	

REF PANTRY Entry Lav LINEN

Width: 48'-0"
Depth: 47'-0"

BR 3
12'8 x 10'2

Fam Rm Below

BATH 2

Balcony

BR 2
12'8 x 12'6

BR 4
14'8 x 9'

SEAT

Second Floor
570 sq. ft.

Ideal Home For Lake, Mountains Or Seaside

1,711 total square feet of living area

Price Code B

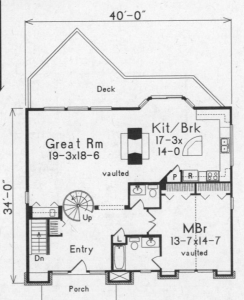

Rear View

Second Floor
397 sq. ft.

open to below

plant shelf

MBr
below

Loft/Br 2
19-3x12-0
vaulted

Dn

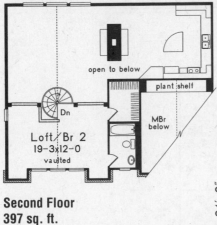

40'-0"

Deck

Great Rm
19-3x18-6
vaulted

Kit/Brk
17-3x
14-0

P   R

34'-0"

Up

MBr
13-7x14-7
vaulted

Dn

Entry

Porch

First Floor
1,314 sq. ft.

Special features

- Colossal entry leads to a vaulted great room with exposed beams, two-story window wall, brick fireplace, wet bar and balcony
- Bayed breakfast room shares the fireplace and joins a sun-drenched kitchen and sundeck
- Vaulted first floor master suite with double entry doors, closets and bookshelves
- Spiral stair and balcony dramatizes a loft that doubles as a spacious second bedroom
- 2 bedrooms, 2 1/2 baths
- Basement foundation

TO ORDER BLUEPRINTS USE THE FORM ON PAGE 15 OR CALL TOLL-FREE 1-877-671-6036
View thousands more home plans online at www.familyhandyman.com/homeplans

219

Big Features In A Small Package

1,941 total square feet of living area

Price Code C

Special features

- Dramatic, exciting and spacious interior
- Vaulted great room brightened by sunken atrium window wall and skylights
- Vaulted U-shaped gourmet kitchen with plant shelf opens to dining room
- First floor half bath features space for stackable washer and dryer
- 4 bedrooms, 2 1/2 baths, 2-car garage
- Walk-out basement foundation

Lower Level 945 sq. ft.

First Floor 996 sq. ft.

1,496 total square feet of living area

Price Code A

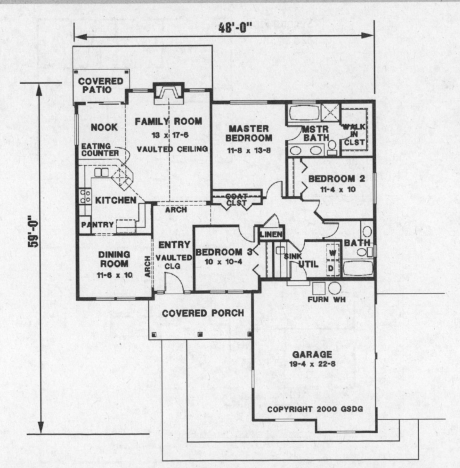

Special features

- Large utility room with sink and extra counterspace
- Covered patio off breakfast nook extends dining to the outdoors
- Eating counter in kitchen overlooks vaulted family room
- 3 bedrooms, 2 baths, 2-car side entry garage
- Crawl space foundation

Wrap-Around Porch Adds Curb Appeal

1,840 total square feet of living area

Price Code C

**Second Floor
826 sq. ft.**

**First Floor
1,014 sq. ft.**

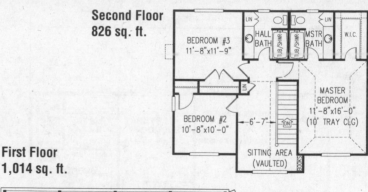

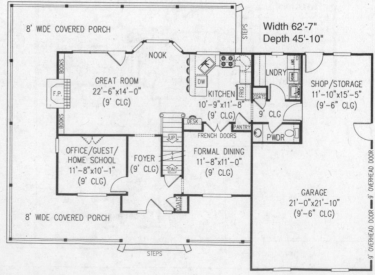

Special features

- All bedrooms located on the second floor for privacy
- Counter dining space provided in the kitchen
- Formal dining room connects to the kitchen through French doors
- 4 bedrooms, 2 1/2 baths, 2-car side entry garage with shop/storage
- Basement, crawl space or slab foundation, please specify when ordering

TO ORDER BLUEPRINTS USE THE FORM ON PAGE 15 OR CALL TOLL-FREE 1-877-671-6036
View thousands more home plans online at www.familyhandyman.com/homeplans

Private Breakfast Room Provides Casual Dining

1,708 total square feet of living area

Price Code B

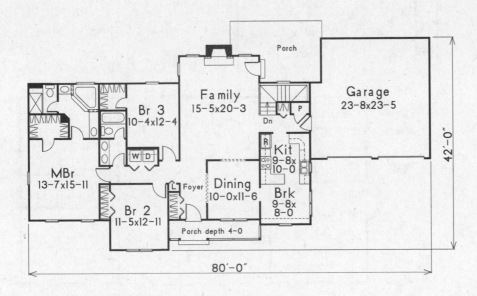

Special features

- Massive family room enhanced with several windows, fireplace and access to porch
- Deluxe master bath accented by step-up corner tub flanked by double vanities
- Closets throughout maintain organized living
- Bedrooms isolated from living areas
- 3 bedrooms, 2 baths, 2-car garage
- Basement foundation, drawings also include crawl space foundation

Open Living Spaces

1,698 total square feet of living area

Price Code B

Special features

- Large and open great room adds spaciousness to the living area

- Cheerful bayed sitting area in the master bedroom

- Compact, yet efficient kitchen

- 3 bedrooms, 2 1/2 baths, 2-car side entry garage

- Basement, crawl space or slab foundation, please specify when ordering

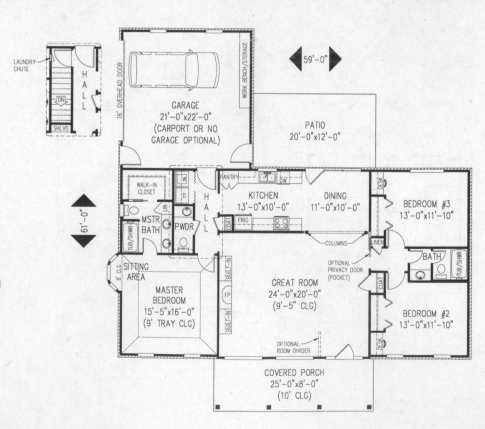

Charming Two-Story With Dormers And Porch

1,711 total square feet of living area

Price Code C

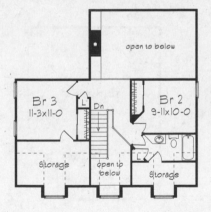

open to below

Second Floor 483 sq. ft.

Br 3
11-3x11-0

L Dn

Br 2
9-11x10-0

Storage

open to below

Storage

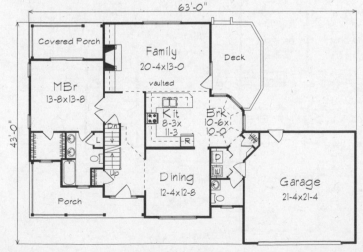

63'-0"

Covered Porch

Family
20-4x13-0

Deck

vaulted

MBr
13-8x13-8

43'-0"

Kit
8-3x
11-3

Brk
10-6x
10-0

L

R

Dining
12-4x12-8

Porch

Garage
21-4x21-4

First Floor 1,228 sq. ft.

Special features

- U-shaped kitchen joins break-fast and family rooms for open living atmosphere
- Master bedroom has secluded covered porch and private bath
- Balcony overlooks family room that features a fireplace and accesses deck
- 3 bedrooms, 2 1/2 baths, 2-car garage
- Basement foundation

TO ORDER BLUEPRINTS USE THE FORM ON PAGE 15 OR CALL TOLL-FREE 1-877-671-6036
View thousands more home plans online at www.familyhandyman.com/homeplans

225

Covered Porches All Around

1,725 total square feet of living area

Price Code B

Special features

- Spectacular arches when entering the foyer
- Dining room has double-doors leading to the kitchen
- Unique desk area off kitchen is ideal for computer work station
- 3 bedrooms, 2 baths, 2-car side entry garage
- Slab or crawl space foundation, please specify when ordering

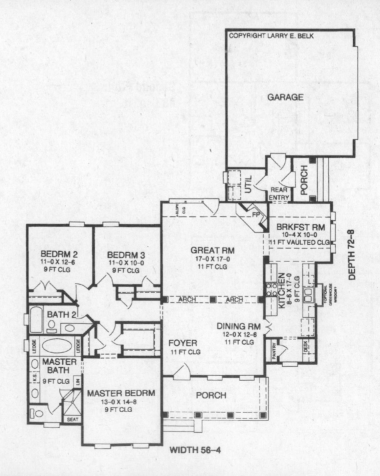

COPYRIGHT LARRY E. BELK

GARAGE

UTIL

REAR ENTRY

PORCH

FP

BRKFST RM
10-4 X 10-0
11 FT VAULTED CLG

BEDRM 2
11-0 X 12-6
9 FT CLG

BEDRM 3
11-0 X 10-0
9 FT CLG

GREAT RM
17-0 X 17-0
11 FT CLG

DEPTH 72-8

KITCHEN
8-6 X 17-0
9 FT CLG

BATH 2

ARCH   ARCH

LEDGE   LEDGE

MASTER BATH
9 FT CLG

FOYER
11 FT CLG

DINING RM
12-0 X 12-6
11 FT CLG

PANTRY   DESK

MASTER BEDRM
13-0 X 14-8
9 FT CLG

PORCH

SEAT

WIDTH 56-4

Special Planning In This Compact Home

977 total square feet of living area

Price Code AA

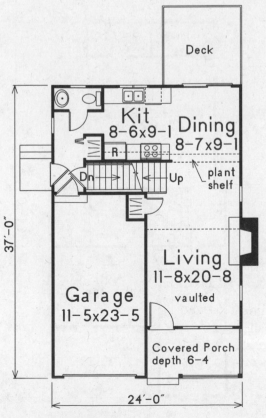

First Floor
545 sq. ft.

Deck

Kit
8-6x9-1

Dining
8-7x9-1

plant shelf

Dn

Up

R

Living
11-8x20-8
vaulted

Garage
11-5x23-5

Covered Porch
depth 6-4

37'-0"

24'-0"

Br 2
9-1x10-1

Dn

L

Br 1
11-5x11-2

Second Floor
432 sq. ft.

Special features

- Comfortable living room features a vaulted ceiling, fireplace, plant shelf and coat closet
- Both bedrooms are located on second floor and share a bath with double-bowl vanity and linen closet
- Sliding glass doors in dining room provide access to the deck
- 2 bedrooms, 1 1/2 baths, 1-car garage
- Basement foundation

TO ORDER BLUEPRINTS USE THE FORM ON PAGE 15 OR CALL TOLL-FREE 1-877-671-6036
View thousands more home plans online at www.familyhandyman.com/homeplans

227

Isolated Master Suite Has Grand Master Bath

1,856 total square feet of living area

Price Code C

Special features

- Living room features include fireplace, 12' ceiling and skylights

- Energy efficient home with 2" x 6" exterior walls

- Common vaulted ceiling creates open atmosphere in kitchen and breakfast room

- Garage with storage areas conveniently accesses home through handy utility room

- Private hall separates secondary bedrooms from living areas

- 3 bedrooms, 2 baths, 2-car side entry garage

- Slab foundation, drawings also include crawl space foundation

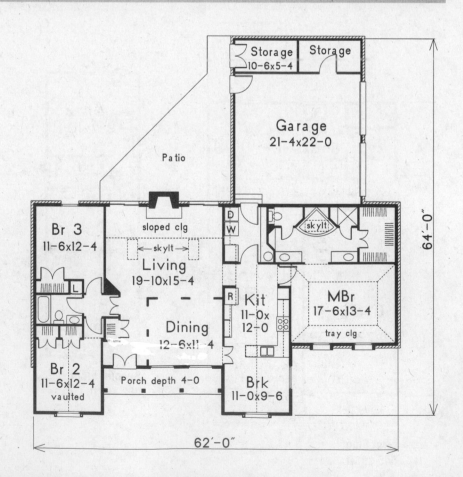

TO ORDER BLUEPRINTS USE THE FORM ON PAGE 15 OR CALL TOLL-FREE 1-877-671-6036
View thousands more home plans online at www.familyhandyman.com/homeplans

Quaint Cottage With Inviting Front Porch

1,020 total square feet of living area　　　　**Price Code AA**

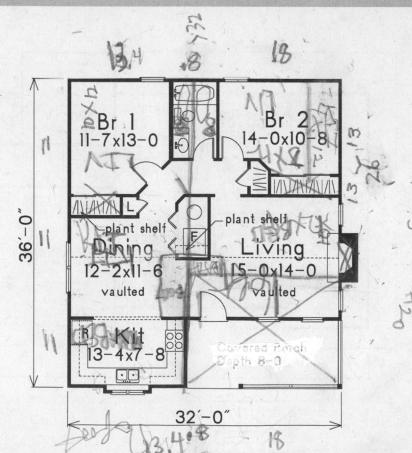

Br 1
11-7x13-0

Br 2
14-0x10-8

L
plant shelf

plant shelf

F

Dining
12-2x11-6
vaulted

Living
15-0x14-0
vaulted

R
Kit
13-4x7-8

Covered Porch
Depth 8-0

36'-0"

32'-0"

Special features

- Living room is warmed by a fireplace
- Dining and living rooms are enhanced by vaulted ceilings and plant shelves
- U-shaped kitchen with large window over the sink
- 2 bedrooms, 1 bath
- Slab foundation

Corner Fireplace In Great Room

1,642 total square feet of living area

Price Code B

Special features

- Built-in cabinet in dining room adds a custom feel
- Secondary bedrooms share an oversized bath
- Master bedroom includes private bath with dressing table
- 3 bedrooms, 2 baths, 2-car garage
- Basement, crawl space or slab foundation, please specify when ordering

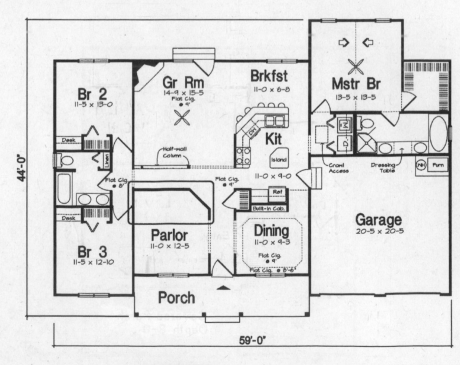

Optional Basement Stairs

Summer Home Or Year-Round

1,403 total square feet of living area

Price Code A

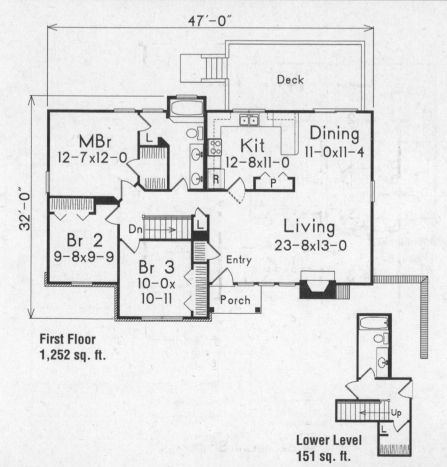

47'-0"

Deck

MBr
12-7x12-0

L

Kit
12-8x11-0

Dining
11-0x11-4

R

P

32'-0"

Br 2
9-8x9-9

Dn

L

Living
23-8x13-0

Br 3
10-0x
10-11

Entry

Porch

First Floor
1,252 sq. ft.

Up

L

Lower Level
151 sq. ft.

Special features

- Impressive living areas for a modest-sized home

- Special master/hall bath has linen storage, step-up tub and lots of window light

- Spacious closets everywhere you look

- 3 bedrooms, 2 baths, 2-car drive under garage and second bath on lower level

- Basement foundation

TO ORDER BLUEPRINTS USE THE FORM ON PAGE 15 OR CALL TOLL-FREE 1-877-671-6036
View thousands more home plans online at www.familyhandyman.com/homeplans

231

Charming Extras Add Character To This Home

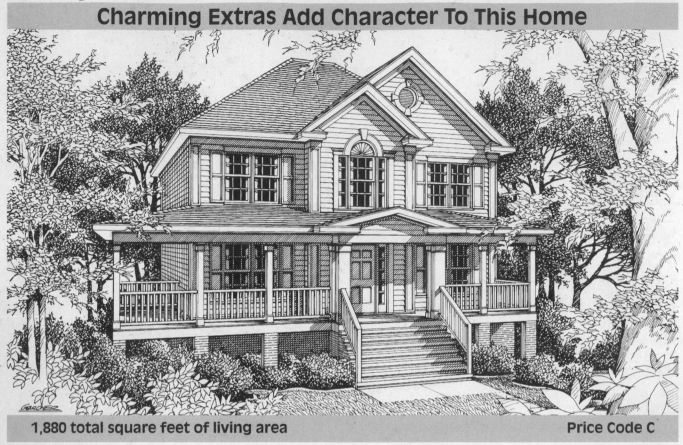

1,880 total square feet of living area

Price Code C

Special features

- Master suite enhanced with coffered ceiling
- Generous family and breakfast areas are modern and functional
- Front porch complements front facade
- 3 bedrooms, 2 1/2 baths, 2-car drive under garage
- Basement foundation

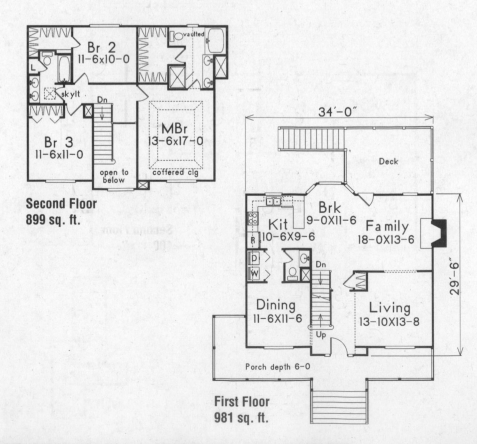

Second Floor
899 sq. ft.

First Floor
981 sq. ft.

232

TO ORDER BLUEPRINTS USE THE FORM ON PAGE 15 OR CALL TOLL-FREE 1-877-671-6036
View thousands more home plans online at www.familyhandyman.com/homeplans

Compact Home, Perfect Fit For Narrow Lot

1,085 total square feet of living area

Price Code AA

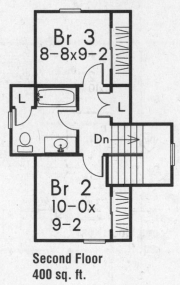

Br 3
8-8x9-2

L

L

Dn

Br 2
10-0x
9-2

Second Floor
400 sq. ft.

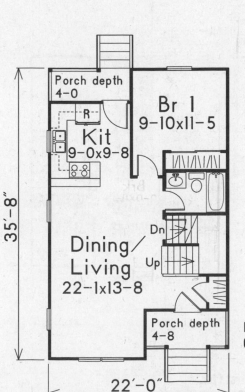

Porch depth
4-0

R

Kit
9-0x9-8

Br 1
9-10x11-5

35'-8"

Dn

Up

Dining/
Living
22-1x13-8

Porch depth
4-8

First Floor
685 sq. ft.

22'-0"

Special features

- Rear porch is a handy access through the kitchen
- Convenient hall linen closet located on the second floor
- Breakfast bar in kitchen offers additional counterspace
- Living and dining rooms combine for an open living atmosphere
- 3 bedrooms, 2 baths
- Basement foundation

TO ORDER BLUEPRINTS USE THE FORM ON PAGE 15 OR CALL TOLL-FREE 1-877-671-6036
View thousands more home plans online at www.familyhandyman.com/homeplans

233

Cozy Hearth Room

1,872 total square feet of living area

Price Code C

Special features

- Three-season room off hearth room extends living area
- Spacious deck can be reached through sliding glass doors in living room
- Kitchen has work desk and access to laundry
- 3 bedrooms, 2 1/2 baths, 3-car garage
- Basement foundation

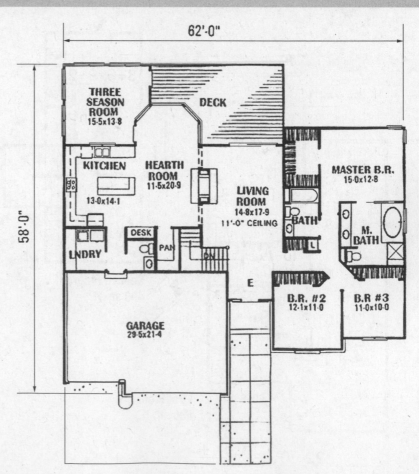

Inviting Covered Corner Entry

1,747 total square feet of living area

Price Code B

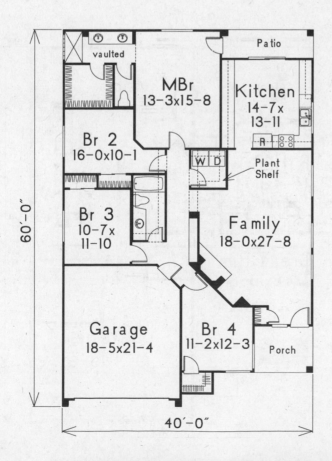

Special features

- Entry opens into large family room with coat closet, angled fireplace and attractive plant shelf
- Kitchen and master bedroom access covered patio
- Functional kitchen includes ample workspace
- 4 bedrooms, 2 baths, 2-car garage
- Slab foundation

Floor plan labels:

- vaulted
- MBr 13-3x15-8
- Patio
- Kitchen 14-7x 13-11
- Br 2 16-0x10-1
- W D
- Plant Shelf
- R
- Br 3 10-7x 11-10
- Family 18-0x27-8
- Garage 18-5x21-4
- Br 4 11-2x12-3
- Porch
- 60'-0"
- 40'-0"

TO ORDER BLUEPRINTS USE THE FORM ON PAGE 15 OR CALL TOLL-FREE 1-877-671-6036
View thousands more home plans online at www.familyhandyman.com/homeplans

235

Breakfast Bay Area Opens To Deck

1,020 total square feet of living area

Price Code AA

Special features

- Kitchen features open stairs, pass-through to great room, pantry and deck access

- Master bedroom features private entrance to bath, large walk-in closet and sliding doors to deck

- Informal entrance into home through the garage

- Great room with vaulted ceiling and fireplace

- 2 bedrooms, 1 bath, 2-car garage

- Basement foundation

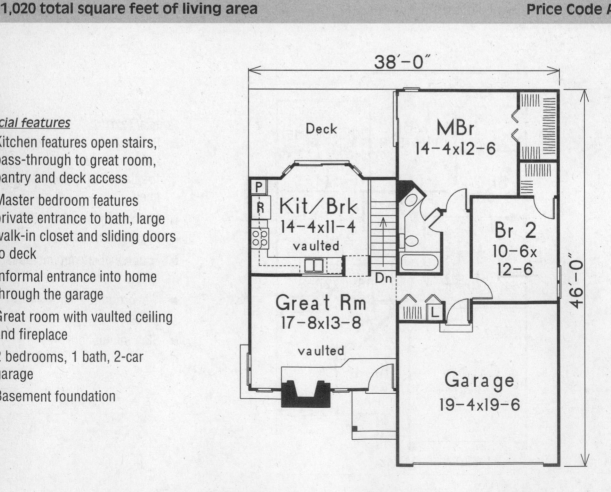

38'-0"

46'-0"

Deck

MBr
14-4x12-6

Kit/Brk
14-4x11-4
vaulted

P
R

Dn

Br 2
10-6x
12-6

Great Rm
17-8x13-8
vaulted

L

Garage
19-4x19-6

2,109 total square feet of living area

Price Code C

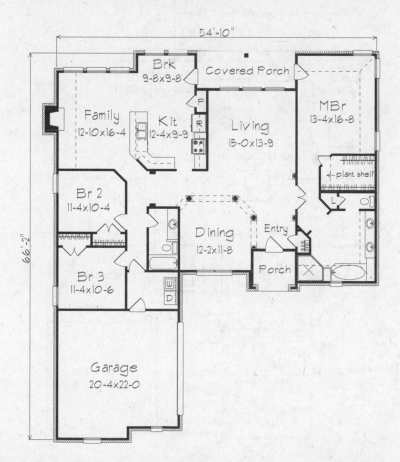

Special features

- 12' ceilings in living and dining rooms

- Kitchen designed as an integral part of the family and breakfast rooms

- Secluded and generous-sized master bedroom includes a plant shelf, walk-in closet and private bath with separate tub and shower

- Stately columns and circle-top window frame dining room

- 3 bedrooms, 2 baths, 2-car side entry garage

- Slab foundation, drawings also include crawl space foundation

TO ORDER BLUEPRINTS USE THE FORM ON PAGE 15 OR CALL TOLL-FREE 1-877-671-6036
View thousands more home plans online at www.familyhandyman.com/homeplans

237

Spacious Family Room For Growing Families

2,147 total square feet of living area

Price Code C

Special features

- Living and dining rooms adjacent to entry foyer for easy access
- Kitchen conveniently located next to sunny breakfast nook
- Master suite includes large walk-in closet and luxurious bath
- Breakfast area offers easy access to deck
- 4 bedrooms, 2 1/2 baths, 2-car garage
- Basement foundation

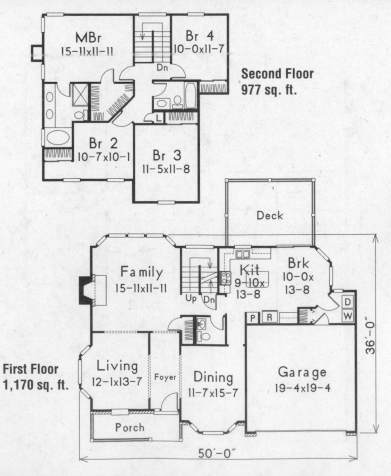

Second Floor 977 sq. ft.

MBr 15-11x11-11
Br 4 10-0x11-7
Br 2 10-7x10-1
Br 3 11-5x11-8

First Floor 1,170 sq. ft.

Deck
Family 15-11x11-11
Kit 9-10x13-8
Brk 10-0x13-8
Living 12-1x13-7
Foyer
Dining 11-7x15-7
Garage 19-4x19-4
Porch

36'-0"
50'-0"

Casual Exterior, Filled With Great Features

1,958 total square feet of living area

Price Code C

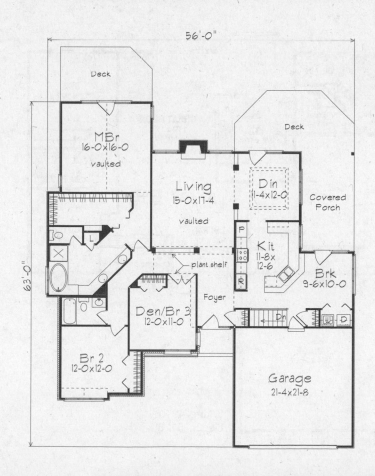

Special features

- Large wrap-around kitchen opens to a bright cheerful breakfast area with access to large covered deck and open stairway to basement
- Kitchen nestled between the dining and breakfast rooms
- Master suite includes large walk-in closet, double-bowl vanity, garden tub and separate shower
- Foyer features attractive plant shelves and opens into living room that includes attractive central fireplace
- 3 bedrooms, 2 baths, 2-car garage
- Basement foundation

Luxurious Master Bath

1,456 total square feet of living area

Price Code A

Special features

- Open floor plan adds spaciousness to this design
- The study can easily be converted a third bedroom
- Corner fireplace in great room is a terrific focal point
- 3 bedrooms, 2 baths, 2-car garage
- Basement foundation

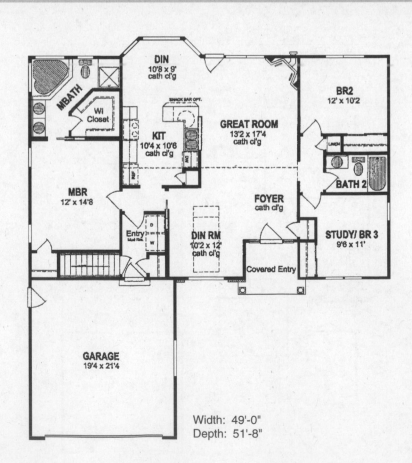

Width: 49'-0"
Depth: 51'-8"

240

TO ORDER BLUEPRINTS USE THE FORM ON PAGE 15 OR CALL TOLL-FREE 1-877-671-6036
View thousands more home plans online at www.familyhandyman.com/homeplans

Cozy Columned Archway Defines Foyer

1,777 total square feet of living area

Price Code B

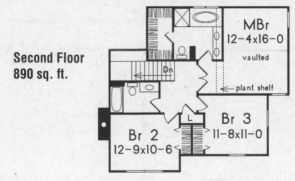

Second Floor 890 sq. ft.

MBr
12-4x16-0
vaulted

plant shelf

Dn

L

Br 3
11-8x11-0

Br 2
12-9x10-6

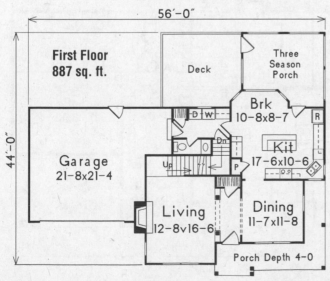

56'-0"

First Floor 887 sq. ft.

44'-0"

Deck

Three Season Porch

D W

Brk
10-8x8-7

R

Dn

Kit
17-6x10-6

Garage
21-8x21-4

Up

P

Living
12-8v16-6

Dining
11-7x11-8

Porch Depth 4-0

Special features

- Large master bedroom and bath with whirlpool tub, separate shower and spacious walk-in closet
- Large island kitchen with breakfast bay and access to the three-season porch
- Convenient laundry room with half bath
- 3 bedrooms, 2 1/2 baths, 2-car garage
- Basement foundation

Open Living Areas Separate Remote Bedrooms

1,868 total square feet of living area

Price Code D

Special features

- Luxurious master bath is impressive with angled quarter-circle tub, separate vanities and large walk-in closet

- Energy efficient home with 2" x 6" exterior walls

- Dining room is surrounded by a series of arched openings which complement the open feeling of this design

- Living room has a 12' ceiling accented by skylights and a large fireplace flanked by sliding doors

- Large storage areas

- 3 bedrooms, 2 baths, 2-car side entry garage

- Slab foundation, drawings also include crawl space foundation

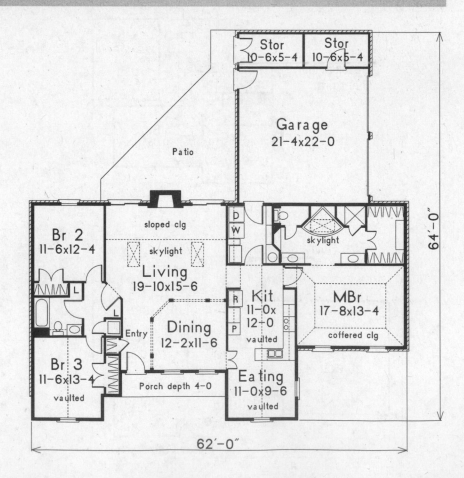

Open Living Centers On Windowed Dining Room

2,003 total square feet of living area

Price Code D

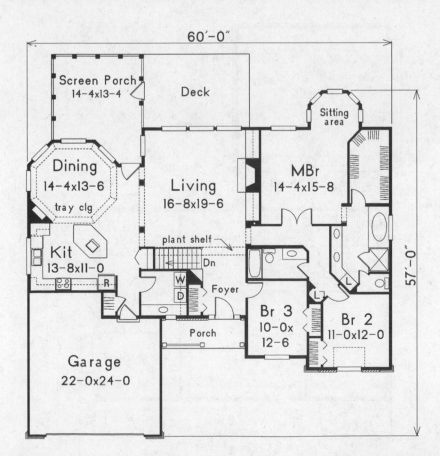

60'-0"

Screen Porch
14-4x13-4

Deck

Sitting area

Dining
14-4x13-6
tray clg

Living
16-8x19-6

MBr
14-4x15-8

Kit
13-8x11-0

plant shelf

Dn

W
D

Foyer

Br 3
10-0x
12-6

Br 2
11-0x12-0

Porch

Garage
22-0x24-0

57'-0"

Special features

- Octagon-shaped dining room with tray ceiling and deck overlook
- L-shaped island kitchen serves living and dining rooms
- Master bedroom boasts luxury bath and walk-in closet
- Living room features columns, elegant fireplace and 10' ceiling
- 3 bedrooms, 2 baths, 2-car garage
- Basement foundation

TO ORDER BLUEPRINTS USE THE FORM ON PAGE 15 OR CALL TOLL-FREE 1-877-671-6036
View thousands more home plans online at www.familyhandyman.com/homeplans

243

Quaint And Cozy

1,191 total square feet of living area

Price Code AA

Special features

- Energy efficient home with 2" x 6" exterior walls

- Master bedroom located near living areas for maximum convenience

- Living room has cathedral ceiling and stone fireplace

- 3 bedrooms, 2 baths, 2-car side entry garage

- Slab or crawl space foundation, please specify when ordering

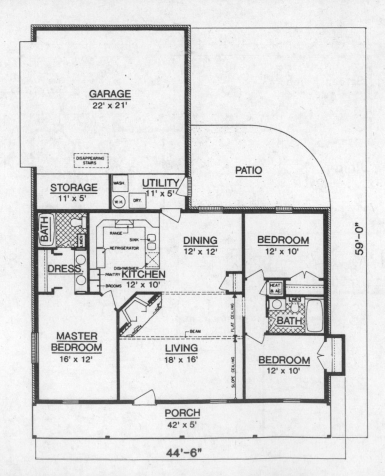

Relax On The Covered Front Porch

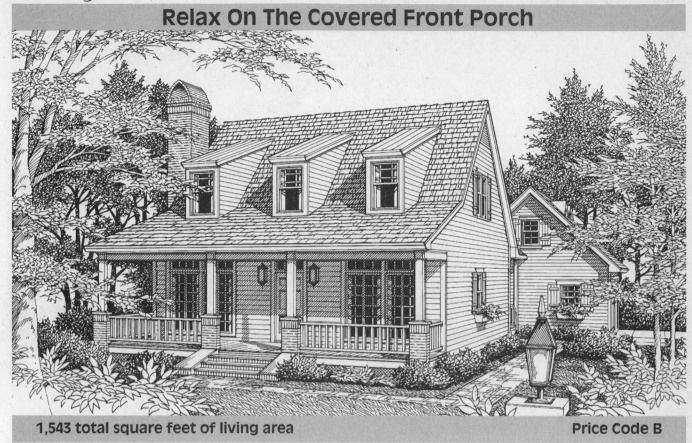

1,543 total square feet of living area

Price Code B

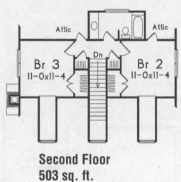

Second Floor
503 sq. ft.

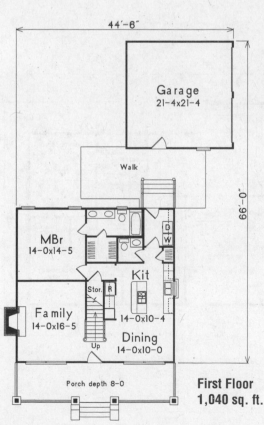

First Floor
1,040 sq. ft.

Special features

- Fireplace serves as the focal point of the large family room
- Efficient floor plan keeps hallways at a minimum
- Laundry room connects the kitchen to the garage
- Private first floor master bedroom has walk-in closet and bath
- 3 bedrooms, 2 1/2 baths, 2-car detached side entry garage
- Slab foundation, drawings also include crawl space foundation

TO ORDER BLUEPRINTS USE THE FORM ON PAGE 15 OR CALL TOLL-FREE 1-877-671-6036
View thousands more home plans online at www.familyhandyman.com/homeplans

245

Lovely Arched Touches On The Covered Porch

1,594 total square feet of living area

Price Code B

Special features

- Corner fireplace in the great room creates a cozy feel
- Spacious kitchen combines with the dining room creating a terrific gathering place
- A handy family and guest entrance is a casual and convenient way to enter the home
- 3 bedrooms, 2 baths, 2-car garage
- Slab or crawl space foundation, please specify when ordering

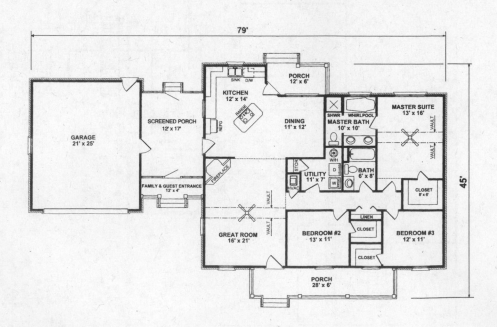

987 total square feet of living area

Price Code AA

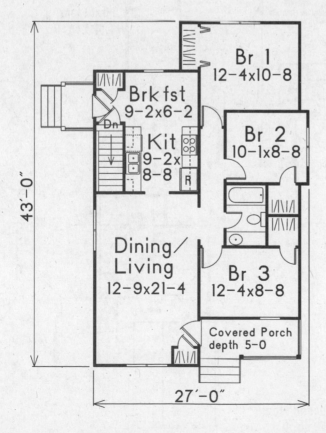

Special features

- Galley kitchen opens into cozy breakfast room
- Convenient coat closets located by both entrances
- Dining/living room combined for expansive open area
- Breakfast room has access to the outdoors
- Front porch great for enjoying outdoor living
- 3 bedrooms, 1 bath
- Basement foundation

Computer Area Is A Handy Feature

2,082 total square feet of living area

Price Code C

Special features

- Master bedroom boasts a deluxe bath and a large walk-in closet

- Natural light floods the breakfast room through numerous windows

- Great room features 12' ceiling, a cozy fireplace and stylish French doors

- Bonus room on the second floor has an additional 267 square feet of living area

- 3 bedrooms, 2 1/2 baths, 2-car garage

- Basement foundation

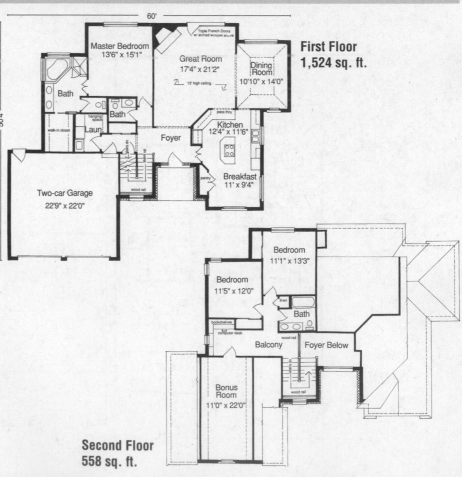

First Floor
1,524 sq. ft.

Second Floor
558 sq. ft.

Columned Breakfast Room Adds Appeal

1,954 total square feet of living area

Price Code D

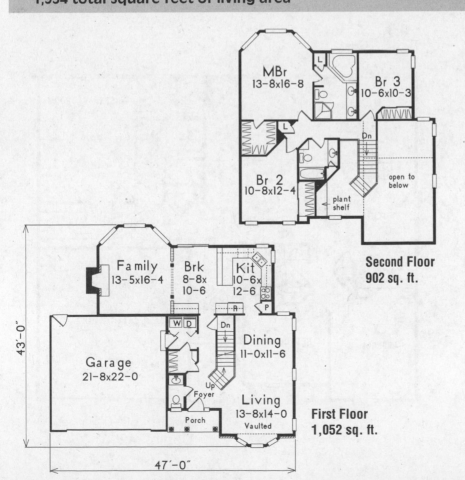

Second Floor 902 sq. ft.

First Floor 1,052 sq. ft.

Special features

- Living and dining areas include vaulted ceilings and combine for added openness
- Convenient access to laundry room from garage
- Appealing bay window in family room attracts light
- Raised jacuzzi tub featured in master bath
- 3 bedrooms, 2 1/2 baths, 2-car garage
- Basement foundation

Corner Fireplace In Grand Room

1,606 total square feet of living area

Price Code B

Special features

- Kitchen has snack bar which overlooks dining area for convenience

- Master bedroom has lots of windows with a private bath and large walk-in closet

- Cathedral vault in great room adds spaciousness

- 3 bedrooms, 2 baths, 2-car garage

- Slab foundation

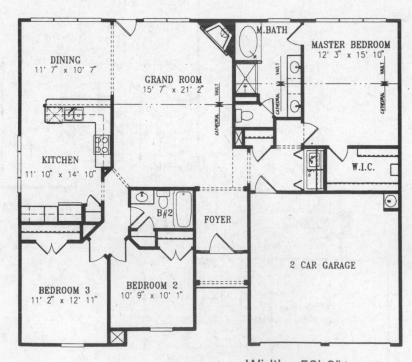

Width: 50'-0"
Depth: 42'-0"

Corner Windows Grace Library

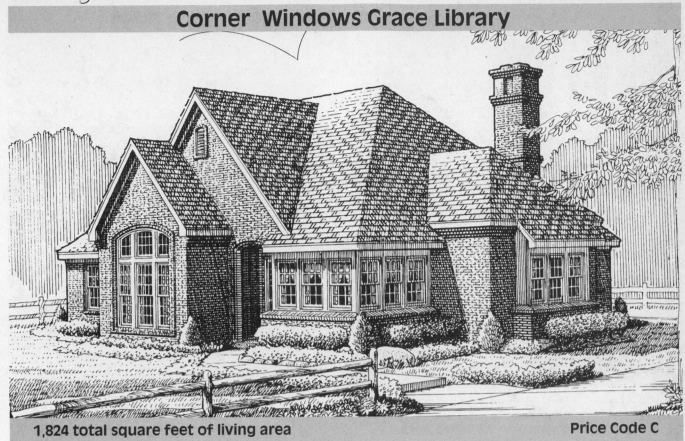

1,824 total square feet of living area

Price Code C

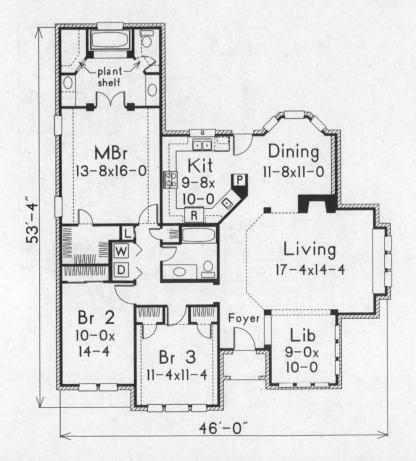

plant shelf

MBr
13-8x16-0

Kit
9-8x
10-0

Dining
11-8x11-0

L
W
D

Living
17-4x14-4

53'-4"

Br 2
10-0x
14-4

Br 3
11-4x11-4

Foyer

Lib
9-0x
10-0

46'-0"

Special features

- Living room features 10' ceiling, fireplace and media center
- Dining room includes bay window and convenient kitchen access
- Master bedroom features large walk-in closet and double-doors leading into master bath
- Modified U-shaped kitchen features pantry and bar
- 3 bedrooms, 2 baths, 2-car detached garage
- Slab foundation

TO ORDER BLUEPRINTS USE THE FORM ON PAGE 15 OR CALL TOLL-FREE 1-877-671-6036
View thousands more home plans online at www.familyhandyman.com/homeplans

251

Victorian-Style Home Features Double Bays

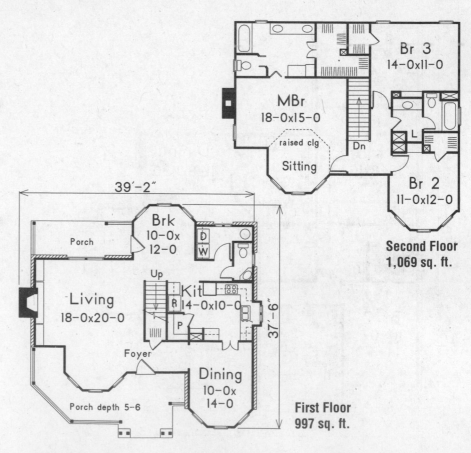

2,066 total square feet of living area

Price Code C

Special features

- Large master bedroom includes sitting area and private bath
- Open living room features a fireplace with built-in book-shelves
- Spacious kitchen accesses formal dining area and breakfast room
- 3 bedrooms, 2 1/2 baths
- Slab foundation

Br 3
14-0x11-0

MBr
18-0x15-0

raised clg

Dn

Sitting

Second Floor
1,069 sq. ft.

Br 2
11-0x12-0

39´-2"

Brk
10-0x
12-0

Porch

Up

Living
18-0x20-0

Kit
14-0x10-0

P

37´-6"

Foyer

Dining
10-0x
14-0

Porch depth 5-6

First Floor
997 sq. ft.

Nostalgic Porch And Charming Interior

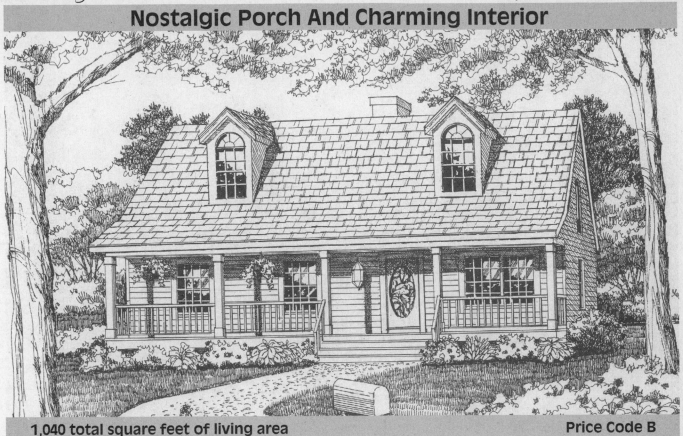

1,040 total square feet of living area

Price Code B

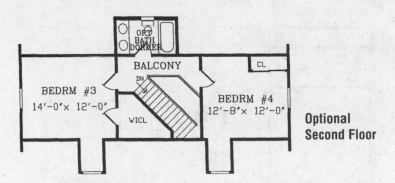

BEDRM #3
14'-0" x 12'-0"

BALCONY

DN

WICL

BEDRM #4
12'-8" x 12'-0"

CL

OPT BATH DORMER

Optional Second Floor

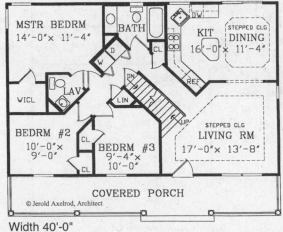

MSTR BEDRM
14'-0" x 11'-4"

BATH

KIT

DINING
16'-0" x 11'-4"

STEPPED CLG

DW

REF

CL

D

W

LAV

WICL

DN

UP

LIN

CL

BEDRM #2
10'-0" x 9'-0"

BEDRM #3
9'-4" x 10'-0"

CL

CL

LIVING RM
17'-0" x 13'-8"

STEPPED CLG

COVERED PORCH

© Jerold Axelrod, Architect

First Floor
1,040 sq. ft.

Width 40'-0"
Depth 32'-0"

Special features

- Affordable home has the ability to accommodate a small or large family

- An island in the kitchen greatly simplifies your food preparation efforts

- A wide archway joins the formal living room to the dramatic angled kitchen and dining room

- Optional second floor has an additional 597 square feet of living area

- 4 bedrooms, 2 baths

- Basement, crawl space or slab foundation, please specify when ordering

TO ORDER BLUEPRINTS USE THE FORM ON PAGE 15 OR CALL TOLL-FREE 1-877-671-6036
View thousands more home plans online at www.familyhandyman.com/homeplans

253

A Trim Arrangement Of Living Areas

1,770 total square feet of living area

Price Code B

Special features

- Distinctive covered entrance leads into spacious foyer
- Master bedroom, living and dining rooms, all feature large windows for plenty of light
- Oversized living room has a high ceiling and large windows that flank the fireplace
- Kitchen includes pantry and large planning center
- Master bedroom has high vaulted ceiling, deluxe bath, and private access outdoors
- 3 bedrooms, 2 baths, 2-car garage
- Slab foundation

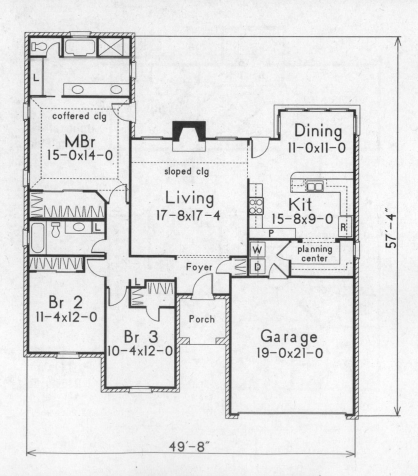

Distinctive Ranch Has A Larger Look

1,360 total square feet of living area

Price Code A

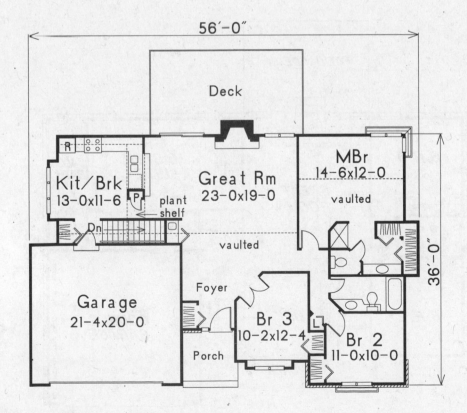

Special features

- Double-gabled front facade frames large windows
- Entry area is open to vaulted great room, fireplace and rear deck creating an open feel
- Vaulted ceiling and large windows add openness to kitchen/breakfast room
- Bedroom #3 easily converts to a den
- Plan easily adapts to crawl space or slab construction, with the utilities replacing the stairs
- 3 bedrooms, 2 baths, 2-car garage
- Basement foundation

Cozy Country Appeal

1,482 total square feet of living area

Price Code A

Special features

- Coffered ceiling in master suite adds a dramatic feel

- Half-wall in breakfast room helps maintain an open flowing floor plan

- Covered front porch creates a place for a quiet retreat

- 3 bedrooms, 2 baths, 2-car garage

- Slab or crawl space foundation, please specify when ordering

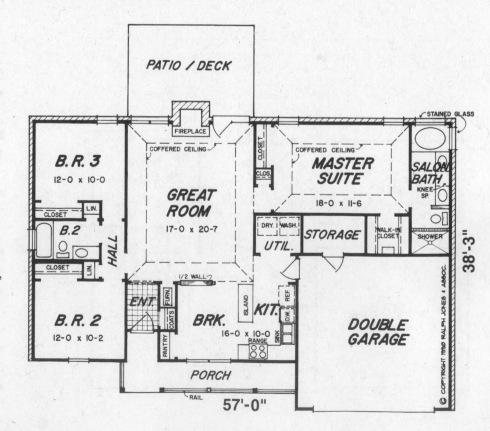

256

TO ORDER BLUEPRINTS USE THE FORM ON PAGE 15 OR CALL TOLL-FREE 1-877-671-6036
View thousands more home plans online at www.familyhandyman.com/homeplans

Gabled, Covered Front Porch

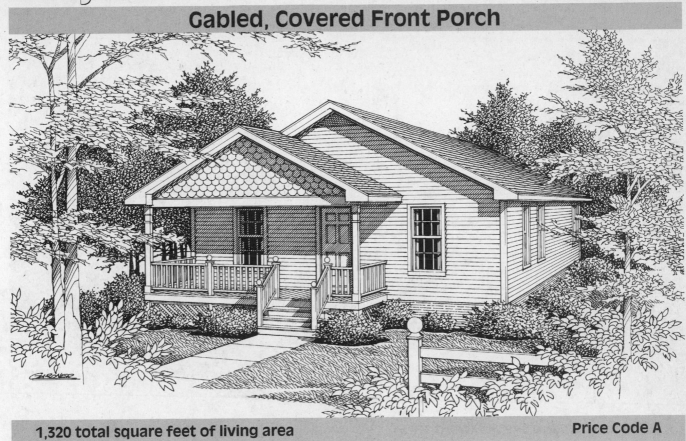

1,320 total square feet of living area

Price Code A

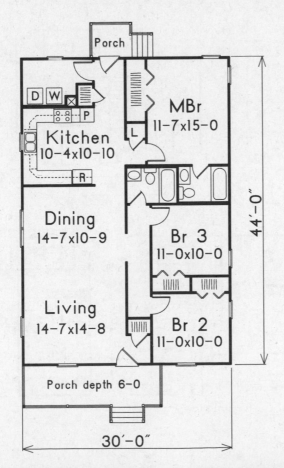

Special features

- Functional U-shaped kitchen features pantry
- Large living and dining areas join to create an open atmosphere
- Secluded master bedroom includes private full bath
- Covered front porch opens into large living area with convenient coat closet
- Utility/laundry room located near the kitchen
- 3 bedrooms, 2 baths
- Crawl space foundation

Trio Of Dormers Adds Light

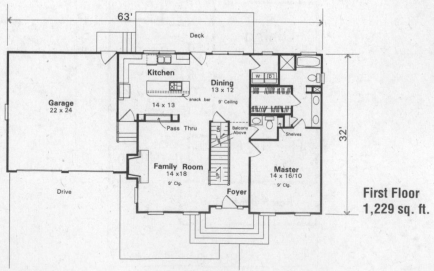

1,780 total square feet of living area

Price Code B

Special features

- Traditional styling with the comforts of home

- First floor master bedroom has walk-in closet and bath

- Large kitchen and dining area open to deck

- 3 bedrooms, 2 1/2 baths, 2-car garage

- Basement, crawl space or slab foundation, please specify when ordering

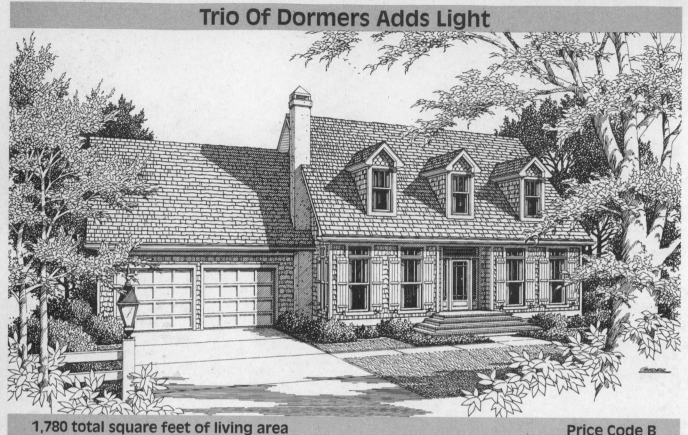

Attic Storage

BR. # 2
11 x 13

BR. #3
11 x 13
8' Ceiling

Foyer Below

Second Floor 551 sq. ft.

Deck

Kitchen
14 x 13

Dining
13 x 12
9' Ceiling

snack bar

Pass Thru

W D

Balcony Above

Shelves

Garage
22 x 24

Family Room
14 x18
9' Clg.

Master
14 x 16/10
9' Clg.

Drive

Foyer

63'

32'

First Floor 1,229 sq. ft.

TO ORDER BLUEPRINTS USE THE FORM ON PAGE 15 OR CALL TOLL-FREE 1-877-671-6036
View thousands more home plans online at www.familyhandyman.com/homeplans

Covered Front Porch Is A Terrific Focal Point

1,934 total square feet of living area

Price Code C

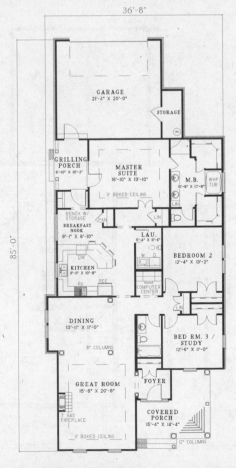

Special features

- Private master suite has access onto covered porch, a private bath and his and hers walk-in closets

- Extra storage in the garage

- Centralized laundry area

- 3 bedrooms, 2 baths, 2-car rear entry garage

- Crawl space or slab foundation, please specify when ordering

Open Living On First Floor

1,584 total square feet of living area

Price Code B

Special features

- Kitchen overlooks family room creating a natural gathering place
- Double vanity in master bath
- Dining room flows into living room
- 3 bedrooms, 2 1/2 baths, 2-car rear entry garage
- Crawl space foundation

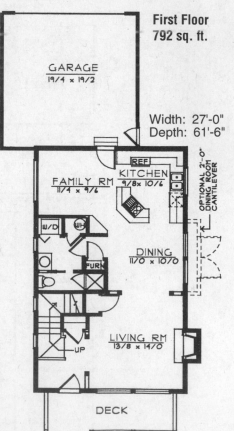

First Floor
792 sq. ft.

GARAGE
19/4 x 19/2

Width: 27'-0"
Depth: 61'-6"

FAMILY RM
11/4 x 9/6

KITCHEN
9/8 x 10/6

REF.

OPTIONAL 2'-0"
DINING ROOM
CANTILEVER

W/D   WH

DINING
11/0 x 10/0

FUR

LIVING RM
13/8 x 14/0

UP

DECK

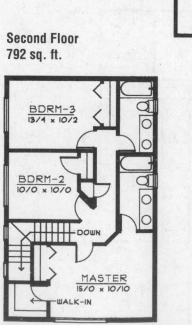

Second Floor
792 sq. ft.

BDRM-3
13/4 x 10/2

BDRM-2
10/0 x 10/0

DOWN

MASTER
15/0 x 10/10

WALK-IN

260

TO ORDER BLUEPRINTS USE THE FORM ON PAGE 15 OR CALL TOLL-FREE 1-877-671-6036
View thousands more home plans online at www.familyhandyman.com/homeplans

Compact Home With Functional Design

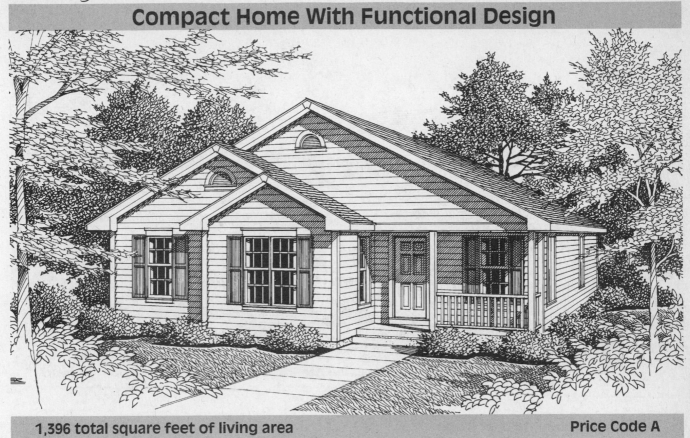

1,396 total square feet of living area

Price Code A

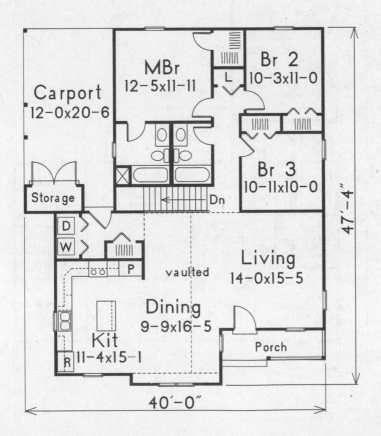

Special features

- Gabled front adds interest to facade
- Living and dining rooms share a vaulted ceiling
- Master bedroom features a walk-in closet and private bath
- Functional kitchen with a center work island and convenient pantry
- 3 bedrooms, 2 baths, 1-car carport
- Basement foundation, drawings also include crawl space foundation

Award Winning Style With This Design

2,156 total square feet of living area

Price Code C

Special features

- Secluded master bedroom has spa-style bath with corner whirlpool tub, large shower, double sinks and a walk-in closet

- Kitchen overlooks rear patio

- Plenty of windows add an open, airy feel to the great room

- 3 bedrooms, 3 baths, 2-car side entry garage

- Basement, crawl space or slab foundation, please specify when ordering

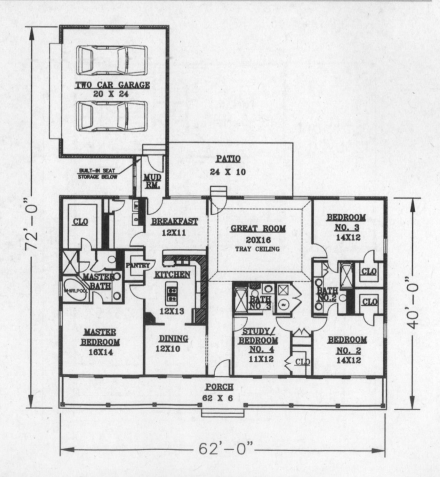

Dormers And Stone Veneer Add Exterior Appeal

1,609 total square feet of living area

Price Code B

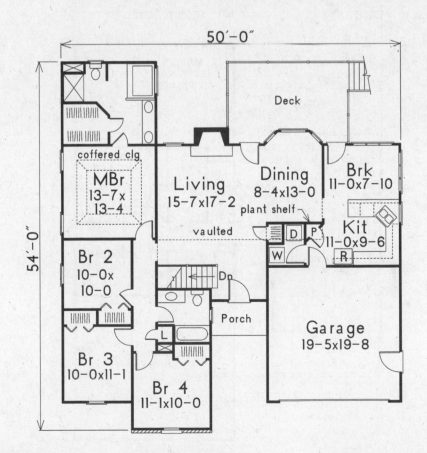

50'-0"

54'-0"

Deck

coffered clg.

MBr
13-7 x
13-4

Living
15-7x17-2

Dining
8-4x13-0

plant shelf

Brk
11-0x7-10

vaulted

D P

Kit
11-0x9-6

W

R

Br 2
10-0x
10-0

Dn

Porch

Garage
19-5x19-8

Br 3
10-0x11-1

L

Br 4
11-1x10-0

Special features

- Efficient kitchen with corner pantry and adjacent laundry room
- Breakfast room boasts plenty of windows and opens onto rear deck
- Master bedroom features tray ceiling and private deluxe bath
- Entry opens into large living area with fireplace
- 4 bedrooms, 2 baths, 2-car garage
- Basement foundation

TO ORDER BLUEPRINTS USE THE FORM ON PAGE 15 OR CALL TOLL-FREE 1-877-671-6036
View thousands more home plans online at www.familyhandyman.com/homeplans

263

Arched Entry Adds Appeal

1,263 total square feet of living area

Price Code A

Special features

- 9' ceilings throughout most of this home
- Kitchen features large island eating bar ideal for extra seating when entertaining
- 3 bedrooms, 2 baths, 2-car side entry garage
- Basement foundation

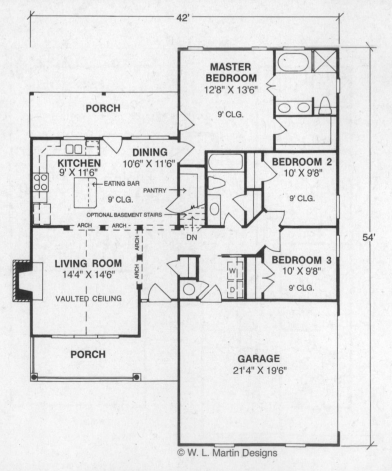

© W. L. Martin Designs

Bay Window In Dining Room

1,225 total square feet of living area

Price Code A

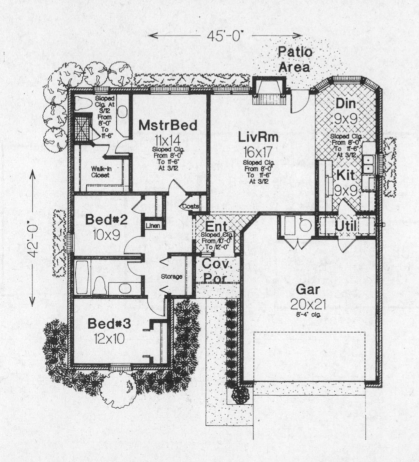

Special features

- Utility room accesses kitchen and garage for convenience
- Extra closets and storage space throughout
- All bedrooms located on one side of the home for privacy
- 3 bedrooms, 2 baths, 2-car garage
- Slab foundation

Roomy Ranch For Easy Living

1,343 total square feet of living area

Price Code A

Special features

- Separate and convenient family and living/dining areas

- Nice-sized master bedroom suite with large closet and private bath

- Foyer with convenient coat closet opens into combined living and dining rooms

- Kitchen has access to the outdoors through sliding glass doors

- 3 bedrooms, 2 baths, 2-car garage

- Crawl space foundation, drawings also include basement foundation

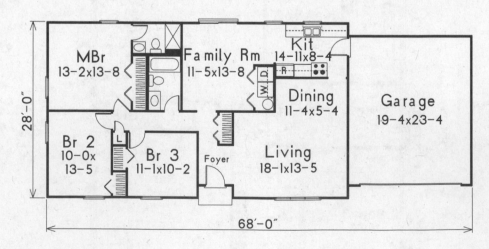

Country Accents Make This Home

1,568 total square feet of living area

Price Code B

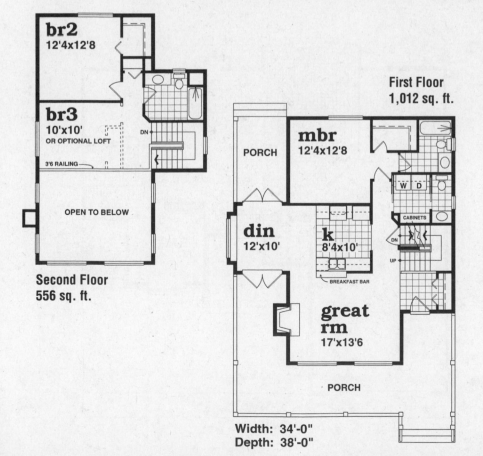

br2
12'4x12'8

br3
10'x10'
OR OPTIONAL LOFT

DN

3'6 RAILING

OPEN TO BELOW

Second Floor
556 sq. ft.

First Floor
1,012 sq. ft.

PORCH

mbr
12'4x12'8

W   D

CABINETS

din
12'x10'

k
8'4x10'

DN

UP

BREAKFAST BAR

great rm
17'x13'6

PORCH

Width: 34'-0"
Depth: 38'-0"

Special features

- Master bedroom is located on first floor for convenience
- Cozy great room has fireplace
- Dining room has access to both the front and rear porches
- Two secondary bedrooms and a bath complete the second floor
- 3 bedrooms, 2 1/2 baths
- Basement or crawl space foundation, please specify when ordering

Plan #706-JA-67596

Elegant Ranch

1,919 total square feet of living area

Price Code C

Special features

- Elegant contemporary floor plan
- Family room is a central gathering place with fireplace and kitchen pass-through
- Master bath has whirlpool tub, double vanity and large walk-in closet
- 3 bedrooms, 2 baths, 2-car garage
- Basement foundation

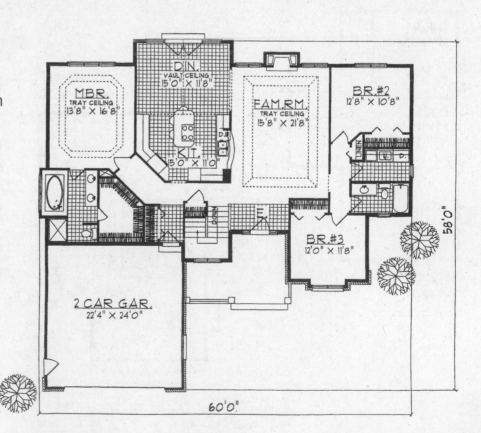

Cozy Cottage Style

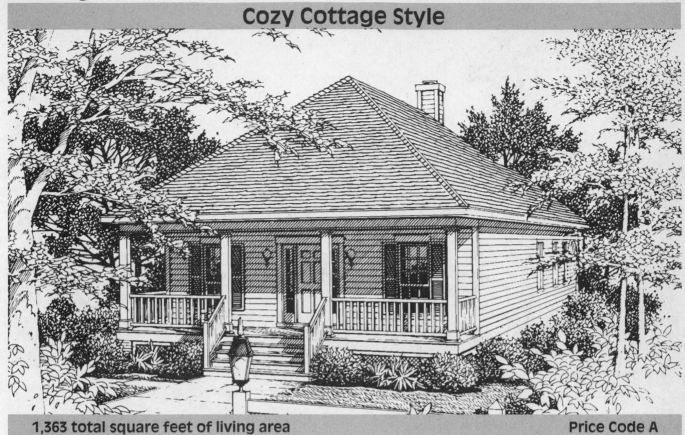

1,363 total square feet of living area

Price Code A

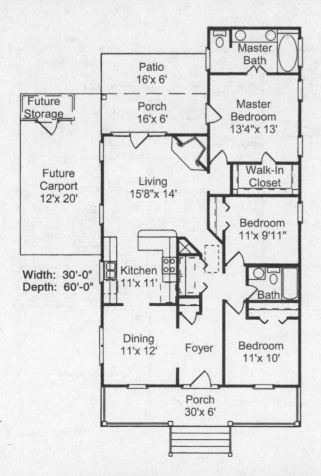

Future Storage

Future Carport 12'x 20'

Width: 30'-0"
Depth: 60'-0"

Patio 16'x 6'

Porch 16'x 6'

Living 15'8"x 14'

Kitchen 11'x 11'

Dining 11'x 12'

Foyer

Porch 30'x 6'

Master Bath

Master Bedroom 13'4"x 13'

Walk-In Closet

Bedroom 11'x 9'11"

Bath

Bedroom 11'x 10'

Special features

- Formal dining area conveniently located next to kitchen
- Master bedroom has private bath and walk-in closet
- Covered porch has patio which allows enough space for entertaining
- 3 bedrooms, 2 baths, optional 1-car carport
- Slab foundation

TO ORDER BLUEPRINTS USE THE FORM ON PAGE 15 OR CALL TOLL-FREE 1-877-671-6036
View thousands more home plans online at www.familyhandyman.com/homeplans

269

Impressive Entry

1,817 total square feet of living area

Price Code C

Special features

- Master suite has its own sitting area flooded with sunlight
- Family room has fireplace flanked by bookshelves
- Open and airy dining room flows into the family room
- 3 bedrooms, 2 baths, 2-car garage
- Slab foundation

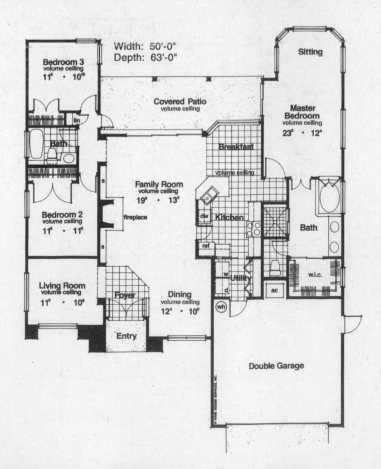

Width: 50'-0"
Depth: 63'-0"

Bedroom 3
volume ceiling
11⁰ · 10¹⁰

Sitting

Covered Patio
volume ceiling

Master Bedroom
volume ceiling
23⁰ · 12⁴

Bath

Breakfast
volume ceiling

lin

Family Room
volume ceiling
19⁰ · 13⁰

Kitchen

dw

Bath

Bedroom 2
volume ceiling
11⁴ · 11⁰

fireplace

ref

Living Room
volume ceiling
11⁰ · 10⁸

Foyer

Dining
volume ceiling
12⁴ · 10⁰

Utility

w.l.c.

w
d

ac

wh

Entry

Double Garage

Graceful Southern Hospitality

1,771 total square feet of living area

Price Code B

**Second Floor
600 sq. ft.**

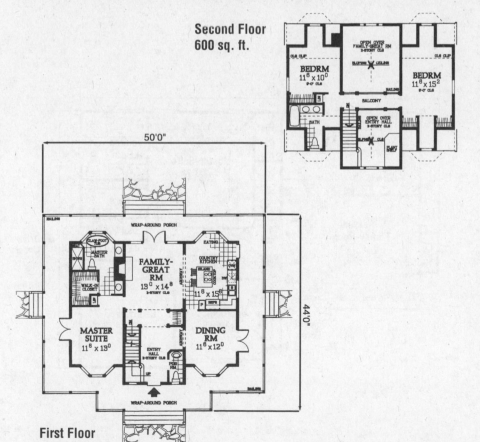

**First Floor
1,171 sq. ft.**

Special features

- Efficient country kitchen shares space with a bayed eating area

- Two-story family/great room is warmed by a fireplace in winter and open to outdoor country comfort in the summer with double French doors

- First floor master suite offers a bay window and access to the porch through French doors

- 3 bedrooms, 2 1/2 baths, optional 2-car detached garage

- Basement foundation

TO ORDER BLUEPRINTS USE THE FORM ON PAGE 15 OR CALL TOLL-FREE 1-877-671-6036
View thousands more home plans online at www.familyhandyman.com/homeplans

271

Plan #706-FB-327

Loaded With Extras

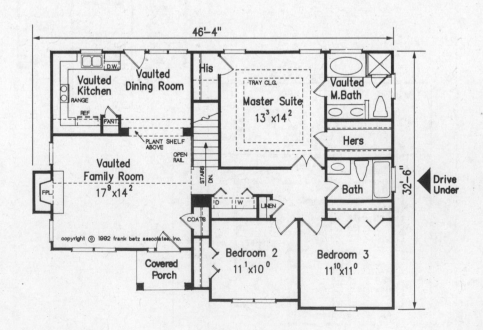

1,281 total square feet of living area

Price Code A

Special features

- Spacious master suite with tray ceiling, double closets and private bath

- Vaulted family room has lots of sunlight and fireplace

- Plant shelf above kitchen and dining room is a nice decorative touch

- 3 bedrooms, 2 baths, 2-car drive under garage

- Walk-out basement foundation

copyright © 1992 frank betz associates. inc.

272

TO ORDER BLUEPRINTS USE THE FORM ON PAGE 15 OR CALL TOLL-FREE 1-877-671-6036
View thousands more home plans online at www.familyhandyman.com/homeplans

The Family Handyman

Double Dormers Add Curb Appeal

1,819 total square feet of living area   **Price Code C**

Second Floor
577 sq. ft.

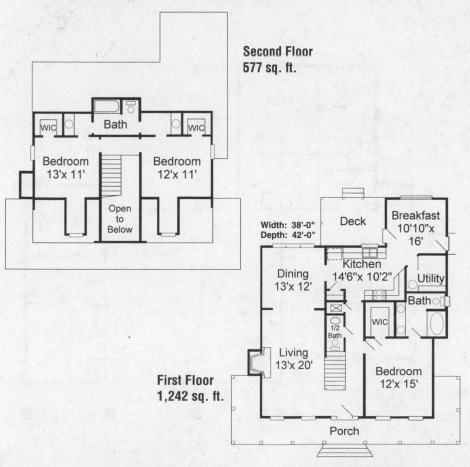

Width: 38'-0"
Depth: 42'-0"

First Floor
1,242 sq. ft.

Special features

- Unique bath layout on the second floor allows for both bedrooms to have their own private sink area while connecting to main bath
- Window wall in dining area floods area with sunlight
- Walk-in closets in every bedroom
- 3 bedrooms, 2 1/2 baths
- Crawl space or slab foundation, please specify when ordering

TO ORDER BLUEPRINTS USE THE FORM ON PAGE 15 OR CALL TOLL-FREE 1-877-671-6036
View thousands more home plans online at www.familyhandyman.com/homeplans

273

Transom Windows Create Impressive Front Entry

1,800 total square feet of living area

Price Code D

Special features

- Energy efficient home with 2" x 6" exterior walls

- Covered front and rear porches add outdoor living area

- 12' ceilings in kitchen, eating area, dining and living rooms

- Private master suite features expansive bath

- Side entry garage with two storage areas

- Pillared styling with brick and stucco exterior finish

- 3 bedrooms, 2 baths, 2-car side entry garage

- Crawl space foundation, drawings also include slab foundation

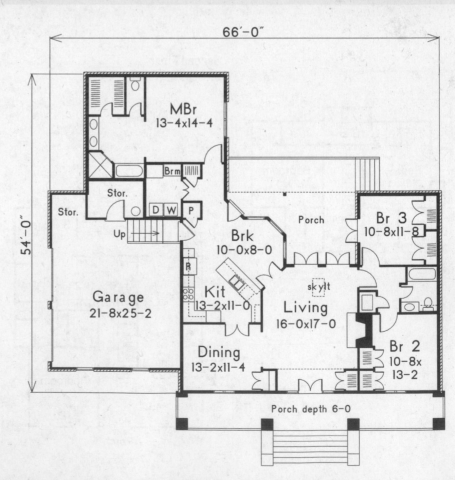

Perfect Ranch With All The Amenities

1,429 total square feet of living area

Price Code A

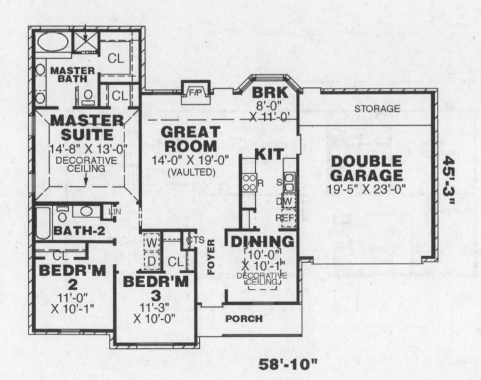

Special features

- Master bedroom features a spacious private bath and double walk-in closets
- Formal dining room has convenient access to kitchen perfect when entertaining
- Additional storage can be found in the garage
- 3 bedrooms, 2 baths, 2-car garage
- Slab foundation

Plan #706-1101

Charming Country Facade

1,643 total square feet of living area   Price Code B

Special features

- Attractive front entry porch gives this ranch a country accent
- Spacious family room is the focal point of this design
- Kitchen and utility room are conveniently located near gathering areas
- Formal living room in the front of the home provides area for quiet and privacy
- Master suite has view to the rear of the home and a generous walk-in closet
- 3 bedrooms, 2 baths, 2-car garage
- Basement foundation, drawings also include crawl space and slab foundations

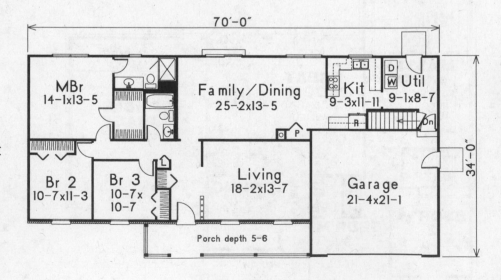

70'-0"

34'-0"

MBr
14-1x13-5

Family/Dining
25-2x13-5

Kit
9-3x11-11

Util
9-1x8-7

Br 2
10-7x11-3

Br 3
10-7x
10-7

Living
18-2x13-7

Garage
21-4x21-1

Porch depth 5-6

TO ORDER BLUEPRINTS USE THE FORM ON PAGE 15 OR CALL TOLL-FREE 1-877-671-6036
View thousands more home plans online at www.familyhandyman.com/homeplans

Comfortable Family Living In This Ranch

1,994 total square feet of living area

Price Code D

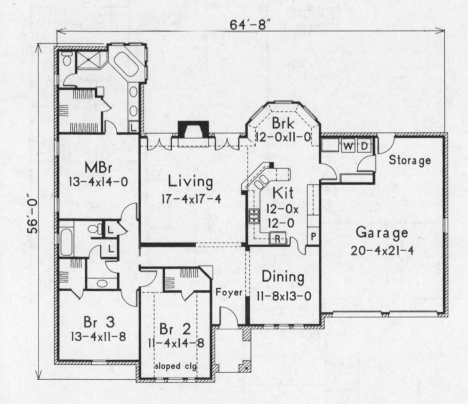

Special features

- Convenient entrance from the garage into the main living area through the utility room

- Standard 9' ceilings, bedroom #2 features a 12' vaulted ceiling and a 10' ceiling in the dining room

- Master bedroom offers a full bath with oversized tub, separate shower and walk-in closet

- Entry leads to formal dining room and attractive living room with double French doors and fireplace

- 3 bedrooms, 2 baths, 2-car garage

- Slab foundation

TO ORDER BLUEPRINTS USE THE FORM ON PAGE 15 OR CALL TOLL-FREE 1-877-671-6036
View thousands more home plans online at www.familyhandyman.com/homeplans

277

Lots Of Charm Throughout

1,902 total square feet of living area

Price Code D

Special features

- A two-story great room is stunning with a fireplace and many windows

- Breakfast nook and kitchen combine creating a warm and inviting place to dine

- Second floor hall overlooks to great room below

- 672 square feet on the second floor includes bonus room above the garage

- 3 bedrooms, 2 1/2 baths, 2-car garage

- Crawl space foundation

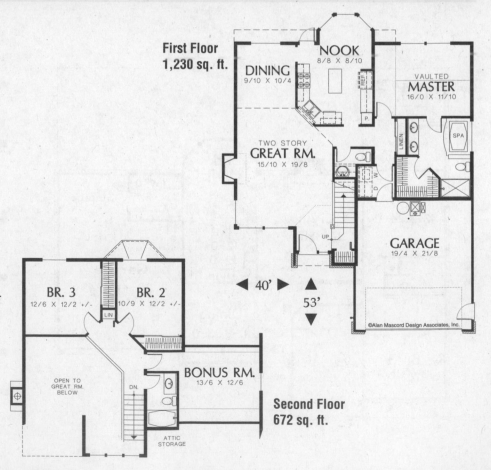

First Floor 1,230 sq. ft.

NOOK 8/8 X 8/10

DINING 9/10 X 10/4

VAULTED MASTER 16/0 X 11/10

TWO STORY GREAT RM. 15/10 X 19/8

SPA

LINEN

GARAGE 19/4 X 21/8

◄ **40'** ►

▲ **53'** ▼

©Alan Mascord Design Associates, Inc.

BR. 3 12/6 X 12/2 +/-

BR. 2 10/9 X 12/2 +/-

LIN

OPEN TO GREAT RM. BELOW

DN.

BONUS RM. 13/6 X 12/6

ATTIC STORAGE

Second Floor 672 sq. ft.

278

TO ORDER BLUEPRINTS USE THE FORM ON PAGE 15 OR CALL TOLL-FREE 1-877-671-6036
View thousands more home plans online at www.familyhandyman.com/homeplans

Country Farmhouse Appeal

1,907 total square feet of living area

Price Code C

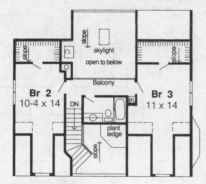

Second Floor
638 sq. ft.

- Br 2
- 10-4 x 14
- Br 3
- 11 x 14
- Balcony
- skylight
- open to below
- slope
- DN
- plant ledge

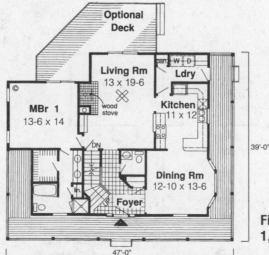

First Floor
1,269 sq. ft.

- Optional Deck
- Living Rm 13 x 19-6
- Ldry
- Kitchen 11 x 12
- MBr 1 13-6 x 14
- wood stove
- Dining Rm 12-10 x 13-6
- Foyer
- DN
- 39'-0"
- 47'-0"

Special features

- Two-story living room is a surprise with skylight and balcony above
- Master bedroom positioned on first floor for convenience
- All bedrooms have walk-in closets
- 3 bedrooms, 2 1/2 baths
- Basement, crawl space or slab foundation, please specify when ordering

TO ORDER BLUEPRINTS USE THE FORM ON PAGE 15 OR CALL TOLL-FREE 1-877-671-6036
View thousands more home plans online at www.familyhandyman.com/homeplans

279

Dramatic Layout Created By Victorian Turret

2,050 total square feet of living area

Price Code C

Special features

- Large kitchen and dining area have access to garage and porch

- Master bedroom suite features unique turret design, private bath and large walk-in closet

- Laundry facilities conveniently located near bedrooms

- 3 bedrooms, 2 1/2 baths, 2-car side entry garage

- Basement foundation, drawings also include crawl space and slab foundations

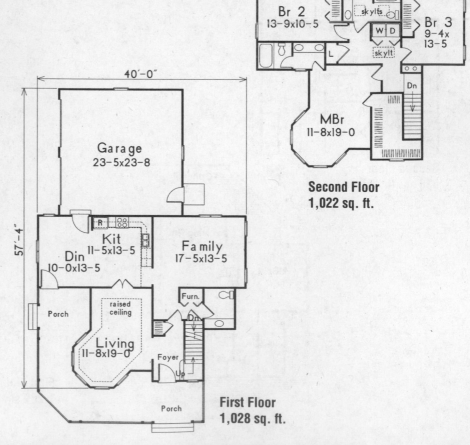

Br 2
13-9x10-5

Br 3
9-4x
13-5

MBr
11-8x19-0

Second Floor
1,022 sq. ft.

40'-0"

57'-4"

Garage
23-5x23-8

Kit
11-5x13-5

Din
10-0x13-5

Family
17-5x13-5

Porch

raised ceiling

Furn.

Living
11-8x19-0

Foyer

Up

Dn

Porch

First Floor
1,028 sq. ft.

Open Breakfast/Family Room Combination

2,135 total square feet of living area

Price Code D

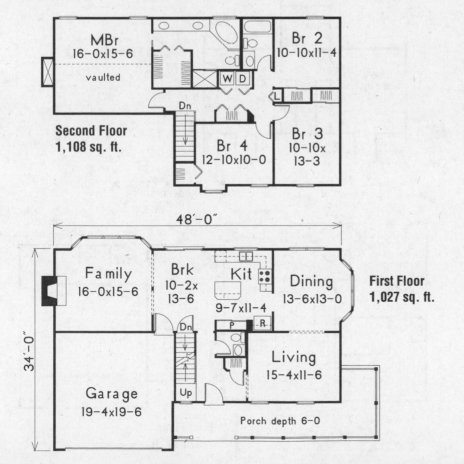

MBr
16-0x15-6
vaulted

Br 2
10-10x11-4

W D

Second Floor
1,108 sq. ft.

Dn

Br 4
12-10x10-0

Br 3
10-10x
13-3

48'-0"

34'-0"

Family
16-0x15-6

Brk
10-2x
13-6

Kit
9-7x11-4

Dining
13-6x13-0

First Floor
1,027 sq. ft.

Dn

P   R

Living
15-4x11-6

Up

Garage
19-4x19-6

Porch depth 6-0

Special features

- Family room features extra space, impressive fireplace and full wall of windows that joins breakfast room creating a spacious entertainment area
- Washer and dryer conveniently located on the second floor
- Kitchen features island counter and pantry
- 4 bedrooms, 2 1/2 baths, 2-car garage
- Basement foundation

TO ORDER BLUEPRINTS USE THE FORM ON PAGE 15 OR CALL TOLL-FREE 1-877-671-6036
View thousands more home plans online at www.familyhandyman.com/homeplans

281

Affordable Country-Style Living

1,945 total square feet of living area

Price Code D

Special features

- Great room has a stepped ceiling and a fireplace

- Bayed dining area with stepped ceiling and French door leading to a covered porch

- Master bedroom has a tray ceiling, a bay window and a large walk-in closet

- 3 bedrooms, 2 1/2 baths, 2-car side entry garage

- Basement, crawl space or slab foundation, please specify when ordering

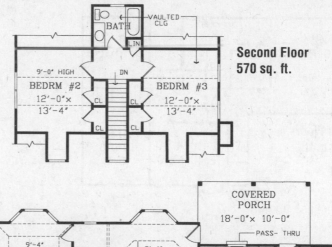

**Second Floor
570 sq. ft.**

9'-0" HIGH

BEDRM #2
12'-0" x
13'-4"

BEDRM #3
12'-0" x
13'-4"

BATH — VAULTED CLG

DN

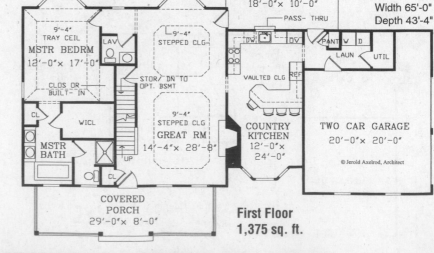

COVERED PORCH
18'-0" x 10'-0"

PASS-THRU

**Width 65'-0"
Depth 43'-4"**

9'-4"
TRAY CEIL

MSTR BEDRM
12'-0" x 17'-0"

LAV

CLOS OR
BUILT-IN

CL

WICL

MSTR BATH

CL

9'-4"
STEPPED CLG

STOR/ DN TO
OPT. BSMT

9'-4"
STEPPED CLG

GREAT RM
14'-4" x 28'-8"

UP

VAULTED CLG

COUNTRY KITCHEN
12'-0" x
24'-0"

PANT W D

LAUN UTIL

REF

TWO CAR GARAGE
20'-0" x 20'-0"

© Jerold Axelrod, Architect

COVERED PORCH
29'-0" x 8'-0"

**First Floor
1,375 sq. ft.**

Covered Porch Adds Appeal

1,480 total square feet of living area

Price Code A

Special features

- Energy efficient home with 2" x 6" exterior walls
- Cathedral ceilings in family and dining rooms
- Master bedroom has walk-in closet and access to bath
- 2 bedrooms, 2 baths
- Basement foundation

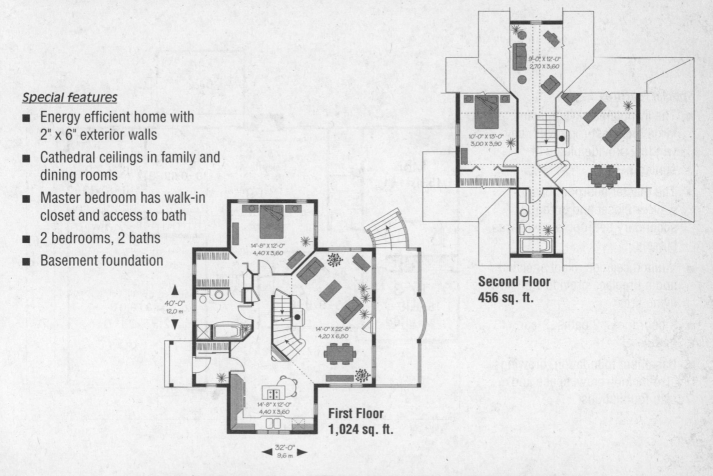

Second Floor
456 sq. ft.

9'-0" X 12'-0"
2,70 X 3,60

10'-0" X 13'-0"
3,00 X 3,90

14'-8" X 12'-0"
4,40 X 3,60

40'-0"
12,0 m

14'-0" X 22'-8"
4,20 X 6,80

14'-8" X 12'-0"
4,40 X 3,60

First Floor
1,024 sq. ft.

32'-0"
9,6 m

TO ORDER BLUEPRINTS USE THE FORM ON PAGE 15 OR CALL TOLL-FREE 1-877-671-6036
View thousands more home plans online at www.familyhandyman.com/homeplans

283

Vaulted Ceilings And Light Add Dimension

1,676 total square feet of living area

Price Code B

Special features

- The living area skylights and large breakfast room with bay window provide plenty of sunlight

- The master bedroom has a walk-in closet and both the secondary bedrooms have large closets

- Vaulted ceilings, plant shelving and a fireplace provide a quality living area

- 3 bedrooms, 2 baths, 2-car garage

- Basement foundation, drawings also include crawl space and slab foundations

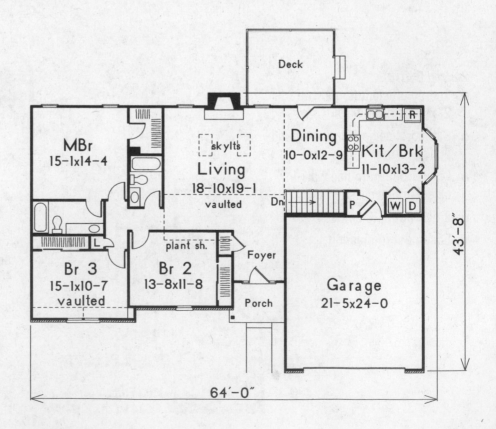

TO ORDER BLUEPRINTS USE THE FORM ON PAGE 15 OR CALL TOLL-FREE 1-877-671-6036
View thousands more home plans online at www.familyhandyman.com/homeplans

Handsome, Compact Ranch

1,296 total square feet of living area

Price Code B

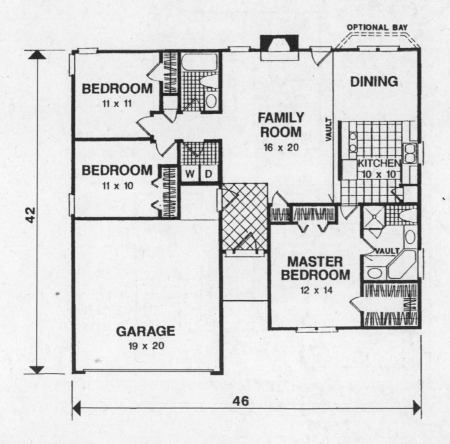

Special features

- Two secondary bedrooms share a bath and have convenient access to the laundry room
- Family room has a large fireplace flanked by sunny windows
- Master bedroom includes privacy as well as an amenity-full bath
- 3 bedrooms, 2 baths, 2-car garage
- Basement, crawl space or slab foundation, please specify when ordering

TO ORDER BLUEPRINTS USE THE FORM ON PAGE 15 OR CALL TOLL-FREE 1-877-671-6036
View thousands more home plans online at www.familyhandyman.com/homeplans

285

Large Utility Room

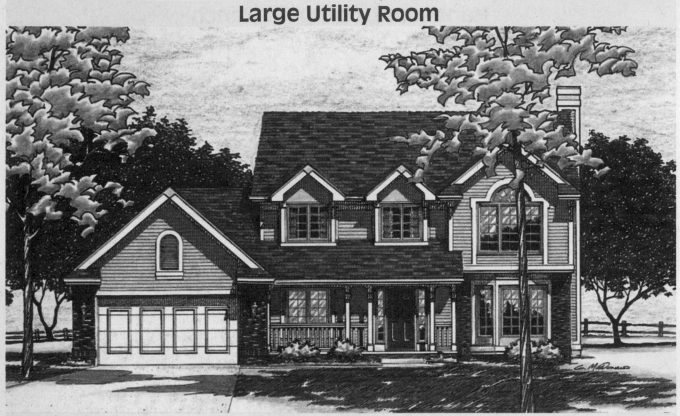

1,998 total square feet of living area

Price Code C

Special features

- Lovely designed family room offers double-door entrance into living area
- Roomy kitchen with breakfast area is a natural gathering place
- 10' ceiling in master bedroom
- 3 bedrooms, 2 1/2 baths, 2-car garage
- Basement foundation

Second Floor
905 sq. ft.

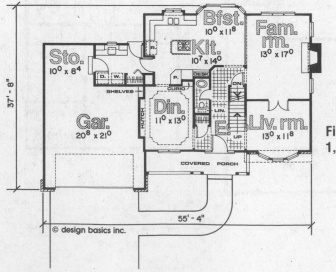

First Floor
1,093 sq. ft.

© design basics inc.

TO ORDER BLUEPRINTS USE THE FORM ON PAGE 15 OR CALL TOLL-FREE 1-877-671-6036
View thousands more home plans online at www.familyhandyman.com/homeplans

Wonderful Two-Story, Charming Yet Practical

2,280 total square feet of living area

Price Code D

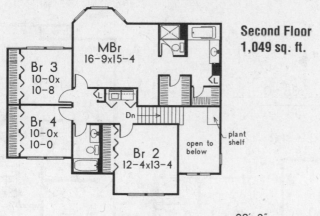

**Second Floor
1,049 sq. ft.**

Br 3
10-0x
10-8

Br 4
10-0x
10-0

MBr
16-9x15-4

L

Dn

L

Br 2
12-4x13-4

open to
below

plant
shelf

Special features

- Laundry area conveniently located on second floor
- Compact yet efficient kitchen
- Unique shaped dining room overlooks front porch
- Cozy living room enhanced with sloped ceiling and fireplace
- 4 bedrooms, 2 1/2 baths, 2-car side entry garage
- Basement foundation

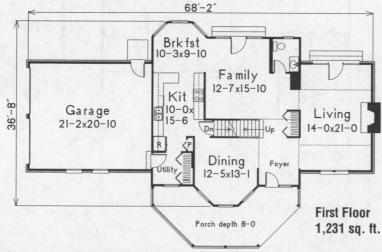

68'-2"

36'-8"

Garage
21-2x20-10

Brk fst
10-3x9-10

Family
12-7x15-10

Kit
10-0x
15-6

Living
14-0x21-0

Dn

Up

R

P

Utility

Dining
12-5x13-1

Foyer

**First Floor
1,231 sq. ft.**

Porch depth 8-0

TO ORDER BLUEPRINTS USE THE FORM ON PAGE 15 OR CALL TOLL-FREE 1-877-671-6036
View thousands more home plans online at www.familyhandyman.com/homeplans

287

Dining With A View

1,524 total square feet of living area

Price Code B

Special features

- Delightful balcony overlooks two-story entry illuminated by oval window

- Roomy first floor master suite offers quiet privacy

- All bedrooms feature one or more walk-in closets

- 3 bedrooms, 2 1/2 baths, 2-car garage

- Basement foundation

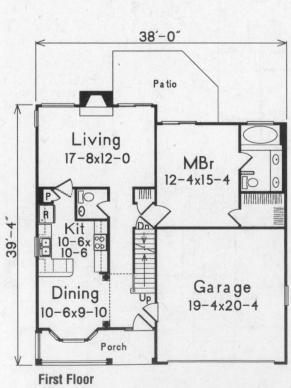

First Floor
951 sq. ft.

38'-0"

39'-4"

Patio

Living
17-8x12-0

MBr
12-4x15-4

Kit
10-6x10-6

Dn

Up

Dining
10-6x9-10

Garage
19-4x20-4

Porch

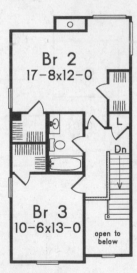

Br 2
17-8x12-0

L

Dn

Br 3
10-6x13-0

open to below

Second Floor
573 sq. ft.

288

TO ORDER BLUEPRINTS USE THE FORM ON PAGE 15 OR CALL TOLL-FREE 1-877-671-6036
View thousands more home plans online at www.familyhandyman.com/homeplans

Country Charm In A Double Feature

Multi-Family

2,986 total square feet of living area

Price Code G

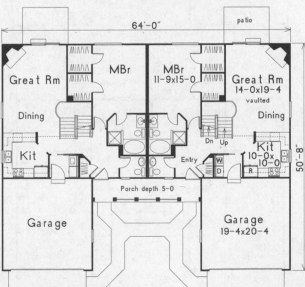

Second Floor
533 sq. ft.
per unit

First Floor
960 sq. ft.
per unit

Special features

- Vaulted great room, kitchen and two balconies define architectural drama

- First floor master suite boasts a lavish bath and double walk-in closets

- Impressive second floor features two large bedrooms, spacious closets, hall bath and balcony overlook

- Each unit has 3 bedrooms, 2 1/2 baths, 2-car garage

- Basement foundation

- Duplex has 1,493 square feet of living space per unit

TO ORDER BLUEPRINTS USE THE FORM ON PAGE 15 OR CALL TOLL-FREE 1-877-671-6036
View thousands more home plans online at www.familyhandyman.com/homeplans

289

Fourplex Is Spacious With Large Living Room

3,648 total square feet of living area

Price Code H

Special features

- Large kitchen adjacent to living room
- Handy linen closet in hallway
- Spacious living area with easy access to patio or balcony
- Centrally located laundry closet for stackable washer and dryer
- Each unit has 2 bedrooms, 1 bath
- Crawl space/slab foundation

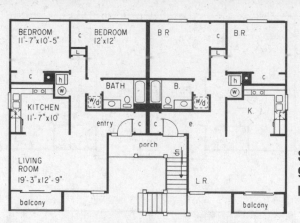

Second Floor
912 sq. ft.
per unit

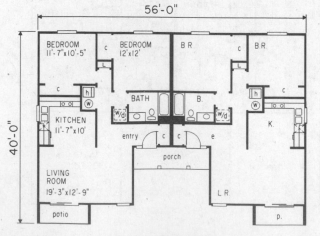

First Floor
912 sq. ft.
per unit

Cottage Appearance Has Cozy Feel

Multi-Family

1,713 total square feet of living area

Price Code D

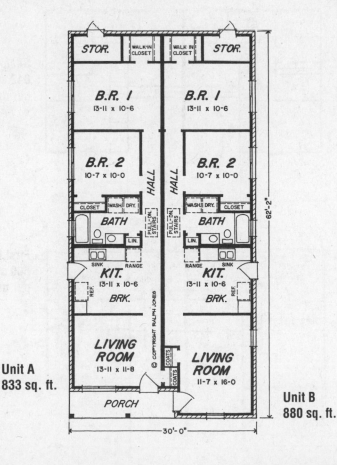

STOR. | WALK-IN CLOSET | WALK-IN CLOSET | STOR.

B.R. 1
13-11 x 10-6

B.R. 1
13-11 x 10-6

B.R. 2
10-7 x 10-0

B.R. 2
10-7 x 10-0

HALL HALL

CLOSET | WASH. DRY. | WASH. DRY. | CLOSET

BATH **BATH**

PULL-DN. STAIRS PULL-DN. STAIRS

LIN. LIN.

SINK RANGE RANGE SINK

KIT.
13-11 x 10-6

KIT.
13-11 x 10-6

REF. REF.

BRK. **BRK.**

© COPYRIGHT RALPH JONES

LIVING ROOM
13-11 x 11-8

LIVING ROOM
11-7 x 16-0

COATS
COATS

62'-2"

Unit A
833 sq. ft.

PORCH

Unit B
880 sq. ft.

30'-0"

Special features

- Kitchen has access outdoors
- Handy washer and dryer closet located in the bath
- Bedrooms at the back of the home for privacy and quiet
- Each unit has 2 bedrooms, 1 bath
- Slab foundation

Duplex Has Inviting Facade

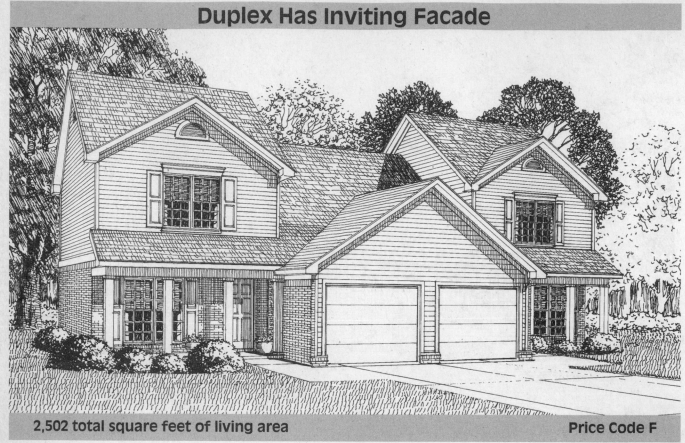

2,502 total square feet of living area

Price Code F

Special features

- Decorative columns separate the dining area from the great room

- All bedrooms located on second floor for privacy

- Each unit has 3 bedrooms, 2 1/2 baths, 1-car garage

- Crawl space or slab foundation, please specify when ordering

- Duplex has 1,251 square feet of living space per unit

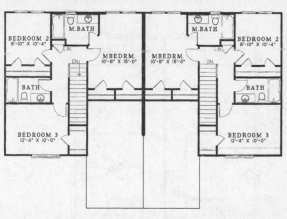

Second Floor 642 sq. ft. per unit

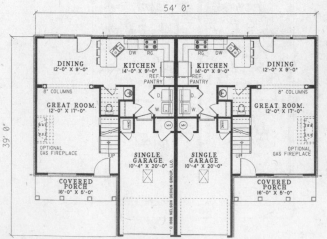

First Floor 609 sq. ft. per unit

Vaulted Ceilings Add Spaciousness To Living Areas

Multi-Family

2,318 total square feet of living area

Price Code F

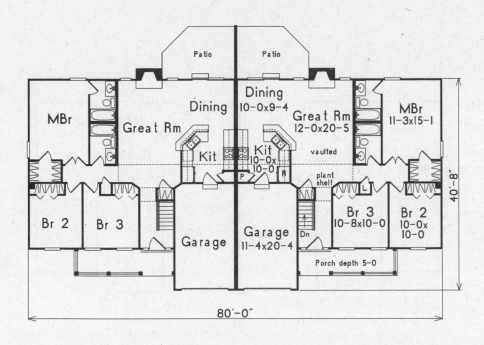

Patio Patio

Dining Dining 10-0x9-4

MBr Great Rm Great Rm 12-0x20-5 MBr 11-3x15-1

Kit Kit 10-0x 10-0 vaulted

P plant shelf

Br 2 Br 3 Br 3 10-8x10-0 Br 2 10-0x 10-0

Garage Garage 11-4x20-4 Dn

Porch depth 5-0

40'-8"

80'-0"

Special features

- Great room area complemented with fireplace and patio access
- Breakfast bar has corner sink which overlooks great room
- Plant shelf graces vaulted entry
- Master suite provides walk-in closet and private bath
- Each unit has 3 bedrooms, 2 baths, 1-car garage
- Basement foundation
- Duplex has 1,159 square feet of living space per unit

Duplex With Cozy Front Porch

1,904 total square feet of living area

Price Code E

Special features

- Convenient laundry area and dining room adjacent to kitchen

- Bedrooms feature ample closet space

- Garage has plenty of space for work/storage area

- Handy coat closets located near garage and living room

- Dining accesses outdoors

- Each unit has 2 bedrooms, 1 bath, 1-car garage

- Partial basement/crawl space foundation

- Duplex has 952 square feet of living space per unit

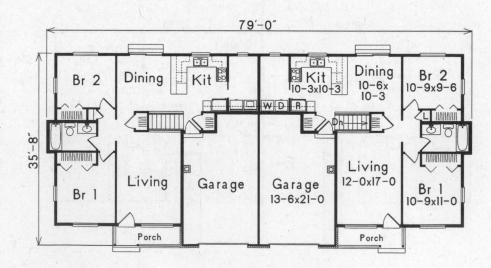

Gables And Arches Adds Drama

Multi-Family

5,810 total square feet of living area

Price Code H

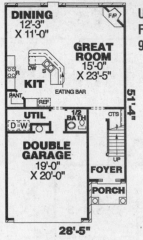

Unit D First Floor 964 sq. ft.

DINING 12'-3" X 11'-0"

GREAT ROOM 15'-0" X 23'-5"

KIT

EATING BAR

PANT

UTIL

1/2 BATH

DOUBLE GARAGE 19'-0" X 20'-0"

FOYER

PORCH

UP

CTS

51'-4"

28'-5"

Unit D Second Floor 1,127 sq. ft.

MASTER SUITE 15'-2" X 15'-6"

BEDR'M 12'-2" X 11'-5"

LIN

CL

BATH

BALCONY

MASTER BATH

BEDR'M 12'-6" X 13'-0"

FOYER BELOW

DN

LIN

CL

Special features

- Unit C has 2 bedrooms, 2 baths, 2-car garage

- Unit D has 3 bedrooms, 2 1/2 baths, 2-car garage

- Unit E has 3 bedrooms, 2 baths, 2-car garage

- All master baths have step up tubs, separate showers, double vanities and walk-in closets

- Slab foundation

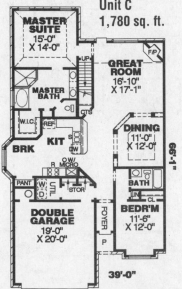

Unit C 1,780 sq. ft.

MASTER SUITE 15'-0" X 14'-0"

MASTER BATH

GREAT ROOM 16'-10" X 17'-1"

UP

CTS

W.I.C.

REF

KIT

BRK

DINING 11'-0" X 12'-0"

BATH

O W/ MICRO

PANT

W/D

STOR

UTIL

DOUBLE GARAGE 19'-0" X 20'-0"

FOYER

BEDR'M 11'-6" X 12'-0"

LIN

CL

66'-1"

39'-0"

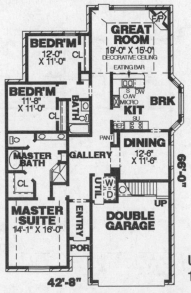

BEDR'M 12'-0" X 11'-0"

GREAT ROOM 19'-0" X 15'-0" DECORATIVE CEILING

EATING BAR

CL

BEDR'M 11'-8" X 11'-0"

BATH

KIT

BRK

CL

MASTER BATH

GALLERY

PANT

DINING 12'-6" X 11'-6"

CL

UTIL

W/D

MASTER SUITE 14'-1" X 16'-0"

ENTRY

POR

DOUBLE GARAGE

UP

66'-0"

42'-8"

Unit E 1,939 sq. ft.

Plan #706-0464

Stylish Living, Open Design

1,992 total square feet of living area

Price Code E

Special features

- Graciously designed ranch duplex with alluring openness

- Vaulted kitchen with accent on spaciousness features huge pantry, plenty of cabinets and convenient laundry room

- Master bedroom includes its own cozy bath and oversized walk-in closet

- Each unit has 2 bedrooms, 2 baths, 1-car garage

- Basement foundation

- Duplex has 996 square feet of living space per unit

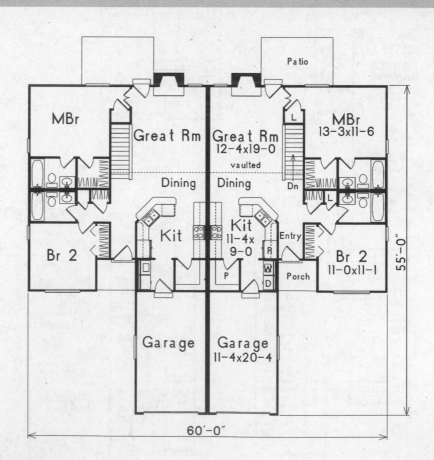

Multi-Family With Residential Look

Multi-Family

3,728 total square feet of living area

Price Code H

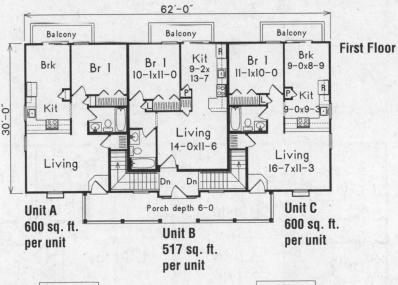

First Floor

62'-0"
30'-0"

Balcony   Balcony   Balcony

Brk   Br 1   Br 1 10-1x11-0   Kit 9-2x 13-7   Br 1 11-1x10-0   Brk 9-0x8-9

Kit   Living 14-0x11-6   Kit 9-0x9-3

Living   Living 16-7x11-3

Dn   Dn

Porch depth 6-0

Unit A
600 sq. ft.
per unit

Unit B
517 sq. ft.
per unit

Unit C
600 sq. ft.
per unit

Lower Level

Patio   Patio

Brk   Br 1   storage   storage   Br 1 11-1x10-0   Brk 9-0x8-9

Kit   storage   storage   Kit 9-0x9-3

storage

Living   storage   Laundry   Up   Living 16-0x10-8

utility

Unit D
592 sq. ft.
per unit

Unit E
592 sq. ft.
per unit

Special features

- This fiveplex home features an extra large porch and roof dormers that make it fit graciously into any residential neighborhood
- Three first floor units have access to their own balcony while the two lower level units each enjoy private patios
- Each unit has 1 bedroom, 1 bath
- Walk-out basement foundation with centrally located storage and laundry room
- Fiveplex has 1,868 square feet of living area on the first floor and 1,860 square feet of living area on the lower level

Compact Duplex With Large Living Area

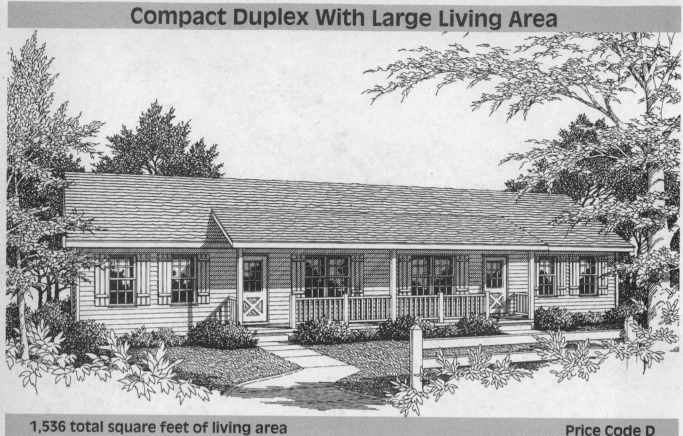

1,536 total square feet of living area

Price Code D

Special features

- Living room joins the kitchen/dining area for an open atmosphere
- L-shaped kitchen with outdoor access and convenient laundry area
- Linen and coat closet
- Welcoming front porch
- Each unit has 2 bedrooms, 1 bath
- Crawl space foundation, drawings also include slab foundation
- Duplex has 768 total square feet of living space per unit

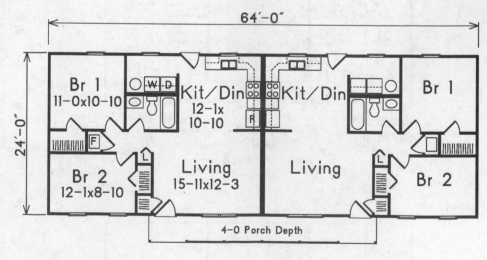

64'-0"

24'-0"

Br 1
11-0x10-10

W D

Kit/Din
12-1x
10-10

Kit/Din

Br 1

F

Br 2
12-1x8-10

Living
15-11x12-3

Living

Br 2

4-0 Porch Depth

Charming Victorian-Style Duplex

Multi-Family

2,172 total square feet of living area

Price Code E

**Second Floor
543 sq. ft.
per unit**

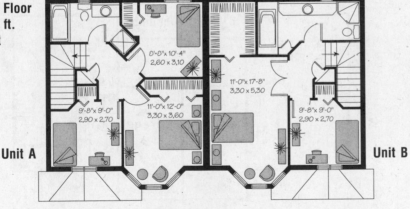

8'-0"x 10'-4"
2,60 x 3,10

11'-0" 17'-8"
3,30 x 5,30

9'-8"x 9'-0"
2,90 x 2,70

11'-0" 12'-0"
3,30 x 3,60

9'-8"x 9'-0"
2,90 x 2,70

Unit A

Unit B

**First Floor
543 sq. ft.
per unit**

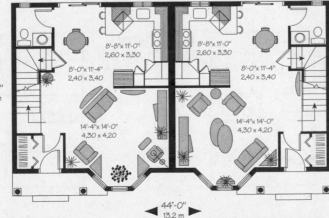

26'-6"
7,95 m

8'-8"x 11'-0"
2,60 x 3,30

8'-0"x 11'-4"
2,40 x 3,40

14'-4"x 14'-0"
4,30 x 4,20

8'-8"x 11'-0"
2,60 x 3,30

8'-0"x 11'-4"
2,40 x 3,40

14'-4"x 14'-0"
4,30 x 4,20

Unit A

Unit B

44'-0"
13,2 m

Special features

- Bay windows on both floors brighten living spaces
- Open living on first floor is a terrific layout for entertaining
- Unit A has 3 bedrooms, 1 1/2 baths
- Unit B has 2 bedrooms, 1 1/2 baths
- Basement foundation
- Duplex has 1,086 square feet of living space per unit

Compact Two-Story Duplex

2,408 total square feet of living area

Price Code F

Special features

- The large great room offers a fireplace and dining area with view of patio
- Each unit enjoys its own private garage, front porch and rear patio
- The second floor bedrooms are large in size and feature spacious walk-in closets
- Each unit has 2 bedrooms, 1 1/2 baths, 1-car garage
- Basement foundation
- Duplex has 1,204 square feet of living space per unit

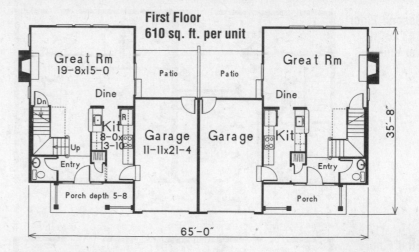

First Floor
610 sq. ft. per unit

Great Rm
19-8x15-0

Patio   Patio

Dine

Dn

Kit
8-0x
3-10

Garage
11-11x21-4

Garage

Great Rm

Dine

Kit

Up

Entry

Entry

Porch depth 5-8

Porch

35-8"

65'-0"

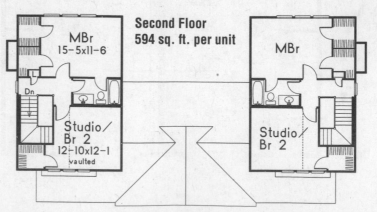

Second Floor
594 sq. ft. per unit

MBr
15-5x11-6

MBr

Dn

Studio/
Br 2
12-10x12-1
vaulted

Studio/
Br 2

300

TO ORDER BLUEPRINTS USE THE FORM ON PAGE 15 OR CALL TOLL-FREE 1-877-671-6036
View thousands more home plans online at www.familyhandyman.com/homeplans

Varied Front Facades Adds Interest

6,410 total square feet of living area

Price Code H

Multi-Family

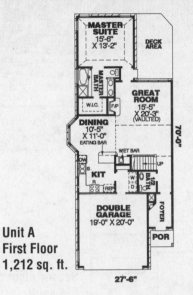

Unit A
First Floor
1,212 sq. ft.

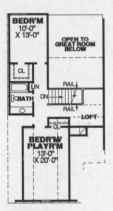

Unit A
Second Floor
750 sq. ft.

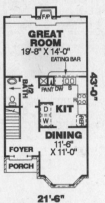

Unit B
First Floor
787 sq. ft.

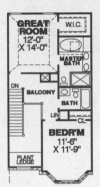

Unit B
Second Floor
684 sq. ft.

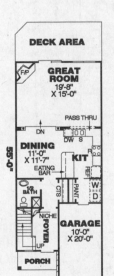

Unit C
First Floor
806 sq. ft.

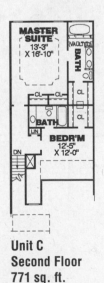

Unit C
Second Floor
771 sq. ft.

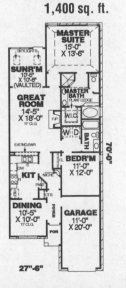

Unit D
1,400 sq. ft.

Special features

- All master bedrooms have private bath and walk-in closet
- Unit A has 3 bedrooms, 2 1/2 baths, 2-car garage
- Unit B has 2 bedrooms, 2 1/2 baths
- Unit C has 2 bedrooms, 2 1/2 baths, 1-car garage
- Unit D has 2 bedrooms, 2 baths, 1-car garage
- Slab foundation

Handsome Arched Entry

3,366 total square feet of living area

Price Code H

Special features

- 9' ceilings throughout the first floor

- Impressive kitchen with center island/snack bar has lots of counterspace and cabinetry

- Master suite has private bath and is conveniently located on the first floor

- Bonus room on the second floor has an additional 265 square feet of living area per unit

- Each unit has 3 bedrooms, 2 1/2 baths, 1-car garage

- Crawl space or slab foundation, please specify when ordering

- Duplex has 1,683 square feet of living space per unit

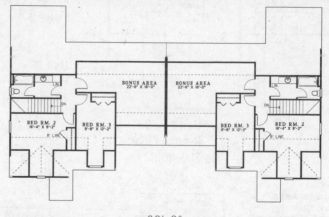

Second Floor 529 sq. ft. per unit

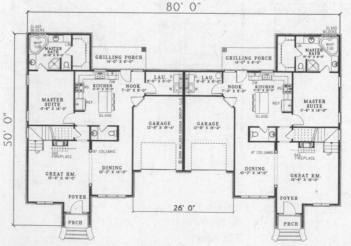

First Floor 1,154 sq. ft per unit

TO ORDER BLUEPRINTS USE THE FORM ON PAGE 15 OR CALL TOLL-FREE 1-877-671-6036

View thousands more home plans online at www.familyhandyman.com/homeplans

Traditional Elegance In A Duplex

Multi-Family

3,258 total square feet of living area

Price Code H

Second Floor
823 sq. ft. per unit

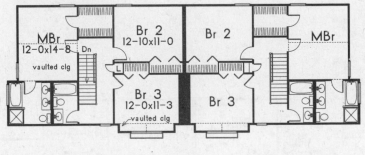

MBr
12-0x14-8
vaulted clg

Br 2
12-10x11-0

Br 2

MBr

Dn

Br 3
12-0x11-3
vaulted clg

Br 3

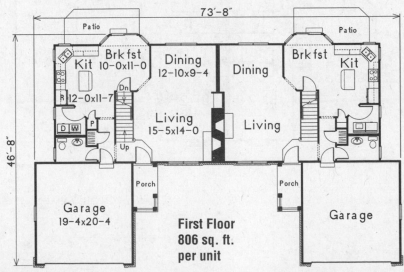

73'-8"

Patio

Patio

Kit
Brk fst
10-0x11-0

Dining
12-10x9-4

Dining

Brk fst

Kit

R 12-0x11-7

Dn

Living
15-5x14-0

Living

Up

D W P

46'-8"

Garage
19-4x20-4

Porch

First Floor
806 sq. ft.
per unit

Porch

Garage

Special features

- Multi-gables, brickwork, windows with shutters and planter boxes create great curb appeal
- Living room has large dining area, a fireplace, entry with coat closet and nearby powder room
- Well-equipped kitchen includes an island snack bar, bayed breakfast room, built-in pantry, corner windows above sink and laundry room
- Second floor has large bedrooms including a vaulted master with luxury bath
- Each unit has 3 bedrooms, 2 1/2 baths, 2-car garage
- Basement foundation
- Duplex has 1,629 square feet of living space per unit

Duplex With Plenty Of Style

1,704 total square feet of living area

Price Code D

Special features

- Smartly designed layout with emphasis on efficiency
- Functional kitchen embraces the sun with its bay window, glass sliding doors and pass-through to living room
- Five generously designed closets offer an abundance of storage
- Each unit has 2 bedrooms, 1 bath, 1-car garage
- Basement foundation
- Duplex has 852 square feet of living space per unit

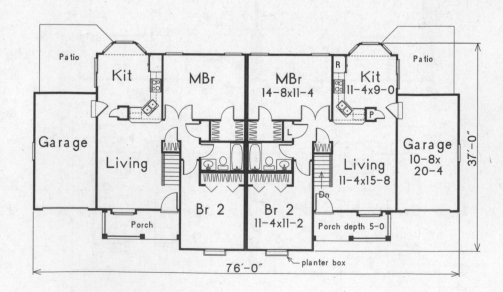

Neat Floor Plan Creates Open Living

Multi-Family

1,796 total square feet of living area

Price Code D

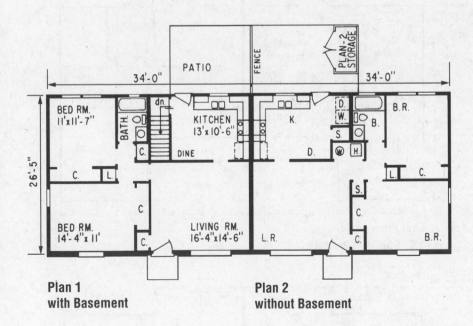

PATIO

FENCE

PLAN-2 STORAGE

34'-0"

34'-0"

BED RM. 11'x11'-7"

BATH.

dn.

KITCHEN 13'x10'-6"

K.

B.R.

D. W.

B.

S.

26'-5"

C.

L.

DINE

D.

W H

L.

C.

S.

C.

BED RM. 14'-4"x11'

C.

LIVING RM. 16'-4"x14'-6"

L.R.

C.

B.R.

Plan 1
with Basement

Plan 2
without Basement

Special features

- Large kitchen is perfect for entertaining
- Plenty of storage space in these units
- Each unit has 2 bedrooms, 1 bath
- Basement foundation, drawings also include crawl space/slab foundation
- Duplex has 898 square feet of living space per unit

Atrium Duplex With Room To Grow

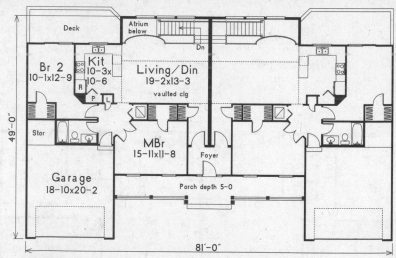

3,666 total square feet of living area

Price Code H

Special features

- Inviting porch and foyer leads to vaulted living room and dining balcony with atrium window wall

- Bedroom #2 doubles as a study with access to deck through sliding glass doors

- Atrium opens to large family room and third bedroom

- Each unit has 3 bedrooms, 2 baths, 2-car garage

- Walk-out basement foundation

- Duplex has 1,833 square feet of living space per unit

Deck
Atrium below
Dn
Br 2
10-1x12-9
Kit
10-3x
10-6
Living/Din
19-2x13-3
vaulted clg
R
Stor
P L
MBr
15-11x11-8
Foyer
Garage
18-10x20-2
Porch depth 5-0
49'-0"
81'-0"

First Floor
1,073 sq. ft. per unit

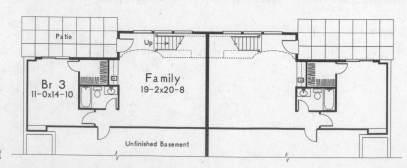

Patio
Up
Br 3
11-0x14-10
Family
19-2x20-8
Unfinished Basement

Lower Level
760 sq. ft. per unit

306

TO ORDER BLUEPRINTS USE THE FORM ON PAGE 15 OR CALL TOLL-FREE 1-877-671-6036
View thousands more home plans online at www.familyhandyman.com/homeplans

Open Living Areas

Multi-Family

2,622 total square feet of living area

Price Code G

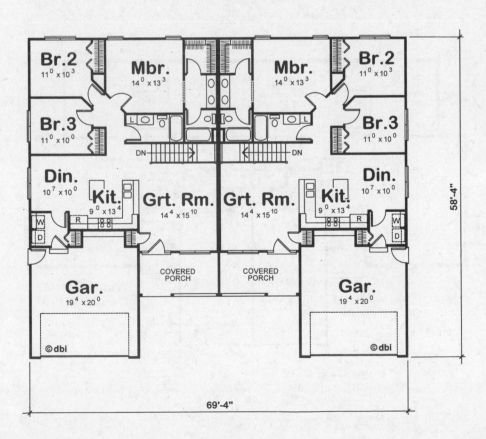

Special features

- Charming covered porch
- Kitchen features snack bar which overlooks great room as well as an island making food preparation easier
- Sunny dining room
- Each unit has 3 bedrooms, 2 baths, 2-car garage
- Basement foundation
- Duplex has 1,311 square feet of living space per unit

Plan #706-DDI-100-107

Perfect Symmetry With This Duplex

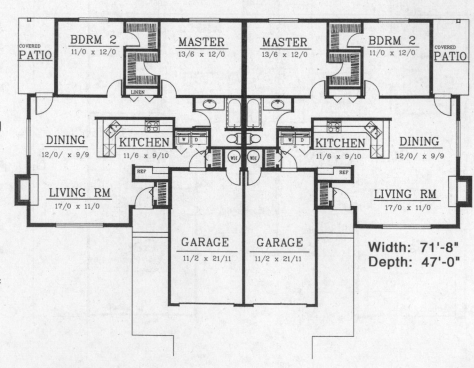

2,068 total square feet of living area

Price Code E

Special features

- Open living area has cozy fireplace and views into dining area and kitchen

- Covered patio directly off dining area

- Both bedrooms have large walk-in closets for additional storage

- Each unit has 2 bedrooms, 1 bath, 1-car garage

- Slab foundation

- Duplex has 1,034 square feet of living space per unit

Width: 71'-8"
Depth: 47'-0"

Sprawling Ranch Design

Multi-Family

© Michael E. Nelson
NELSON DESIGN GROUP, LLC

3,419 total square feet of living area

Price Code H

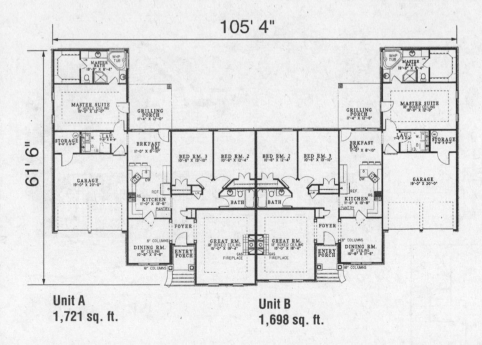

105' 4"

61' 6"

Unit A
1,721 sq. ft.

Unit B
1,698 sq. ft.

Special features

- 9' ceilings throughout this design

- Master suite has many luxuries including private bath, walk-in closet and grilling porch access

- Great room has convenient gas fireplace and 12' boxed ceiling creating a cozy, warm atmosphere

- Each unit has 3 bedrooms, 2 baths, 2-car garage

- Crawl space or slab foundation, please specify when ordering

2-Car Garage Apartment

Plan #706-15037

Special features

- 628 square feet
- Building height - 26'-6"
- Roof pitch - 8/12, 9/12
- Ceiling heights - First floor 9'-0"
  Second floor 8'-0"
- 16' x 7' overhead door
- 1 bedroom, 1 bath
- Vaulted living room has fireplace
- Complete list of materials

Price Code P13

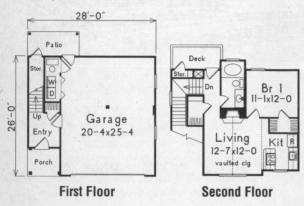

First Floor　　**Second Floor**

3-Car Apartment Garage Has Flair

Plan #706-15040

Special features

- 929 square feet
- Building height - 27'-0"
- Roof pitch - 6.5/12, 10/12
- Ceiling heights - First floor - 9'-0"
  Second floor - 8'-0"
- 16' x 8', 9' x 8' overhead doors
- 2 bedrooms, 1 bath, 3-car side entry garage
- Complete list of materials

Price Code P13

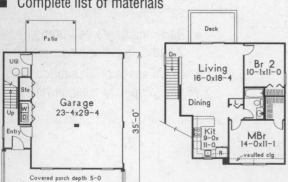

Second Floor

First Floor

TO ORDER BLUEPRINTS USE THE FORM ON PAGE 320 OR CALL TOLL-FREE 1-877-671-6036
View thousands more home plans online at www.familyhandyman.com/homeplans

2-Car Garage Apartment

Plan #706-15034

Special features

- 654 square feet
- Building height - 24'-0"
- Roof pitch - 7/12
- Ceiling height - 8'-0"
- 16' x 7' overhead door
- 1 bedroom, 1 bath
- Living room is open to a pass-through kitchen and sliding glass doors to an outside balcony
- Complete list of materials

Price Code P13

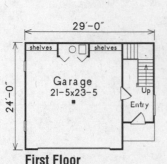

First Floor

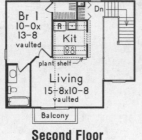

Second Floor

2-Car Garage Apartment

Plan #706-15504

Special features

- 840 square feet
- Building height - 25'-8"
- Roof pitch - 7/12
- Ceiling heights - First floor - 9'-0"
  Second floor - 8'-0"
- 1 bedroom, 1 bath
- Two 9' x 7' overhead doors
- Cozy covered entry
- Complete list of materials

Price Code P11

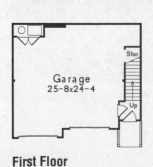

First Floor

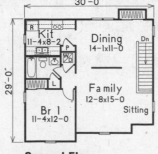

Second Floor

3-Car Garage Apartment   Plan #706-15515

Special features

- 676 square feet
- Building height - 22'-0"
- Roof pitch - 12/12
- Ceiling height - 8'-0"
- 1 bedroom, 1 bath
- Complete list of materials

Price Code P11

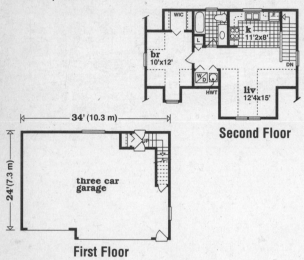

Second Floor

First Floor

3-Car Garage Apartment   Plan #706-15031

Special features

- 1,040 square feet
- Building height - 23'-0"
- Roof pitch - 5/12
- Ceiling height - 8'-0"
- Three 9' x 7' overhead doors
- 2 bedrooms, 1 bath
- Complete list of materials

Price Code P12

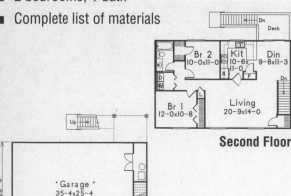

Second Floor

First Floor

TO ORDER BLUEPRINTS USE THE FORM ON PAGE 320 OR CALL TOLL-FREE 1-877-671-6036
View thousands more home plans online at www.familyhandyman.com/homeplans

2-Car Garage Apartment   Plan #706-15510

Special features

- 633 square feet
- Building height - 24'-0"
- Roof pitch - 9/12
- Ceiling height - 8'-0"
- 1 bedroom, 1 bath
- Two 8' x 7' overhead doors
- Storage throughout including built-in shelves
- Complete list of materials

Price Code P13

◄ 28' ►

GARAGE
23/0 X 25/0

UP

First Floor

26'

BR.
12/0 X 10/0

DN

W/D

LIVING
16/6 X 12/4

SHELVES

Second Floor

2-Car Garage Apartment - Gambrel Roof   Plan #706-15026

Special features

- 604 square feet
- Building height - 21'-4"
- Roof pitch - 4/12, 12/4.75
- Ceiling height - 8'-0"
- Two 9' x 7' overhead doors
- Charming dutch colonial style
- Spacious studio provides extra storage space
- Complete list of materials
- Step-by-step instructions

Price Code P10

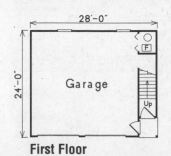

28'-0"

24'-0"

Garage

Up

F

First Floor

Kitchen

Dining

R

Dn

Studio
17-4x14-7

L

Second Floor

TO ORDER BLUEPRINTS USE THE FORM ON PAGE 320 OR CALL TOLL-FREE 1-877-671-6036
View thousands more home plans online at www.familyhandyman.com/homeplans

313

2-Car Garage Apartment - Tudor Style   Plan #706-15015

Special features

- 784 square feet
- Building height - 24'-6"
- Roof pitch - 6/12
- Ceiling height - 8'-0"
- Two 9' x 7' overhead doors
- 1 bedroom, 1 bath
- Outside covered stairs shelter from the elements
- Complete list of materials
- Step-by-step instructions

Price Code P9

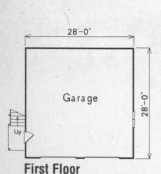

First Floor

Second Floor

2-Car Garage Apartment - Western Style   Plan #706-15020

Special features

- 784 square feet
- Building height - 24'-6"
- Roof pitch - 6/12
- Ceiling height - 8'-0"
- Two 9' x 7' overhead doors
- 1 bedroom, 1 bath
- Open living area spacious and functional
- Complete list of materials
- Step-by-step instructions

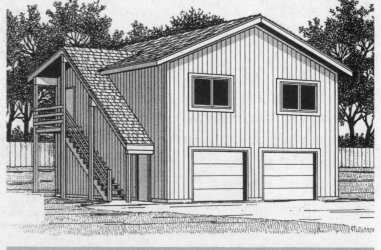

Price Code P9

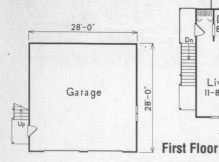

First Floor

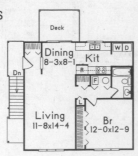

Second Floor

3-Car Garage Apartment

Plan #706-15519

Special features

- 1,032 square feet
- Building height - 24'-0"
- Roof pitch - 5/12, 10/12
- Ceiling height - 8'-0"
- 2 bedrooms, 1 bath
- Complete list of materials

Price Code P12

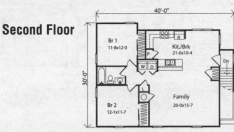

Second Floor

40'-0"

Br 1
11-8x12-0

Kit/Brk
21-0x10-4

Br 2
12-1x11-7

Family
20-0x15-7

30'-0"

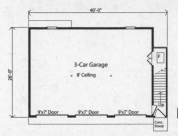

40'-0"

3-Car Garage
8' Ceiling

26'-0"

9'x7' Door   9'x7' Door   9'x7' Door

Up

Conc. Stoop

First Floor

2-Car Garage Apartment - Cape Cod

Plan #706-15028

Special features

- 566 square feet
- Building height - 22'-0"
- Roof pitch - 12/12, 4.5/12
- Ceiling heights - First floor - 8'-0"
                    Second floor - 7'-7"
- Two 9' x 7' overhead doors
- Charming dormers add appeal to this design
- Comfortable open living area
- Complete list of materials
- Step-by-step instructions

Price Code P10

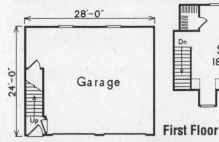

28'-0"

Garage

24'-0"

Up

First Floor

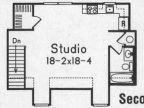

Dn

Studio
18-2x18-4

R

Second Floor

3-Car Garage Apartment With Storage Plan #706-15508

Special features

- 973 square feet
- Building height - 24'-8"
- Roof pitch - 6/12
- Ceiling height - 8'-0"
- 2 bedrooms, 1 bath
- 16' x 7' and 9' x 7' overhead doors
- Convenient breakfast room near the kitchen
- Complete list of materials

Price Code P12

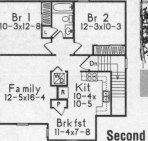

Br 1
10-3x12-8

Br 2
12-3x10-3

Family
12-5x16-4

Kit
10-4x
10-5

Dn

Brk fst
11-4x7-8

Second Floor

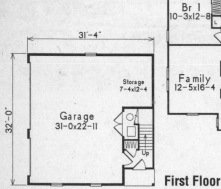

Storage
7-4x12-4

Garage
31-0x22-11

31'-4"

32'-0"

Up

First Floor

2-Car Garage Studio Apartment Plan #706-15027

Special features

- 576 square feet
- Building height - 21'-6"
- Roof pitch - 4/12
- Ceiling height - 8'-0"
- Two 9' x 7' overhead doors
- Contemporary style with outdoor entrance
- Complete list of materials
- Step-by-step instructions

Price Code P9

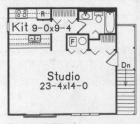

Kit 9-0x9-4

Studio
23-4x14-0

Dn

Second Floor

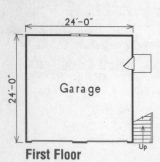

24'-0"

24'-0"

Garage

Up

First Floor

2-Car Garage Apartment

Plan #706-15520

Special features

- 568 square feet
- Building height - 26'-0"
- Roof pitch - 12/12
- Ceiling heights - First floor - 9'-0"
  Second floor - 8'-0"
- 1 bedroom/sleeping area, 1 bath
- Complete list of materials

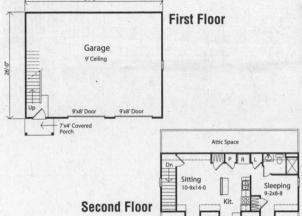

First Floor

34'-0"

26'-0"

Garage
9' Ceiling

Up

9'x8' Door   9'x8' Door

7'x4' Covered Porch

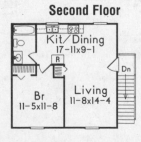

Second Floor

Attic Space

Dn   P R L

Sitting
10-9x14-0

Kit.

Sleeping
9-2x8-8

Price Code P12

2-Car Garage Apartment

Plan #706-15030

Special features

- 576 square feet
- Building height - 21'-5"
- Roof pitch - 4/12
- Ceiling height - 8'-0"
- Two 9' x 7' overhead doors
- 1 bedroom, 1 bath
- Loft has roomy kitchen and dining area
- Private side exterior entrance
- Complete list of materials
- Step-by-step instructions

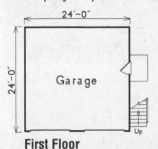

24'-0"

24'-0"

Garage

Up

First Floor

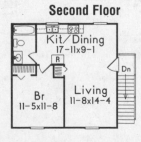

Second Floor

Kit/Dining
17-11x9-1

R

Br
11-5x11-8

Living
11-8x14-4

Dn

Price Code P9

2-Car Garage Apartment - Gambrel Roof   Plan #706-15029

Special features

- 438 square feet
- Building height - 21'-3"
- Roof pitch - 6/12, 12/6
- Ceiling heights - First floor - 8'-0"
  Second floor - 7'-9"
- Two 9' x 7' overhead doors
- Simple, yet spacious studio design
- Large windows warm inside
- Complete list of materials
- Step-by-step instructions

Price Code P9

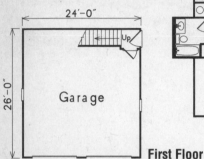

24'-0"

26'-0"

Garage

First Floor

Studio
14-11x22-3

Second Floor

2-Car Garage Apartment   Plan #706-15517

Special features

- 484 square feet
- Building height - 25'-0"
- Ceiling height - 8'-0"
- Roof pitch - 7/12
- 1 bedroom, 1 bath
- Complete list of materials

Price Code P11

Width: 24'-0"
Depth: 22'-0"

two~car
garage

First Floor

din
9'x8'

k
8'6x6

10'6'x9'
liv

DECK

12'x9'
br

Second Floor

3-Car Garage Apartment - Cape Cod   Plan #706-15032

Special features

- 813 square feet
- Building height - 22'-0"
- Roof pitch - 12/12, 4.25/12
- Ceiling height - 8'-0"
- Three 9' x 7' overhead doors
- Studio, 1 bath
- Spacious studio apartment has kitchen and bath
- Complete list of materials

Price Code P12

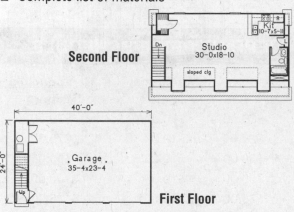

3-Car Garage Apartment   Plan #706-15505

Special features

- 949 square feet
- Building height - 24'-10"
- Roof pitch - 6/12
- Ceiling heights - First floor - 9'-0"
                    Second floor - 8'-0"
- 1 bedroom, 1 bath
- Three 9' x 7' overhead doors
- Sitting area has an attractive window seat
- Complete list of materials

Price Code P12

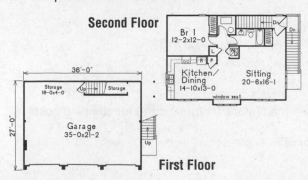

TO ORDER BLUEPRINTS USE THE FORM ON PAGE 320 OR CALL TOLL-FREE 1-877-671-6036
View thousands more home plans online at www.familyhandyman.com/homeplans

How To Order

For fastest service, Call Toll-Free
1-877-671-6036
24 hours a day

Three Easy Ways To Order

1. CALL toll free 1-877-671-6036 for credit card orders. MasterCard, Visa, Discover and American Express are accepted.
2. FAX your order to 1-314-770-2226.
3. MAIL the Order Form to:

HDA, Inc.
4390 Green Ash Drive
St. Louis, MO 63045

QUESTIONS?
Call Our Customer Service Number
314-770-2228

ORDER FORM

Please send me -

PLAN NUMBER 706BT - ____________

PRICE CODE ______ (see Plan Page)
(for plans on pgs. 310-319)

Reproducible Masters (see chart at right) $ ________
Initial Set of Plans $ ________
Additional Plan Sets (see chart at right)
____ (Qty) at $ ______ each $ ________

SUBTOTAL $ ________
SALES TAX (MO residents add 6%) $ ________
☐ Shipping / Handling (see chart at right) $ ________
(each additional set add $2.00 to shipping charges)

TOTAL ENCLOSED (US funds only) $ ________

☐ Enclosed is my check or money order payable to HDA, Inc. (Sorry, no COD's)

I hereby authorize HDA, Inc. to charge this purchase to my credit card account (check one):

☐ MasterCard ☐ VISA ☐ DISCOVER NOVUS ☐ AMERICAN EXPRESS Cards

Credit Card number ____________________

Expiration date ____________________

Signature ____________________

Name ____________________
(Please print or type)

Street Address ____________________
(Please **do not** use PO Box)

City ____________________

State __________ Zip ____________________

Daytime phone number (____) - ____________

Thank you for your order!

IMPORTANT INFORMATION TO KNOW BEFORE YOU ORDER

- **Exchange Policies -** Since blueprints are printed in response to your order, we cannot honor requests for refunds. However, if for some reason you find that the plan you have purchased does not meet your requirements, you may exchange that plan for another plan in our collection. At the time of the exchange, you will be charged a processing fee of 25% of your original plan package price, plus the difference in price between the plan packages (if applicable) and the cost to ship the new plans to you.

  Please note: Reproducible drawings can only be exchanged if the package is unopened, and exchanges are allowed only within 90 days of purchase.

- **Building Codes & Requirements -** At the time the construction drawings were prepared, every effort was made to ensure that these plans and specifications meet nationally recognized codes. Our plans conform to most national building codes. Because building codes vary from area to area, some drawing modifications and/or the assistance of a professional designer or architect may be necessary to comply with your local codes or to accommodate specific building site conditions. We advise you to consult with your local building official for information regarding codes governing your area.

BLUEPRINT PRICE SCHEDULE

Price Code	1-Set	Additional Sets	Reproducible Masters
P4	$20.00	$10.00	$70.00
P5	$25.00	$10.00	$75.00
P6	$30.00	$10.00	$80.00
P7	$50.00	$10.00	$100.00
P8	$75.00	$10.00	$125.00
P9	$125.00	$20.00	$200.00
P10	$150.00	$20.00	$225.00
P11	$175.00	$20.00	$250.00
P12	$200.00	$20.00	$275.00
P13	$225.00	$45.00	$440.00

Plan prices guaranteed through December 31, 2004.
Please note that plans are not refundable.

SHIPPING & HANDLING CHARGES

EACH ADDITIONAL SET ADD $2.00 TO SHIPPING CHARGES

U.S. SHIPPING

Regular *(allow 7-10 business days)* $5.95
Priority *(allow 3-5 business days)* $15.00
Express* *(allow 1-2 business days)* $25.00

CANADA SHIPPING

Standard *(allow 8-12 business days)* $15.00
Express* *(allow 3-5 business days)* $40.00

OVERSEAS SHIPPING/INTERNATIONAL

Call, fax, or e-mail (plans@hdainc.com) for shipping costs.

* For express delivery please call us by 11:00 a.m. CST